AFRO-AMERICAN LITERARY STUDIES IN THE 1990s

Black Literature and Culture

A series edited by Houston A. Baker, Jr.

AFRO-AMERICAN LITERARY STUDY IN THE 1990s

Edited by

Houston A. Baker, Jr., *and* Patricia Redmond

The University of Chicago Press

Chicago and London

An earlier version of Deborah E. McDowell's "Boundaries: Or Distant Relations and Close Kin" appeared in Nellie Y. McKay, ed., *Critical Essays on Toni Morrison,* © 1988 Twayne Publishers, a division of G. K. Hall and Co., Boston; material from that version is used with permission. In Kimberley Benston's "Performing Blackness: Re/Placing Afro-American Poetry," A. B. Spellman's poem "Did John's Music Kill Him?" is used courtesy of the author. Arnold Rampersad's "Biography and Afro-American Culture" appeared as "Psychology and Afro-American Biography" in *The Yale Review* 78, no. 1, © Yale University, and as "The Challenge of Writing Black Biography" in Leo Hamalian and James V. Hatch, eds., *Artist and Influence 1986,* vol. 7 (Hatch-Billops Collection, Inc.).

The University of Chicago Press, Chicago 60637
The University of Chicago Press, Ltd., London
© 1989 by The University of Chicago
All rights reserved. Published 1989
Paperback edition 1992
Printed in the United States of America

98 97 96 95 94 93 92   5 4 3 2

Library of Congress Cataloging-in-Publication Data

Afro-American literary study in the 1990s / edited by
    Houston A. Baker, Jr. and Patricia Redmond.
        p.   cm.—(Black literature and culture)
      Bibliography: p.
      Includes index.
      1. American literature—Afro-American authors—History
    and criticism—Theory etc.   2. American literature—20th
    century—History and criticism—Theory etc.   3. Afro-
    Americans—Intellectual life—20th century.   4. Afro-
    Americans in literature.   I. Baker, Houston A.
    II. Redmond, Patricia.   III. Series.
      PS153.N5A345   1989
    810.9'896073—dc20   89-31971
                                                                    CIP
    ISBN 0-226-03537-9 (cloth)
    ISBN 0-226-03543-3 (paperback)

Contents

Introduction

Houston A. Baker, Jr., and Patricia Redmond

The essays collected in this volume constitute the proceedings of a three-day conference held in April 1987 for leading scholars of Afro-American literature. Sponsored by the Albert M. Greenfield professorship and the Center for the Study of Black Literature and Culture at the University of Pennsylvania, the conference brought together twenty-one Afro-Americanists to present and consider a series of theoretical and critical papers devoted to major genres and areas of Afro-American literature and criticism. The conference was called "The Study of Afro-American Literature: An Agenda for the 1990s," and its purpose was to allow Afro-American literary scholars to discuss the past and future of the field in a forum designed to encourage sustained critical dialogue.

In publishing these proceedings, we who took part in the conference hope to release into the larger Afro-American and literary communities some of the insights and energy that became ours during a remarkable three days. Seven principal papers and fourteen discussants' responses are included here. The essays are the record of critical conversations conducted among a small group of colleagues. To read them as a collection is to eavesdrop on the development of consensus and controversy as scholars set an agenda for Afro-American literary studies in the 1990s.

That such an agenda is being set, that scholars of Afro-American literature are debating together the shape of their future work, is both an indication of critical achievement and a tremendous challenge. The conference in April 1987 was historic: never before had leading Afro-American critics formally convened to set an agenda for the field. Of course, there is a long and full history of Afro-American and, indeed, African diasporic conferences and conventions devoted to questions of creative intellectual endeavor and scholarship. But that history is both a general and a public one. Our retreat was not aimed at social change; nor was it open to the public. We came together as a select community of specialists with a specific disciplinary aim, aware that our work was

1

among the most important scholarly activities presently engaged in by
the academy.

Still it is important to note that the scholarly collaboration that occurred at our retreat was not new to Afro-American literary study.
Collaboration has always been a necessity for those who have chosen to
study the excluded and invisible traditions of Afro-America. Only
through the work of communities, both political and intellectual, has it
been possible to define and institutionalize Afro-American studies in
general, and to make a place in the conservative world of literary scholarship for the study of Afro-American texts.

The most forceful example of such collaboration from the nineteenth
century is that offered by the vast network of black abolitionists described so eloquently by the historian Benjamin Quarles. Men and
women from various backgrounds and various stations in life were
bound in their outspokenness to a common end of black liberation.
Their formal and informal approaches to the job of liberation were
coextensive, interdependent, and conjoined. Similarly, at the turn of the
nineteenth and early in the twentieth century, an emergent group of
Afro-American professionals, creative artists, educators, and intellectuals
strove—often collaboratively—to define institutions supportive of what
they regarded as an *imperium in imperia*—an Afro-American nation
within the United States of America. It was this group that helped to
form and gave generative energy to the Harlem Renaissance of the
1920s. More recently, there was the vibrant Black Arts movement of the
1960s and 1970s.

What so palpably characterized such historical collaborations was a
desire for national self-definition and self-determination in combination
with a sense of black marginality in need of accommodation by a dominant, white culture. In all cases—whether directly or subtly—white men
and women played dominant (and sometimes dominating) roles as leaders, editors, employers, agents, publishers, patrons, and so on—seldom
as what might be called "organic" participants in the general, collaborative enterprise. Their roles, in fact, offered some measure of the very
tension between self-determination and, loosely, integration or accommodation intrinsic to the collaboration.

What was unique about the collaborative moment signaled by our
conference was its aim of refiguring historical patterns by quite clearly
defining Afro-American literary study as a, for want of a better word,
dominant category of American intellectual life—an enterprise brought
to such a status by the sound efforts of Afro-American scholars, writers,
and critics themselves. The uniqueness of the participation of white

scholars and critics in the project was not their presence in itself but their unqualified status of earned participation in a still evolving work. The definition of collaboration as an enterprise that dissolves boundaries and seeks genuinely to write a nontraditional version of scholarly work comes to fruition in today's community of Afro-Americanists. And by "community" we do not mean a mellow, suburban homogeneity. Debate—the open forum and town meeting, as it were—is fundamental to genuine community, as are diversity of points of view and myriad sites of cultural and political tension. Perhaps our best definition of the collaboration marking our conference is, to repeat a phrase, *earned participation*. Those who forward the work of Afro-American literary study through laborious research, ample scholarly production, and demonstrable commitment earn participation—indeed, keep alive always both the community itself and questions of its definition at any given moment.

For such a group as the Afro-Americanists just described, the collaborative project of this conference was, then, in some respects a natural undertaking and in others a particularly difficult challenge. With a heritage of collaborative activity, Afro-American scholars are deeply aware of its benefits; however, as recently established academics, we are subject to institutional pressures that make genuine collaboration very difficult.

Academic institutions have traditionally rewarded intellectual individualism. This practice has worked well for many scholars and for the academic community as a whole. The assumptions supporting it lie close to central principles of the academy: those of us who cherish academic freedom are also likely to honor scholars who think independently and produce original work. And, because so much valuable, and original, scholarship has been and continues to be produced in this context, its specific detriments—such as disincentives to collaboration—are not easy to address.

Afro-Americanists to date have been largely exempt from this system's disadvantages, simply because they have been denied its privileges. Excluded from the centers of academic power, they have developed an intellectual culture that functions within a traditional academic setting but also compensates for the academy's indifference or hostility to their work. As noted, a hallmark of this culture has been collaboration. From alternative scholarly presses to informal conversations, the scholarly networks of literary Afro-Americanists have, by necessity, generally included many members of the community and involved those members in regular and intense intellectual discussion.

This is not to say that the academic world in general is devoid of intellectual exchange, nor is it to romanticize the conditions of marginality. The point here is structural: as Linda Brodkey has explained in her study of academic discourse, academic networks are formed in response to social and economic needs. Academic groups whose work is often given the chance of a "hearing" and whose scholarly contributions are often positively valued do not need collaborative networks to maintain scholarly progress. Members of these groups are likely to form what Brodkey (following Larissa Lomnitz) terms egocentric networks— loosely knit and intermittently maintained professional relationships. Marginal academics, on the other hand, have reason to form and maintain stronger sets of professional bonds (exocentric networks).[1]

The essays in this volume grow out of and contribute to an exocentric network. First presented in an intimate collegial setting, many of them are frankly personal. Yet they are also critically, politically, and historically sophisticated. Their authors hold positions in some of the nation's most prestigious institutions. (Or, as Hortense Spillers says in her response, we are "the representative agency of some of the most powerful and complicitous arrangements and institutions in America.") At issue in this collection, then, as in the conference that produced it, is the fate of collaborative practice as Afro-Americanists gain acceptance in the academic world. Reading these erudite and insightful pieces, composed as contributions to a collaborative agenda, one is tempted to claim that Afro-American literary scholars should have no difficulty maintaining their distinctive professional networks as they acquire more professional influence.

But as students of Afro-American experience, we are no strangers to the problems of assimilation. Just as we are not likely to assume that our limited though substantial scholarly progress signifies an absence of racism in our institution, we also cannot neglect the challenging fact that our rising but uncertain status in the academy brings with it pressures to conform to highly individualistic models of academic interaction. Can collaborative practice survive the 1990s?

None of the essays in this volume presumes to answer this question, but as a collection they suggest what survival might look like. They are printed here in the order in which they were presented in April 1987; some of the vitality of the program is, of course, lost, as we cannot reproduce the lively and often contentious exchanges that occurred between speakers. Still, to eavesdrop on this performance is to be privy to

1. Linda Brodkey, *Academic Writing as a Social Practice* (Philadelphia: Temple University Press, 1987), p. 39.

the triumphs and struggles of contemporary collaborative practice among Afro-American literary scholars. They began, on April 9, with the issue of canon.

Henry Louis Gates, Jr., opened the conference presentations by announcing the recently commissioned Norton anthology of Afro-American literature. Gates's essay discusses the anthology as a milestone in the project of canon formation. The Norton anthology will mean that our literature can no longer be excluded from classrooms with the excuse that its texts are unavailable. The anthology is an opportunity to see that a canon of Afro-American literature is accessible to instructors and students at any institution which might teach Afro-American texts. What will this anthology, this canon, include? Gates says that the project must be self-consciously executed. We must be aware that we, as scholars, make canons.

Gates's own approach to canon-formation is through a parable and a discussion of three previous attempts at Afro-American canon production by way of anthology formation. The parable tells of the ways in which the relations between (white) power and (black) art and criticism have shaped the agenda for Afro-American literary studies since the beginning of the enterprise. The record of canon-making in anthologies shows this tension in action—in the expressly political aims of the anthologists and in the similarly political racism of white publishers and publics.

Gates concludes his look at Afro-American anthologies by turning to *Black Fire*, the "blackest canon of all." Here was a tradition defined by formal innovations and themes; the black vernacular was the emphasis, as was the urge toward black liberation. In canon formation and in critical activity, Gates calls for an affirmation of the vernacular like that in *Black Fire*. The Afro-American canon Gates would construct would stress vernacular roots and the formal relationships that obtain among texts in the black tradition—relations of revision, echo, call and response, antiphony, and so on. And criticism as well should find in black expression resources for its development as a form of inquiry. Although we must, according to Gates, use the most sophisticated critical methods available, we must also come to understand "how certain forms of difference and the languages we employ to define those supposed differences not only reinforce each other but tend to create and maintain each other." Our theoretical task is to avoid "the mistake of accepting the empowering language of white critical theory as 'universal' or as our own language, the mistake of confusing the enabling mask of theory with our own black faces."

Barbara Johnson responds to Gates's call for canons and theory that affirm the vernacular by analyzing the complexity and paradoxical nature of the project as it is revealed through Gates's own discourse. To figure Western critical theory as an "enabling mask" contrasted with "our own black faces" is to set the Afro-American theoretical enterprise in the context of the historically problematic relation between language and the body. Johnson asks: "How can one find a language that neither denies the oppression of bodies nor proclaims an essentialized relation *to* bodies? How can the notion of the *mask* help us avoid both the false universalization of linguistic theory and the false essentialism of a simple continuity between bodies and languages?"

Johnson notes that the terms "black" and "white" often imply a binary model of mutual exclusion, a model that is neither empowering nor historically accurate. Moreover, the term "vernacular" itself belies this mutual exclusion: vernacular's root, the latin "verna," means "a slave born in his master's home," thus signifying a difference *within,* not a realm outside. Johnson's conclusion—that vernacular theory must "'co-opt' (in Soyinka's words) rather than expel or deny the white man within"—lead her to propose that a linguistic model is more appropriate than a geometric one to describe the "'signifying black difference' that Gates intends to theorize."

Turning again to Gates's critical language, Johnson considers his use of the expression "our own." (She observes that it appears in his text no fewer than nineteen times). In Gates's text, "our own" is what Roman Jakobson calls "a shifter," an expression with different meanings in different contexts. Johnson finds that the ambiguity of the shifter illustrates a split between the performative and the cognitive in Gates's language: "our own" is, as Johnson puts it "interested in proclaiming the fact of its own enunciation. But the information given about the collectivity implied is vague."

Johnson questions who "we" are, pointing out that a subject position is synthetic, taking nourishment from more than one source. She closes her argument by recalling Gates's public acknowledgment in a recent scholarly essay of his mother's voice. The essay illustrates what Johnson is interested in throughout Gates's current piece: the paradoxes of mimesis and of the supplementary voice. That Gates himself was unable to deliver this paper at the conference (because of the death of his mother), and that Hortense Spillers read his remarks to the group makes "the circle of voices all the more poignant."

While Donald Gibson, in responding to Gates's address, has praise for Gates's critical work, he is also anxious to ensure that enthusiasm for the vernacular does not do to certain black writers what the New Criticism did to Longfellow, Whittier, Lowell, and Holmes. Gibson notes that we may have gone further in the process of canon-formation than Gates implies. He also questions the relation, implicit in Gates's parable, between the formation of criticism and canon. Whatever the shape of our criticism and canon, Gibson wishes to see both "carry forward the tradition of black writing that has seen it as functional, as having more to do with our social and political well-being than with our need for enjoyment or entertainment."

The social and the political are founding concerns of Afro-American feminist criticism, and Deborah McDowell discusses in "Boundaries: Or Distant Relations and Close Kin" how awareness of these never-static realities makes it impossible to essentialize or homogenize black women. The "black woman" is the dominant focus of black feminist discourse, and this, according to McDowell, is a vital political necessity. Still, what is necessary for the future is a close scrutiny of concepts such as "black womanhood," "black female identity," and "black experience."

McDowell demonstrates her commitment to such scrutiny with an extended reading of Toni Morrison's *Sula,* a work that questions and complicates the concept of identity. As Morrison's text—"fragmentary, episodic, and elliptical"—resists any unity other than that provided by the reader, the act of reading becomes analogous to the construction of self in the novel. McDowell draws on reader response as well as contemporary feminist theory as she argues that, just as the self is fluid and formed in relations with others, so identification in reading is a process of dialogue between the self and "the 'otherness' of writers, texts, literary characters, and interpretive communities."

McDowell's work inspired two very different responses. Hortense Spillers's response relies upon her basic agreement with the argument in "Boundaries." Rather than question or quarrel with McDowell's thesis, Spillers considers some of its implications. Confronting *Sula* in all of its subversive and discomfiting ambiguity requires "confronting the convergences of difference among our commonly-shared cultural practices." We do not as yet, according to Spillers, have any way of "signing" to ourselves our own ambivalence. This ambivalence is the result of our being "the representative agency of some of the most powerful and complicitous arrangements and institutions in America." Spillers urges Afro-American literary scholars to articulate the spaces of contradiction that they occupy.

Michael Awkward's response takes issue with McDowell's critical theory and practices. Awkward is troubled by the application of poststructuralist critical tools to *Sula*. Noting that McDowell herself, in earlier work, had thought it important to allow the critical concerns of black women's novels to emerge organically from the texts themselves, Awkward finds that poststructuralism is ill-suited to recognize the positive search in black female texts for a black female wholeness.

Somewhat similar attention to the implications of Afro-American narrative voice and narrative strategy marks the three essays in this volume concerned with the novel. But here, rather than a focus on the analogies between critical theory and the Afro-American construction of character, the concern is with history.

William Andrews's paper, "Toward a Poetics of Afro-American Autobiography," is a call for study of the formal qualities of Afro-American autobiographies and for expansion of the field itself. Paying more attention to the shape of autobiographies is not, in Andrews's agenda, placing form and theme in any sort of binary opposition. Rather it is proceeding in accord with Jameson's claim that all texts can be read as having "an ideology of form" and it is allowing the necessary rethinking of the relationships between theme and form in this genre. Expanding the canon of Afro-American autobiography means recognizing the politics that influenced this canon from the beginning. Slave narratives are usually seen as the roots of Afro-American autobiography but, as Andrews points out, one particular *kind* of slave narrative has been privileged in Afro-American literary history. The antebellum slave narratives are considered by critics to be *the* slave narratives; for a number of political reasons (which Andrews outlines), postbellum slave narratives are virtually ignored. Andrews argues that we must attend to this lacuna in black literary history: "We cannot read the history of Afro-American autobiography as though it validates a certain model of black selfhood or approved notions of black experience."

Both Sandra Pacquet and Geneviève Fabre, who responded to Andrews's paper, concur with him on the need for critical reflection on the Afro-American autobiographical canon. But Pacquet does express some reservations: she is deeply enthusiastic about the currently canonical texts (such as Douglass's 1845 *Narrative* and Wright's *Black Boy*), and she attributes her confidence in the durability of these texts not to an unwillingness to recognize new additions so much as a reluctance to retreat from the social political framework that inspired the shaping of the canon, without a clear understanding of what will replace it as a measure of aesthetic value. Pacquet also observes the crucial points of connection between Afro-American and Caribbean autobiography.

Fabre's response comes from the perspective of a European scholar.

She charts the French interest in slave narrative as parallel to the American canonization process, making note of the significant French scholarship in the field. Fabre applauds Andrews for his scholarly work (*To Tell A Free Story*) and comments on the correspondence between his formal (as well as thematic) analysis and the preoccupations of Hispanic and other minority writers who call for their own literary space within the American scene. Finally, she stresses the function of slave narratives as "lieux de mémoire"; their aesthetic, political and social function is crucial. They must continue to be discovered and examined so that they can "stimulate the understanding and the collective imagination, generating new creative acts."

Richard Yarborough's paper briefly traces the use of the first-person point of view in Afro-American fiction. "Why have so few Afro-American fiction writers before the mid-twentieth century used the first-person point of view?" Yarborough suggests the possibility that the avoidance of the first person in most nineteenth-century texts reflects an insecure identity on the part of the writers. He also observes that for nineteenth-century black authors, fiction itself was a problem: "Why use *fiction* as a weapon in the battle to gain a hearing for the *true* version of the Afro-American experience?"

Robert Stepto agrees both with Yarborough's identification of patterns in the Afro-American point of view and his assessment of the authorial anxieties likely to derive from first-person narration. However, he believes that Yarborough needs to consider not just the writer's feelings, but also the peculiar pressure antebellum blacks experienced in writing for American audiences. Stepto speculates that first-person narration might have been a deliberating form for blacks since this was the form of the slave narrative. There were models available to the early Afro-American fiction writer that made third-person narration more attractive than first-person. Stepto sets forth some of these, and concludes by mentioning the possible influence of *Uncle Tom's Cabin* on Brown's *Clotel*. The links between these novels lead Stepto to urge that comparative Americanist study remain part of the Afro-American literary agenda in the next decade.

In response to Yarborough's thoughts on the absence of first-person narration, Eleanor Traylor draws attention to cases of multiple narration in the fiction of the period. Even though, as Yarborough points out, there is an authorial presence in many of these novels, this presence, Traylor explains, seems to manifest itself as a plurality looking from several points of vantage. Traylor asks the same "Why?" of this narrative technique as Yarborough asks of the absence of first-person fictions. She concludes that the form of multiple narration is liberating: the reader is encouraged to join in the narrative act, to engage in a powerful act of re-creation. These narratives thus allow us "to claim our heritage and 'repeat into the silence' our own regenerative identity."

In Baker's essay, "There Is No More Beautiful Way: Theory and the Poetics of Afro-American Women's Writing" he argues that the most theoretically sophisticated act for the Afro-American scholar is an auto-biographical one. Theory is not, as some have recently claimed, antithetical to the spirit of Afro-American texts; on the contrary, the articulation of culture at the "metalevel" (which constitutes the domain of theory) is basic in the Afro-American historical experience. Baker proposes an Afro-American theoretical project rooted in personal experience. This he calls personal poetry in the critical field, and he links its emphasis on individual response to late nineteenth-century British aestheticism.

For Afro-American women's writing, personal poetry in the critical field can draw upon what Bachelard terms poetic images (poetic images are the origin of consciousness, the impetus for expression to create being) to comprehend the ways in which readers may interact with these women's texts and arrive at their guiding spirit, or consciousness. Baker reads Alice Walker's garden in her critical essay "In Search of Our Mother's Gardens" as a poetic image of this sort: by writing her mother's vernacular garden as a literate poetic image, Walker opens the field of Afro-American women's consciousness in its founding radiance and claims for herself an enduring spiritual legacy. To move with Walker (and other Afro-American women writers) through her poetic images is to move toward a unique inscription of the Afro-American self as woman and a refiguration of the African body that emerges from the standard male theoretical story.

That a felicitous poetic image is still an image is Mae Henderson's concern in response to this paper. Henderson analyzes the function of the visual metaphor in Baker's poetics. Citing Luce Irigaray, Henderson explains that the gaze relegates women to passivity; she will be the beautiful object. Theory built upon imagistic fields connotes woman as spectacle; it puts women "at the mercy of what the Other(s) determines is the appropriate 'scopic field,'" the grid which distinguishes the "pathological or aversive" from the "felicitous" and is "the disturbing aspect of Baker's critical approach." "What happens," she asks, "when the eye is averted from the 'nonfelicitous' image?"

Kimberly Benston's paper, "Performing Blackness: Re/placing Afro-American Poetry," locates the failure of criticism to provide the kind of sophisticated and provocative account of Afro-American poetry that has been developed for narrative and drama in critical preoccupation with an unproductive polarization. Those critical works which aspire to a theoretical overview of Afro-American poetry unfortunately set the poetry against one of two criteria: either the poem is considered in relation to a privileged notion of blackness or the poem is tested for conformity to a universally applicable norm of "the poetic" which is supposed to exist both in and outside of any notion of blackness.

Benston wishes to move beyond the critical impasse resulting from this polarized methodology, but he sees this move as exegetically and politically complex. The polarization in criticism, according to Benston, concerns a very real historical and ideological issue: "What is the continuing meaning of the Black Arts movement of the 1960s and 1970s; on what terms shall we calculate its aims, achievements, and legacy?" Furthermore, this question is, to Benston, a derivative of the literature's own contemporary struggle for self-definition. He proceeds to a reading of Ellison's sermon on the "blackness of blackness" in the Prologue of *Invisible Man* and Clay's climactic speech in Baraka's *Dutchman*. Read by Benston, these texts offer a mechanism, "an enabling allegory . . . for resituating the critical opposition of 'blackness' and 'universality' on a ground internal to Afro-American discourse."

How might this enabling allegory be realized in practice? Here Benston turns to two experts—one critical, one poetic—for illumination. In Stephen Henderson's introduction to *Understanding the New Black Poetry* and in A. B. Spellman's "Did John's Music Kill Him?" Benston finds pointers toward an answer to this question. His conclusion, drawing upon these pointers, is a proposal that we come to see Afro-American poetry not as a static alignment of proclamations but as a performative activity that sees itself in struggle with other practices. This agenda coincides with Benston's view that we must reconsider the nature of textuality in Afro-American poetry through further exploration of the vernacular (an area that Benston notes is already receiving intense, often brilliant scrutiny).

As Cheryl Wall examines Benston's analysis of the inadequacies in Afro-American poetic criticism, she finds his own paper making significant progress. Wall praises Benston's "clarifying insight" that the critical debate parallels an argument in the poetry itself. She has, however, a reservation: "suggestive and useful" as Benston's allegory is, "it is nevertheless more applicable to the literature of the period it invokes . . . than to more recent writing." Wall finds in the work of recent Afro-American women poets "an attempt to move beyond the 'blackness is and blackness ain't' debate Benston so adroitly configures." Wall's attention to the alternative vision of female poetry brings us to a concluding statement on the necessity of canon revision. To accomplish Benston's agenda of new paradigms, we need a canon—one that can bring together for us the multitude of new poetic voices that speak to each other in ways we have not recognized.

Stephen Henderson—dialogically engaged with Benston in the "Performing Blackness" paper—engages him again here in a brief but provocative response to his paper. Henderson observes the correspondence between Benston's diagnosis of the state of criticism and his own remarks in 1979 at the Melvin Butler Poetry Festival in Baton Rouge, Louisiana. At that time, Henderson described a challenge for black poetry. As Henderson charted it, the challenge consisted of three parts: (1) a cultural base (the folk and popular roots of the poetry) (2) the challenge of the tradition, and (3) the challenge of the modern world—which, Henderson observes, "requires the kind of sophisticated criticism Benston calls for today." To explore blackness in the way Benston suggests, Henderson turns to two textual challenges: lines from Skip James, the blues man, and Carolyn Rodgers' "Poems for Some Lonely Black Woman." Both of these texts reveal much when their employment of the vernacular is analyzed; both are an exploration of the conflicting dimensions of blackness at issue in Benston's text.

The concluding exchange of the conference focused on Arnold Rampersad's "Biography and Afro-American Literature." Rampersad's paper explores the lack of psychological sophistication in biographies of American blacks. Why are biographies of blacks so hesitant to employ psychology? Rampersad finds one reason in the cultural perception that psychology is a flagrant violation of the intimate; another in the Afro-American biographer's awareness of his or her relation to the Afro-American audience, many of whom might resent (for understandable political reasons) the psychoanalytic method and its conclusions. Should this hesitancy be overcome? Rampersad's answer is yes—"one explains very little if one does not attempt to explain the mind"—and the insights of psychology, however partial or politically inadequate, are the best available tool.

Rampersad acknowledges the clumsiness of the tool: Freud may be all wrong for blacks, and any psychology and psychiatry, to the degree that they work with scientific terminology, are inappropriate languages for the discipline of biography. But, says Rampersad, this leaves us not with the excuse of ignoring psychology but "with the burden of recognizing the validity of psychology and of using its methods to understand our subject." Being black in America is, Rampersad notes, "above all a psychological state." To examine the effects of racism on the subject, we must examine the effects of racism on the mind, and for this we need "some model derived . . . from the works of Freud, or from some conscious opposition to Freud."

Of Rampersad's three respondents, two, Nellie McKay and Robert O'Meally, endorse (with some qualifications) his agenda for the use of psychology in Afro-American biography, while, one, Michel Fabre, is decidedly more reluctant. Nellie McKay's cautionary acceptance is based upon her conviction that what literary biographers do with the tools of psychology is very different from what is done by scientific practitioners of the field. Citing Leon Edel, she calls the biographer's task "literary psychology," and emphasizes the care that needs to be taken in translation as one discipline is imported into the practices of another. O'Meally casts a vote for Rampersad and science, provided that the psychologically interested biographer takes care with the complexities of what the Harvard psychiatrist Chester Pierce calls racism's microaggressions (the change flung on the counter or the delayed promotion, in contrast to the macroaggressions such as lynching) and avoid the many reductive interpretations that can result from a too formulaic application of psychological principles.

For Michel Fabre, the "choice of methodology is ideological." While he agrees that ignoring psychoanalysis leaves the biographer without valuable instruments, he doubts that it is possible to borrow instruments piecemeal without subscribing to their underpinning ideology. Fabre believes that "the best literary biographies have not been written by social scientists or psychologists but by literary critics-cum-historians"— those like Rampersad himself. Fabre admires Rampersad's biographical work: it is an example of a biographer avoiding reductive "keys"; it takes the risk of multiple interpretations, a risk Fabre is anxious to defend "against the too frequently totalitarian assumptions of a narrowly 'scientific' exploration of a writer's life and works."

Collaboration that results in a scholarly volume extends the range of participation to a diverse readership. What we hope is that readers of our various exchanges will both profit intellectually from them and join us in the risks and possibilities that they suggest. Our hope is not that we have provided a complete or definitive statement of what ought to be done. Drama and other genres of expression, for example, form no part of our consideration. Our statements and exchanges are, rather, tentative statements of what we think *is* the state of Afro-American literary study at the moment and a projection of some of the states that it might occupy— with our readers' generous and thoughtful cooperation, response, and collaboration—in what appears to us a promising future.

1

Canon-Formation, Literary History, and The Afro-American Tradition: From the Seen to the Told

Henry Louis Gates, Jr.

I want to address the first topic of this conference in three parts: first, I want to present a parable about canon-formation at crucial moments of cultural liminality in the black tradition, a parable in which the figures of Alexander Crummell, John C. Calhoun, Greg Tate, and Wole Soyinka play their parts. I have chosen to share this parable because I believe that we are at just such a moment of literary liminality in the African-American tradition; at that old crossroads—presided over by Esu-Elegbara—where tradition and the present, Africa and the West, Afro-America and America, black, indeed, and white face each other in confrontation. The potential at such a moment of liminality is wondrous, and I believe that such a moment must be named. After narrating this parable, I next want to discuss, briefly, three previous attempts—of several attempts—at canon-formation in the Afro-American tradition. I choose to do so by discussing the idea of the black anthology as canon-formation, and I have four anthologies in mind. The first is William G. Allen's 1849 volume, entitled *Wheatley, Banneker, and Horton*. The second is *Negro Caravan*, published in 1941 and edited by Sterling Brown, Arthur Davis, and Ulysses Lee. Third is *Black Fire*, published in 1968 by Amiri Baraka (LeRoi Jones) and Larry Neal.[1] Finally, I want to discuss in broad

---

1. William G. Allen, *Wheatley, Banneker, and Horton; With Selections From the Poetical Works of Wheatley and Horton, and the Letter of Washington to Wheatley, and of Jefferson to Banneker* (Boston: Daniel Laing, Jr., 1849); Sterling A. Brown, Arthur P. Davis, Ulysses Lee, eds., *The Negro Caravan: Writings by American Negroes* (New York: The Citadel Press, 1941); LeRoi Jones and Larry Neal, eds., *Black Fire: An Anthology of Afro-American Writing* (New York: William Morrow, 1968). All subsequent references to these works will be given parenthetically in the text.

outline the editing of the Norton Anthology of Afro-American Literature, a project commissioned by Norton and still in an early stage of organization.

But before I attempt to discuss any of these things, I want to talk about Houston A. Baker, Jr., the person who conceived the idea of bringing us all together in this conference, despite our methodological, theoretical, and ideological differences, to reflect upon the *moment* of Afro-American cultural history that *we* are shaping virtually by all that we do here, each day. It was Houston Baker who had the brilliant insight and entrepreneurial energy to bring us together in isolation so that we can be ourselves and *name* this critical moment among ourselves. Houston's position as the leading and most prolific theorist of Afro-American literature is, it seems to me, beyond debate. His capacity to remain fresh, to produce a seminal book every other year (and two books are coming in this year alone), to train graduate students, and to lecture widely in this country and in Europe inspires and encourages me, and indeed serves as an inspiration to us all. Houston both works hard and produces brilliant ideas and observations, and that combination is unassailable. My own admiration for him and his work only continues to be enlarged. He is for me a true friend and colleague, one whom I trust implicitly.

I

Alexander Crummell, a pioneering nineteenth-century pan-Africanist, statesman, and missionary who spent the bulk of his creative years as an Anglican minister in Liberia, was also a pioneering intellectual and philosopher of language, founding the American Negro Academy in 1897 and serving as the intellectual godfather of W. E. B. Du Bois. In his first annual address as president of the academy, delivered on December 28, 1898, Crummell selected as his topic "The Attitude of the American Mind Toward the Negro Intellect."[2] Given the occasion of the first annual meeting of the great intellectuals of the race, he could not have chosen a more timely or appropriate topic.

Crummell wished to attack, he said, "the denial of intellectuality in the Negro; the assertion that he was not a human being, that he did not belong to the human race," assertions, he continued, which set out "to prove that the Negro was of a different species from the white man"

2. Alexander Crummell, "The Attitude of the American Mind Toward the Negro Intellect," Occasional Papers, No. 3 (Washington, D.C.: The American Negro Academy, 1898). All subsequent references will be given parenthetically in the text.

(p. 10). Crummell argues that the desire "to becloud and stamp out the intellect of the Negro" led to the enactment of "laws and statutes, closing the pages of every book printed to the eyes of Negroes; barring the doors of every school-room against them!" This, he concludes, "was the systematized method of the intellect of the South, to stamp out the brains of the Negro!", a program which created an "almost Egyptian darkness [which] fell upon the mind of the race, throughout the whole land" (p. 10).

Crummell next shared with his audience a conversation he had over-heard in 1833 or 1834, when he was "an errand boy in the Anti-slavery office in New York City":

> A distinguished illustration of this ignoble sentiment can be given. In the year 1833 or 4 the speaker was an errand boy in the Anti-slavery office in New York City.
>
> On a certain occasion he heard a conversation between the Secretary and two eminent lawyers from Boston,—Samuel E. Sewell and David Lee Child. They had been to Washington on some legal business. While at the Capitol they happened to dine in the company of the great John C. Calhoun, the senator from South Carolina. It was a period of great ferment upon the question of Slavery, States' Rights, and Nullification; and consequently the Negro was the topic of conversation at the table. One of the utterances of Mr. Calhoun was to this effect—"That if he could find a Negro who knew the Greek syntax, he would then believe that the Negro was a human being and should be treated as a man." (pp. 10–11)

"Just think of the crude asininity," Crummell concluded rather gener-ously, "of even a great man" (p. 11). For John C. Calhoun—who held during his lifetime the offices of U.S. congressman, secretary of war, vice president, senator, and secretary of state, and who stood firmly to his dying day a staunch advocate of states' rights and a symbol of an unre-constructed South—the person of African descent would never be a full member of the human community, fit to be anything but a slave, until one individual black person—just one—demonstrated mastery of the subtleties of Greek syntax, of all things! Perhaps fearing that this goal would be too easily achieved, Calhoun later added mastery of the bino-mial theorem to his list of black Herculean tasks.

The salient sign of the black person's humanity—indeed, the only sign for Calhoun—would be the mastering of the very essence of West-ern civilization, of the very foundation of the complex fiction upon which white Western culture had been constructed, which for John C. Calhoun turned out to have been Greek syntax. It is highly likely that "Greek syntax," for Calhoun, was merely a hyperbolic figure of speech, a trope of virtual impossibility, the first to leap to mind during an impassioned debate over states' rights and the abolition of slavery. Calhoun, perhaps, felt driven to the hyperbolic mode because of the long racist tradition, in Western letters, of demanding that black people *prove* their full humanity, a tradition to which Calhoun was heir. We know this tradition all too well, dotted as it is with the names of great intellectual Western racialists, such as Francis Bacon, David Hume, Immanuel Kant, Thomas Jefferson, and Hegel, to list only a few. Whereas each of these figures demanded that blacks write poetry to prove their humanity, Calhoun—speaking in a post–Phillis Wheatley era—took refuge in Greek syntax.

And, just as Phillis Wheatley's mistress and master had urged her to write poetry to refute racialists such as Hume and Kant, Calhoun's outrageous demand would not fall upon the deaf ears of an inarticulate intellectual inferior. In typical Afro-American fashion, a brilliant black intellectual accepted Calhoun's challenge, just as Wheatley had accepted her challenge almost a century before. The anecdote that Crummell shared with his fellow black academicians, it turns out, was his shaping scene of instruction. For Crummell, Calhoun's challenge was his reason for jumping on a boat, sailing to England, and matriculating at Queens College, at the University of Cambridge, where he mastered the intricacies of Greek syntax in a broader field of study, theology. Calhoun, we suspect, was not impressed.

But even after both John C. Calhoun and racial slavery had been long dead, Alexander Crummell never escaped the lesson he had learned as an errand boy at the anti-slavery office. Crummell never stopped believing that mastering the master's tongue was the *sole* path to civilization and to intellectual freedom and social equality for the black person. It was the acquisition of Western "culture," he argued, which the black person "must claim as his rightful heritage, as a man: not stinted training, not a caste education, not," he concludes prophetically, "a Negro curriculum" (p. 16). As he argues so passionately in his well-known speech of 1860, entitled "The English Language in Liberia,"[3] the acquisition of the English language, along with the simultaneous acquisition of Christianity, is the wonderful sign of God's providence encoded in the nightmare of African enslavement in the racist wilderness of the New World:

3. Alexander Crummell, "The English Language in Liberia," in *The Future of Africa* (New York: Charles Scribner, 1862), pp. 9–57. All subsequent references will be given parenthetically in the text.

The acquisition of [the English language] is elevation. It places the native man above his ignorant fellow, and gives him some of the dignity of civilization. New ideas are caught up, new habits formed, and superior and elevating wants are daily increased. (p. 35)

Crummell accepted fully an argument central to the Enlightenment, that written and spoken language-use was the tangible sign of reason; and it was the possession of reason, as Francis Bacon put it in *The New Organon,* "that . . . made man a god to man." Crummell's first anonymous epigraph states this relation clearly:

Language, in connection with reason, to which it gives its proper activity, use, and ornament, raises man above the lower orders of animals, and in proportion as it is polished and refined, contributes greatly . . . to exalt one nation above another, in the scale of civilization and intellectual dignity. (p. 8)

English, for Crummell, was "in proportion . . . polished and refined" in an *inverse* ratio as the African vernacular languages were tarnished and unrefined. And, while the fact that black people spoke English as a first language was "indicative of sorrowful history," a sign of "subjection and conquest," it was also "one of those ordinances of Providence, designed as a means for the introduction of new ideas into the language of a people; or to serve as a transitional step from low degradation to a higher and nobler civilization" (p. 18).

English, for Crummell, was "the speech of Chaucer and Shakespeare, of Milton and Wordsworth, of Bacon and Burke, of Franklin and Webster," and its potential mastery was "this one item of compensation" which "the Almighty has bestowed upon us" in exchange for "the exile of our fathers from their African homes in America" (p. 10). English was "a transforming agency, which is gradually subverting the native languages of our tribes," he maintains with great approval, as the imperialistic forces of Great Britain "introduce trade and civilization, pioneer letters and culture, and prepare the way for the *English Language* and Religion" (pp. 34, 32; Crummell's emphasis). It is "this noble language," he concludes on an unmistakable air of triumph, which is "gradually lifting up and enlightening our heathen neighbors" (p. 32). In the English language are embodied "the noblest theories of liberty" and "the grandest ideas of humanity" (p. 51). By the slave mastering the master's tongue, these great and grand ideas will become African ideas, because "ideas conserve men, and keep alive the vitality of nations. . . . With the noble tongue which Providence has given us, it will be difficult for us to be divorced from the spirit, which for centuries has been speaking through it" (p. 52). "And this," Crummell proclaims, "is our language," and it is "upon the many treasures of this English tongue" that he has "dwell[ed] with delight" (p. 29).

In direct and dark contrast to the splendor and wonders of the English language, Crummell pits the African vernacular languages. "The refined and cultivated English language" is "alien alike from the speech of [our] sires and the soil from whence they sprung" (p. 11). "Let us," he continues, inquire "into the respective values of our native and acquired tongue. . . . The worth of our fathers' language, will, in this way, stand out in distinct comparison with the Anglo-Saxon, our acquired speech" (p. 19). Black vernacular languages, for Crummell, embody "definite marks of inferiority connected with them all, which place them at the widest distances from civilized languages." Crummell then lists these shared "marks of inferiority" of the black vernacular:

Of this whole class of languages, it may be said, in the aggregate that (a) "They are," to use the words of Dr. Leighton Wilson, "harsh, abrupt, energetic, indistinct in enunciation, meager in point of words, abound with inarticulate nasal and guttural sounds, possess but few inflections and grammatical forms, and are withal exceedingly difficult of acquisition." This is his description of the Grebo; but it may be taken, I think, as, on the whole, a correct description of the whole class of dialects which are entitled "Negro." (b) These languages, moreover, are characterized by lowness of ideas. As the speech of rude barbarians, they are marked by brutal and vindictive sentiments, and those principles which show a predominance of the animal propensities. (c) Again, they lack those ideas of virtue, of moral truth, and those distinctions of right and wrong with which we, all our life long, have been familiar. (d) Another marked feature of these languages is the absence of clear ideas of Justice, Law, Human Rights, and Governmental Order, which are so prominent and manifest in civilized countries. And (e) lastly—Those supernal truths of a personal, present Deity, of the moral government of God, of man's immortality, of the judgment, and of Everlasting Blessedness, which regulate the lives of Christians, are either entirely absent, or else exist, and are expressed in an obscure and distorted manner. (pp. 19–20)

So much for the black vernacular!

Any attempt even to render the master's discourse in our own black discourse in an egregious error, Crummell continues, because to do so is merely to translate sublime utterances "in broken English—a miserable caricature of their noble tongue" (p. 50). Such was the case when the English, in the West Indies, translated the Bible from the rich cadences of King James into the "crude, mongrel, discordant jargon" of the black vernacular. No, translation just won't do, because "a language without its characteristic features, stamp, and spirit, is a lifeless and unmeaning thing." The attempt to translate from English to the black vernacular is "so great a blunder." We must abandon forever both indigenous African vernacular languages as well as the neo-African vernacular languages that our people have produced in the New World:

All low, inferior, and barbarous tongues are, doubtless, but the lees and dregs of noble languages, which have gradually, as the soul of a nation has died out, sunk down to degradation and ruin. We must not suffer this decay on these shores, in this nation. We have been made, providentially, the deposit of a noble trust; and we should be proud to show our appreciation of it. Having come to the heritage of this language we must cherish its spirit, as well as retain its letter. We must cultivate it among ourselves; we must strive to infuse its spirit among our reclaimed and aspiring natives. (p. 50)

I cite the examples of John C. Calhoun and Alexander Crummell as metaphors for the relation between the critic of black literature and the broader, larger institution of literature. However, lest anyone believe that the arguments of Calhoun, Kant, Jefferson, Hume, or Hegel have been relegated to their prober places in the garbage can of history, she or he need only recall the recent works of Japanese prime minister Nakasone, when he remarked that America will *never* be the intellectual equal of Japan because the presence of Chicanos, Puerto Ricans, and blacks lowers the country's collective IQ! (to which Ronald Reagan responded, when queried, that before responding he needed to see Nakasone's remarks "in context"!).

Calhoun and Crummell are my metaphors for acts of empowerment. Learning the master's tongue, for our generation of critics, has been an act of empowerment, whether that critical language be New Criticism, so-called humanism, structuralism, Marxism, poststructuralism, feminism, new historicism, or any other "ism" that I have forgotten. Each of these critical discourses arises from a specific set of texts within the Western tradition. At least for the past decade, many of us have busied ourselves with the necessary task of learning about these movements in criticism, drawing upon their modes of reading to explicate the texts in our tradition. This has been an exciting time for critics of Afro-American literature, producing perhaps not as much energy as did, say, the Harlem Renaissance or the Black Arts movement, but certainly producing as many critical essays and books about black literature, and yes, even jobs and courses in white English departments. Even with the institutionalization of the racism inherent in "Reaganomics" and with the death of black power, there have never been more jobs available in Afro-American literature in white colleges and universities than there are today, as even a cursory glance at the MLA job list will attest. (Last year alone, thirty-seven such positions were advertised.) In a few years, we shall at last have our very own Norton anthology, a sure sign that the teaching of Afro-American literature already has been institutionalized and will continue to be so, as only the existence of a well-marketed, affordable anthology can ensure. Our pressing question now becomes this: in what languages shall we choose to speak, and write, our own criticisms? What are we now to do with the enabling masks of empowerment which we have donned as we have practiced one mode of white criticism or another?

In the December 9, 1986, issue of the *Voice Literary Supplement,* in an essay entitled "Cult-Nats Meet Freaky-Deke,"[4] Greg Tate argues cogently and compellingly that

black aestheticians need to develop a coherent criticism to communicate the complexities of our culture. There's no periodical on black cultural phenomena equivalent to *The Village Voice* or *Artforum,* no publication that provides journalism on black visual art, philosophy, economics, media, literature, linguistics, psychology, sexuality, spirituality, and pop culture. Though there are certainly black editors, journalists, and academics capable of producing such a journal, the disintegration of the black cultural nationalist movement and the brain-drain of black intellectuals to white institutions have destroyed the vociferous public dialogue that used to exist between them. (p. 5)

While I would argue that *Sage, Calaloo,* and *BALF* are indeed fulfilling that function for academic critics, I am afraid that the truth of Tate's claim is irresistible. But Tate's real and very important contribution to the future of black criticism is to be found in his most damning allegation: "What's unfortunate," he writes,

is that while black artists have opened up the entire "text of blackness" for fun and games, not many black critics have produced writing as fecund, eclectic, and freaky-deke as the art, let alone the culture, itself. . . . For those who prefer exegesis with a polemical bent, just imagine how critics as fluent in black and Western culture as the postliberated artists could strike terror into that bastion of white supremacist thinking, the Western art [and literary] worlds. (p. 5)

To which I can only say, echoing Shug in *The Color Purple,* "Amen. Amen." Only by reshaping the critical canon with our own voices in our own images can we meet Tate's challenge head-on, because the black tradition theorizes about itself in the vernacular.

Before I return to those metaphors of progress, elevation, and intel-

---

4. Greg Tate, "Cult-Nats Meet Freaky Deke," *Voice Literary Supplement,* December 9, 1986. All subsequent references will be given parenthetically in the text.

lectual equality with which I began, John C. Calhoun and Alexander Crummell, let us consider another example of the black artist at the peculiar liminal crossroads where the black world of letters meets the white. If mastering the forms of Western poetry to refute the racist logocentrism epitomized by John C. Calhoun motivated Phillis Wheatley to break forever the silence of the black voice in the court of Western letters, and motivated Crummell to sail to Cambridge to master Greek syntax, how did Wole Soyinka respond to becoming the first black recipient of the Nobel Prize in literature, that sacred icon of Western intellectual and artistic attainment which many of us thought would be withheld from us for still another century, and which many of us take to be another nuclear warhead dropped upon the last bastion of white racism—that is, their theories of our intellectual inferiority? Soyinka, born in Abeokuta, Nigeria, which Crummell had predicted to be one of the places in West Africa at which the English language would reach perfection as spoken by black people (p. 36), responded not as Crummell did to the racism which led him to Cambridge, by extolling the virtues of the English language over the African vernacular languages, which Crummell thought to reflect the animal propensities of an inferior, barely human intellect, but by recalling the irony that this single event in the history of black literature occurred while Nelson Mandela was languishing in prison and while Western capitalism was guaranteeing the survival and indeed the growth of the prison-house of apartheid. Dedicating his laureate speech to Nelson Mandela, Soyinka proceeded to attack the existence of apartheid and the complicity of the West in its continuation, as a nervous Swedish Academy shifted its weight uneasily.

Soyinka was most concerned to analyze the implications of African artistry and intellect being acknowledged before the white world, at long last, through this curious ritual called the Nobel Prize, endowed by the West's King of Dynamite and weaponry. Soyinka refused to address his black audience; rather, he addressed his white auditors and indeed the racist intellectual tradition of Europe as exemplified by Hegel, Hume, Locke, Voltaire, Frobenius, Kant, and others, who "were unabashed theorists of racial superiority and denigrators of the African history and being" (p. 10).[5]

---

5. Wole Soyinka, "This Past Must Address This Present," Nobel Laureate Address, December 8, 1986. All citations are taken from the manuscript, and will be given parenthetically in the text.

The blacks of course are locked into an unambiguous condition: on this occasion I do not need to address *us*. We know, and we embrace our mission. It is the *other* that this precedent seizes the opportunity to address, and not merely those who live outside, on the fringes of conscience. . . .

Some atavistic bug is at work here which defies all scientific explanation, an arrest in time within the evolutionary mandate of nature, which puts all human experience of learning to serious question! We have to ask ourselves then, what event can speak to such a breed of people? How do we reactivate that petrified cell which houses historic apprehension and development? Is it possible perhaps that events, gatherings such as this might help? Dare we skirt the edge of hubris and say to them: Take a good look. Provide your response. In your anxiety to prove that this moment is not possible, you have killed, maimed, silenced, tortured, exiled, debased and dehumanized hundreds of thousands encased in this very skin, crowned with such hair, proudly content with their very being. (pp. 8–9)

Soyinka's brilliant rhetorical gesture was to bring together an uncompromising renunciation of apartheid and a considered indictment of the racist tradition in Western letters which equates the possession of reason with the reflection of the voice and the face of the master, a tradition which overwhelmed Alexander Crummell, standing as he did at a point of liminality between Western culture and African culture. Citing the work of Locke, Hume, Hegel, Montesquieu, and a host of others as "dangerous for your racial self-esteem!" (p. 19), Soyinka marshalled a most impressive array of citations to chart the racist tradition in Western letters which would deny to the black world the particularity of its discourse, as typified for Soyinka by the following sentiment of the expressionist Johannes Becher: "Negro tribes, fever, tuberculosis, venereal epidemics, intellectual psychic defects—I'll vanquish them" (p. 16). To underscore the failure of the Western intellectual to escape his or her own myopic racism in even the most sublime encounters with the Black Other, Soyinka compares Becher's exhortation with the commentary of Leo Frobenius upon encountering the most sacred, and most brilliantly rendered, bronze of the Yoruba people:

And was it by coincidence that contemporaneously with this stirring manifesto, yet another German enthusiast, Leo Frobenius—with no claims whatever to being part of, or indeed having the least interest in the Expressionist movement, was able to visit Ile-Ife, the heartland and cradle of the Yoruba race and be profoundly stirred by an object of beauty, the product of the Yoruba mind and hand, a classic expression of that serene portion of the world resolution of that race. In his own words: "Before us stood a head of marvelous beauty, wonderfully cast in antique bronze, true to the life, encrusted with a patina of glorious dark green. This was, in very deed, the Olokun, Atlantic Africa's Poseidon." Yet listen to what he had to write about the very people whose handiwork had lifted him into these realms of universal sublimity: "Profoundly stirred, I stood for many minutes before the remnant of the erstwhile Lord and Ruler of the Empire of Atlantis. My companions were no less astounded. As though we had agreed to do so, we held our peace. Then I looked around and saw—the blacks—the circle of the sons of the 'venerable priest,' his Holiness the Oni's friends, and his intelligent officials. I was moved to silent melancholy at the thought that this assembly of degenerate and feeble-minded posterity should be the legitimate guardians of so much loveliness." A direct invitation to a free-for-all race for dispossession, justified on the grounds of the keeper's unworthiness, it recalls other schizophrenic conditions which are mother to, for instance, the far more lethal, dark mythopoeia of [the Nazis]. (pp. 16–17)

"He is breaking an open door," one member of the Swedish Academy said to me while Soyinka spoke. "Why would he choose to indict apartheid at an historic moment such as this?" Soyinka choose to do so to remind the world that no black person can be truly free until we are freed from even the *probability* of racial oppression, and that even Nobel Prizes in literature are useful only when its first black recipient reminds the world of that fact, and of the history of the use of race and reason as tropes of oppression in Western letters. As critics and Artists, Soyinka argues, we must utilize the creative and critical tools at hand to stomp racism out. This is our first great task.

But what else contributes to the relation, then, between (white) power and the (black) critic? Soyinka's terms, and my title, might suggest that ours is the fate of perpetual negation, that we are doomed merely to "oppose," to serve within the academy as black signs of opposition to a political order in which we are the subjugated. We must oppose, of course, when opposition is called for. But our task is much more complex. Again, to define this task, I can do no better than to cite Soyinka: "And when we borrow an alien language to sculpt or paint in, we must begin by co-opting the entire properties of that language as correspondences to properties in our matrix of thought and expression."[6] And this, it seems to me, is the challenge of black canon-formation at the present time. Soyinka's own brilliant achievement in the drama is to have done just this, to have redefined the very concept of "tragedy" by producing a synthesis of African and European tragic forms. At all points, his "English" is Yoruba-informed, Yoruba-based. To assume that we can wear the masks, and speak the languages, of Western literary theory without accepting Soyinka's challenge is to ac-

6. Cited in "Nigeria: The New Culture," *New York Post*, February 17, 1987, Supplement, p. 1.

cept, willingly, the intellectual equivalent of neocolonialism, placing ourselves in a relationship of discursive indenture.

It is the challenge of the black tradition to critique this relation of indenture, an indenture that obtains for our writers and for our critics. We must master, as even Jacques Derrida understands, how "to speak the other's language without renouncing [our] own."[7] When we attempt to appropriate, by inversion, "race" as a term for an essence—as did the negritude movement ("We feel, therefore we are," as Leopold Senghor argued of the African)—we yield too much: in this case, *reason* as the basis of a shared humanity. Such gestures, as Anthony Appiah observes, are futile and dangerous because of their further inscription of new and bizarre stereotypes. How do we meet Soyinka's challenge in the discourse of criticism?

The Western critical tradition has a canon, as the Western literary tradition does. I once thought it our most important gesture to *master* the canon of criticism, to *imitate* and *apply* it, but I now believe that we must turn to the black tradition itself to develop theories of criticism indigenous to our literatures. Alice Walker's revision of Rebecca Cox Jackson's parable of white interpretation (written in 1836) makes this point most tellingly. Jackson, a Shaker eldress and black visionary, claimed like John Jea to have been taught to read by the Lord. She writes in her autobiography that she dreamed a white man came to her house to teach her how to *interpret* and understand the word of God, now that God had taught her to read:

A white man took me by my right hand and led me on the north side of the room, where sat a square table. On it lay a book open. And he said to me. "Thou shall be instructed in this book, from Genesis to Revelations." And then he took me on the west side, where stood a table. And it looked like the first. And said, "Yea, thou shall be instructed from the beginning of creation to the end of time." And then he took me on the east side of the room also, where stood a table and book like the two first, and said, "I will instruct thee—yea, thou shall be instructed from the beginning of all things to the end of all things. Yea, thou shall be well instructed. I will instruct."

And then I awoke, and I saw him as plain as I did in my dream. And after that he taught me daily. And when I would be reading and come to a hard word, I would see him standing by my side and he would teach me the word right. And often, when I would be in meditation and looking into things which was hard to understand, I would find him by me, teaching and giving me understanding. And

7. Jacques Derrida, "The Last Word in Racism," in *"Race," Writing, and Difference*, ed. H. L. Gates, Jr. (Chicago: University of Chicago Press, 1986), p. 333.

oh, his labor and care which he had with me often caused me to weep bitterly, when I would see my great ignorance and the great trouble he had to make me understand eternal things. For I was so buried in the depth of the tradition of my forefathers, that it did seem as if I never could be dug up.[8]

In response to Jackson's relation of interpretive indenture to "a white man," Walker, in *The Color Purple*, records an exchange between Celie and Shug about turning away from "the old white man" which soon turns into a conversation about the elimination of "man" as a mediator between a woman and "everything":

Still, it is like Shug say, you have to git man off your eyeball, before you can see anything a'tall.

Man corrupt everything, say Shug. He on your box of grits, in your head, and all over the radio. He try to make you think he everywhere. Soon as you think he everywhere, you think he God. But he ain't. Whenever you trying to pray, and man plop himself on the other end of it, tell him to git lost, say Shug.[9]

Celie and Shug's omnipresent "man," of course, echoes the black tradition's synechdoche for the white power structure, "the man."

For non-Western, so-called noncanonical critics, getting the "man off your eyeball" means using the most sophisticated critical theories and methods available to reappropriate and redefine our own "colonial" discourses. We must use these theories and methods insofar as they are relevant to the study of our own literatures. The danger in doing so, however, is best put by Anthony Appiah in his definition of what he calls "the Naipaul fallacy":

It is not necessary to show that African literature is fundamentally the same as European literature in order to show that it can be treated with the same tools; . . . nor should we endorse a more sinister line . . . : the post-colonial legacy which requires us to show that African literature is worthy of study precisely (but only) because it is fundamentally the same as European literature.[10]

---

8. Rebecca Cox Jackson, "A Dream of Three Books and a Holy One," *Gifts of Power: The Writings of Rebecca Cox Jackson, Black Visionary, Shaker Eldress*, ed. Jean McMahon Humez (Amherst: University of Massachusetts Press), pp. 146–47.

9. Alice Walker, *The Color Purple* (New York: Harcourt Brace Jovanovich, 1982), p. 179.

10. Anthony Appiah, "Strictures on Structures: The Prospects for a Structuralist Poetics of African Fiction," in *Black Literature and Literary Theory*, ed. H. L. Gates, Jr. (New York: Methuen, 1984), pp. 146, 145. All subsequent references to this work, abbreviated as "S," will be included in the text.

We *must* not, Appiah concludes, ask "the reader to understand Africa by embedding it in European culture" (S, p. 146).

We must, I believe, analyze the ways in which writing relates to race, how attitudes toward racial differences generate and structure literary texts by us *and* about us. We must determine how critical methods can effectively disclose the traces of ethnic differences in literature.

But we must also understand how certain forms of difference and the *languages* we employ to define those supposed differences not only reinforce each other but tend to create and maintain each other. Similarly, and as important, we must analyze the language of contemporary criticism itself, recognizing especially that hermeneutic systems are not universal, color-blind, apolitical, or neutral. Whereas some critics wonder aloud, as Appiah notes, whether or not "a structuralist poetics is inapplicable in Africa because structuralism is European" (S, p. 145), the concern of the Third World critic should properly be to understand the ideological subtext which any critical theory reflects and embodies, and the relation which this subtext bears to the production of meaning. No critical theory—be it Marxist, feminist, post-structuralist, Kwame Nkrumah's "consciencism," or whatever—escapes the specificity of value and ideology, no matter how mediated these may be. To attempt to appropriate our own discourses by using Western critical theory uncritically is to substitute one mode of neocolonialism for another. To begin to do this in our own tradition, theorists have turned to the black vernacular tradition—to paraphrase Jackson, they have begun to dig into the depths of the tradition of our foreparents—to isolate the signifying black difference through which to theorize about the so-called discourse of the Other.

Even Crummell recognized that Western economic and political subjugation has inflicted upon us a desire to imitate, to please, to refashion our public discursive images of our black selves after that of the colonizer: "he will part," Crummell with great satisfaction concludes of the colonized African, "at any moment, with the crude uncouth utterances of his native tongue, for that other higher language, which brings with its utterance, wealth and gratification" (pp. 34–35).

This, it seems to me, is the trap, the tragic lure, to which those who believe that critical theory is a color-blind, universal discourse, or a culturally neutral tool like a hammer or a screwdriver, have unwittingly succumbed. And by succumbing to this mistake, such critics fail to accept the wonderful opportunity offered to our generation of critics as heirs to the Black Arts movement, the great achievement of which, as Greg Tate correctly concludes, was to define a "black cultural *difference*" and "pro-

duce a post-liberated black aesthetic [which is] responsible for the degree
to which contemporary black artists and intellectuals feel themselves
heirs to a culture every bit as def [sic] as classical Western civilization.
This cultural confidence," he concludes, "has freed up more black artists
to do work as wonderfully absurdist as black life itself" (p. 5).

As Tate concludes, where is the black critical theory as great as this
greatest black art? Our criticism is destined merely to be derivative, to be
a pale shadow of the white master's critical discourse, until we become
confident enough to speak in our own black languages as we theorize
about the black critical endeavor.

We must redefine "theory" itself from within our own black cultures,
refusing to grant the racist premise that theory is something that white
people do, so that we are doomed to imitate our white colleagues, like
reverse black minstrel critics done up in whiteface. We are all heirs to
critical theory, but we black critics are heirs as well to the black vernacular
tradition. Our task now is to invent and employ our own critical theory,
to assume our own propositions, and to stand within the academy as
politically responsible and responsive parts of a social and cultural African-American whole. Again, Soyinka's words about our relation to the
black tradition are relevant here:

> That world which is so conveniently traduced by Apartheid thought is of
> course that which I so wholeheartedly embrace—and this is my choice—among
> several options—of the significance of my presence here. It is a world that nour-
> ishes my being, one which is so self-sufficient, so replete in all aspects of its
> productivity, so confident in itself and in its destiny that it experiences no fear in
> reaching out to others and in responding to the reach of others. It is the heart-
> stone of our creative existence. It constitutes the prism of our world perception
> and this means that our sign need not be and has never been permanently turned
> inwards. If it were, we could not so easily understand the enemy on our doorstep,
> nor understand how to obtain the means to disarm it. When this society which is
> Apartheid South Africa indulges from time to time in appeals to the outside
> world that it represents the last bastion of civilization against the hordes of
> barbarism from its North, we can even afford an indulgent smile. It is sufficient,
> imagines this state, to raise the spectre of a few renegade African leaders, psycho-
> paths and robber barons whom we ourselves are victims of—whom we
> denounce before the world and overthrow when we are able—this Apartheid
> society insists to the world that its picture of the future is the reality that only its
> policies can erase. This is a continent which only destroys, it proclaims, it is
> peopled by a race which has never contributed anything positive to the world's
> pool of knowledge. A vacuum, that will suck into its insatiable jaw the entire
> fruits of centuries of European civilization, then spew out the resulting mush
> with contempt. How strange that a society which claims to represent this

endangered face of progress should itself be locked in centuries-old fantasies, blithely unaware of, or indifferent to the fact that it is the last, institutionally functioning product of archaic articles of faith in Euro-Judaic thought. (pp. 11–12)

As deconstruction and other post-structuralisms, or even an aracial Marxism and other "articles of faith in Euro-Judaic thought," exhaust themselves in a self-willed racial never-never land in which we see no true reflections of our black faces and hear no echoes of our black voices, let us—at long last—master the canon of critical traditions and languages of Africa and Afro-America. Even as we continue to reach out to others in the critical canon, let us be confident in our own black traditions and in their compelling strength to sustain systems of critical thought that are as yet dormant and unexplicated. We must, in the truest sense, turn inward even as we turn outward to redefine every institution in this profession— the English Institute, the MLA, the School of Criticism—in our own images. We must not succumb, as did Alexander Crummell, to the tragic lure of white power, the mistake of accepting the empowering language of white critical theory as "universal" or as our own language, the mistake of confusing the enabling mask of theory with our own black faces. Each of us has, in some literal or figurative manner, boarded a ship and sailed to a metaphorical Cambridge, seeking to master the master's tools, and to outwit this racist master by compensating for a supposed lack. In my own instance, being quite literal-minded, I booked passage some fourteen years ago on the *QE II!* And much of my early work reflects my desire to outwit the master by trying to speak his language as fluently as he. Now, we must, at last, don the empowering mask of blackness and talk *that* talk, the language of black difference. While it is true that we must, as Du Bois said so long ago, "know and test the power of the cabalistic letters of the white man," we must also know and test the dark secrets of a black and hermetic discursive universe that awaits its disclosure through the black arts of interpretation. For the future of theory and of the literary enterprise in general, in the remainder of this century, is black, indeed.

II

How does this matter of the black canon of criticism affect our attempts to define canon(s) of black literature? I believe, first of all, that until we free ourselves of the notion that we are "just Americans," as Ellison might put it, and that what is good and proper for Americanists is good and proper for Afro-Americanists, we shall remain indentured servants to white masters, female and male, and to the Western tradition, yielding the most fundamental right that any tradition possesses, and that is the right to define itself, its own terms for order, its very own presuppositions. If we recall the etymology of the word "theory" from the Greek *theoria*, we can understand why the production of black text-specific theory is essential to our attempts to form black canons: theoria, as Wlad Godzich points out in his introduction to Paul de Man's *The Resistance to Theory*, "is a public, institutional act of certification which assumes the authority to 'effect the passage from the seen to the told'; and provides the basis for public discourse. Theory, then, is—like rhetoric—a form of cognition modeled upon (public) utterance rather than upon (private) perception."[11] When we mindlessly borrow another tradition's theory, we undermine this passage from the seen to the told—from what we see to how we tell it—this basis for our own black public discourse, this relation between cognition and utterance.

Lord knows that this relationship between the seen and the told— that gap of difference between what we see among and for ourselves and what we choose to tell in (a white, or integrated) public discourse—has been remarkably complex in our tradition, especially in attempts to define the canon of black literature at any given time.

Curiously enough, the very first evidence of the idea of the "canon" in relation to the Afro-American literary tradition occurs in 1849, in a speech delivered by Theodore Parker. Parker was a theologian, a Unitarian clergyman, and a publicist for ideas; Perry Miller described him as "the man who next only to Emerson . . . was to give shape and meaning to the Transcendental movement in America." In a speech on "The Mercantile Classes" delivered in 1846, Parker had lamented the sad state of "American" letters:

Literature, science, and art are mainly in [poor men's] hands, yet are controlled by the prevalent spirit of the nation. . . . In England, the national literature favors the church, the crown, the nobility, the prevailing class. Another literature is rising, but is not yet national, *still less canonized*. We have no American literature which is permanent. Our scholarly books are only an imitation of a foreign type; they do not reflect our morals, manners, politics, or religion, not even our rivers, mountains, sky. They have not the smell of our ground in their breath.[12]

11. Wlad Godzich, "Foreword," in Paul de Man, *The Resistance to Theory* (Minneapolis: University of Minnesota Press, 1986), pp. xiv–xv, cited in Barbara Jones Guetti, "Resisting the Aesthetic," forthcoming in *Diacritics*.

12. Theodore Parker, *Social Classes in a Republic*, ed. Samuel A. Eliot (Boston: American Unitarian Association, 1907), p. 32. Emphasis added.

Parker, to say the least, was not especially pleased with American letters and their identity with the English tradition. Did he find any evidence of a truly American discourse?

The real American literature is found only in newspapers and speeches, perhaps in some novel, hot, passionate, but poor and extemporaneous. That is our national literature. Does that favor man—represent man? Certainly not. All is the reflection of this most powerful class. The truths that are told are for them, and the lies. Therein the prevailing sentiment is getting into the form of thoughts.

Parker's analysis, of course, is "proto-Marxian," embodying as it does the reflection-theory of base and superstructure. It is the occasional literature, "poor and extemporaneous," wherein "American" literature dwells.

Three years later, in his major oration on "The American Scholar," Parker at last found an entirely original genre of American literature:

Yet, there is one portion of our permanent literature, if literature it may be called, which is wholly indigenous and original. The lives of the early martyrs and confessors are purely Christian, so are the legends of saints and other pious men; there was nothing like this in the Hebrew or heathen literature, cause and occasion were alike wanting for it. So we have one series of literary productions that could be written by none but Americans, and only here; I mean the Lives of Fugitive Slaves. But as these are not the work of the men of superior culture they hardly help to pay the scholar's debt. Yet all the original romance of Americans is in them, not in the white man's novel.[13]

Parker was right about the originality, the peculiarly *American* quality, of the slave narratives. But he was wrong about their inherent inability to "pay the scholar's debt"; scholars had only to learn to *read* the narratives for their debt to be paid in full, indeed many times over. As Charles Sumner said in 1852, the fugitive slaves and their narratives "are among the heroes of our age. Romance has no storms of more thrilling interest than theirs. Classical antiquity has preserved no examples of adventurous trial more worthy of renown."[14] Parker's and Sumner's views reveal that the popularity of the narratives in antebellum America most certainly did not reflect any sort of common critical agreement about their nature and status as art. Still, the implications of these observations for black canon-

13. Theodore Parker, *The American Scholar*, ed. George Willis Cooke (Boston: American Unitarian Association, 1907), p. 37.
14. Charles Sumner, cited in *The Slave's Narrative*, ed. Charles T. Davis and H. L. Gates, Jr. (New York: Oxford University Press, 1985), p. xv.

formation would take three-quarters of a century to be realized. The first attempt to define a black canon that I have found is that by Armand Lanusse, who edited *Les Cenelles,* an anthology of black French verse published at New Orleans in 1845—the first black anthology, I believe, ever published. Lanusse's "Introduction" is a defense of poetry as an enterprise for black people, in their larger efforts to defend the race against "the spiteful and calumnious arrows shot at us," at a target defined as the collective black intellect (p. xxxviii).[15] Despite this stated political intention, these poems imitate the styles and themes of the French Romantics and never engage directly the social and political experience of black Creoles in New Orleans in the 1840s. *Les Cenelles* argues for a political effect—that is, the end of racism—by publishing apolitical poems, poems which share as their silent second texts the poetry written by Frenchmen three thousand miles away. We are like the French—so, treat us like Frenchmen. An apolitical art was being put to uses most political.

Four years later, in 1849, William G. Allen published an anthology in which he canonized Phillis Wheatley and George Moses Horton. Like Lanusse, Allen sought to refute intellectual racism by the act of canon-formation. "The African's called inferior," he writes. "But what race has ever displayed intellect more exaltedly, or character more sublime?" (p. 3). Pointing to the achievements of Pushkin, Placido, and Augustine, as the great African tradition to which Afro-Americans are heir, Allen claims Wheatley and Horton as the exemplars of this tradition, Horton being "decidedly the superior genius," no doubt because of his explicitly racial themes, a judgment quite unlike that which propelled Armand Lanusse into canon-formation. As Allen puts it:

> Who will now say that the African is incapable of attaining to intellectual or moral greatness? What he now is, degrading circumstances have made him. Past clearly evinces. The African is strong, tough and hardy. Hundreds of years of oppression have not subdued his spirit, and though Church and State have combined to enslave and degrade him, in spite of them all, he is increasing in strength and power, and in the respect of the entire world. (p. 7)

Here, then, we see the two poles of black canon-formation, established firmly by 1849: is "black" poetry racial in theme, or is black poetry any sort of poetry written by black people? This quandary has been at play in the tradition ever since.

15. Armand Lanusse, ed., *Les Cenelles: A Collection of Poems by Creole Writers of the Early Nineteenth Century,* translated and edited by Regine Latortue and Gleason R. W. Adams (1845; reprint, Boston: G. K. Hall, 1979). The original publisher was H. Lauve.

I do not have the time here to trace in detail the history of this tension over definitions of the Afro-American canon and the direct relation between the production of black poetry and the end of white racism. I want merely to point to such seminal attempts at canon-formation in the twenties as James Weldon Johnson's *The Book of American Negro Poetry* (1922), Alain Locke's *The New Negro* (1925), and V. F. Calverton's *An Anthology of American Negro Literature* (1929), each of which defined as its goal the demonstration of the existence of the black tradition as a political defense of the racial self against racism. As Johnson put it so clearly:

. . . the matter of Negro poets and the production of literature by the colored people in this country involves more than supplying information that is lacking. It is a matter which has a direct bearing on the most vital of American problems.

A people may be great through many means, but there is only one measure by which its greatness is recognized and acknowledged. The final measure of the greatness of all peoples is the amount and standard of the literature and art that they have produced. The world does not know that a people is great until that people produces great literature and art. No people that has produced great literature and art has ever been looked upon by the world as distinctly inferior.

The status of the Negro in the United States is more a question of national mental attitude toward the race than of actual conditions. And nothing will do more to change that mental attitude and raise his status than a demonstration of intellectual parity by the Negro through the production of literature and art.[16]

Calverton's anthology made two significant departures from this model, both of which are worth considering, if only briefly. Calverton's was the first attempt at black canon-formation to provide for the influence and presence of black vernacular literature in a major way. "Spirituals," "Blues," and "Labor Songs" each comprise a genre of black literature for him. We all understand the importance of this gesture and its influence upon the editors of *The Negro Caravan*. Calverton, as well, announces in his introductory essay, "The Growth of Negro Literature," that his selection principles have been determined by his sense of the history of black literary forms, leading him to make selections because of their formal "representative value," as he puts it. "Certain nineteenth-century poems, for instance," he explains, "which have been included are pathetically naive and sentimental; yet in the development of Negro literature they undoubtedly have their place, and therefore, have been used . . . to represent what the Negro in America has

---

16. James Weldon Johnson, ed. *The Book of American Negro Poetry, Chosen and Edited with an Essay on the Negro's Creative Genius* (New York: Harcourt, Brace, 1922), p. vii.

achieved in the art of literary forms." These forms, he continues, are *black* forms, virtually self-contained in a hermetic black tradition, especially in the vernacular tradition. It is worth repeating Calverton's conclusions at length:

The Negro, in the eyes of the critics, is an oddity, and as an artist and intellectual is stranger far than fiction. Their explanation of his recent success is based mainly upon what they consider an aspect of patronage on the part of the reading public and the publisher. His work is greeted from the point of view of race and not of art. He is pampered as a Negro, and his work is praised often when it ought to be attacked. As a consequence, they are convinced that in a few years, as this illusion in reference to his work has begun to vanish, the interest in Negro literature will cease, and the urge in favor of its creation will correspondingly disappear.

Upon close analysis, these interpretations are seen to be at once irrelevant and futile. . . . his contributions to American art and literature are far more free of white influence than American culture is of English. Indeed, we may say that the contributions of the Negro to American culture are as indigenous to our soil as the legendary cowboy or gold-seeking frontiersman. And, in addition, it is no exaggeration whatsoever to contend that they are more striking and singular in substance and structure than any contributions that have been made by the white man to American culture. In fact, they constitute America's chief claim to originality in its cultural history. In song, the Negro spirituals and to a less extent the Blues; in tradition, Negro folk-lore; and in music, Negro jazz—these three constitute the Negro contribution to American culture. In fact, it can be said, that they constitute all that is unique in our cultural life. . . . After all, the Negro, in his simple, unsophisticated way, has developed out of the American *milieu* a form of expression, a mood, a literary genre, a folk tradition, that are distinctly and undeniably American. This is more than the white man has done. The white man in America has continued, and in an inferior manner, a culture of European origin. He has not developed a culture that is definitely and unequivocally American. In respect of originality, then, the Negro is more important in the growth of American culture than the white man. His art is richer, more spontaneous, and more captivating and convincing in its appeal.

The social background of Negro life in itself was sufficient to inspire an art of no ordinary character. Indeed, the very fact that the Negro, by the nature of his environment, was deprived of education, prevented his art from ever becoming purely imitative. Even where he adopted the white man's substance, as in the case of religion, he never adopted his forms. He gave to whatever he took a new style and a new interpretation. In truth, he made it practically into a new thing. There were no ancient conventions that he, in his untutored zeal, felt duty-bound to respect, and no age-old traditions that instructed him, perforce, as to what was art and what was not. He could express his soul, as it were, without concern for grammar or the eye of the carping critic. As a result, his art is, as is all art that springs from the people, an artless art, and in that sense is the most genuine art of the world. While the white man has gone to Europe for his models, and is seeking still a European approval of his artistic endeavors, the Negro in his art forms has never gone beyond America for his background and has never sought the acclaim of any culture other than his own. This is particularly true of those forms of Negro art that come directly from the people. It is, of course, not so true of a poet such as Phillis Wheatley or of the numerous Negro poets and artists of to-day, who in more ways than one have followed the traditions of their white contemporaries rather than extended and perfected the original art forms of their race. Of course, in the eighteenth century, when Phillis Wheatley wrote, these Negro art forms were scarcely more than embryonic. Today, on the other hand, their existence has become a commonplace to the white writer as well as the black.[17]

Return, or turn, to the black vernacular, Calverton argues, to unearth the veiled structures of black difference.

If Calverton's stress upon the black vernacular heavily influenced the shaping of *The Negro Caravan*—certainly one of the most important anthologies in the tradition—his sense of the black canon as a formal, self-contained entity most certainly did not. As the editors put it in the Introduction to the volume:

> The editors therefore do not believe that the expression "Negro literature" is an accurate one, and in spite of its convenient brevity, they have avoided using it. "Negro literature" has no application if it means structural peculiarity, or a Negro school of writing. The Negro writes in the forms evolved in English and American literature. "A Negro novel," "a Negro play" are ambiguous terms. If they mean a novel or a play by Negroes, then such works as *Porgy* and *The Green Pastures* are left out. If they mean works about Negro life, they include more works by white authors than by Negro, and these works have been most influential upon the American mind. The editors consider Negro writers to be American writers, and literature by American Negroes to be a segment of American literature. They believe that it would be just as misleading to classify Clifford Odet's plays about Jewish life as "Jewish literature" or James T. Farrell's novels of the Chicago Irish as "Irish literature" or some of William Saroyan's tales as "Armenian literature."
>
> The chief cause for objection to the term is that "Negro literature" is too easily placed by certain critics, white and Negro, in an alcove apart. The next step is a double standard of judgment, which is dangerous for the future of Negro writers. "A Negro novel," thought of as a separate form, is too often condoned as "good enough for a Negro." That Negroes in America have had a hard time, and that inside stores of Negro life often present unusual and attractive reading matter are incontrovertible facts; but when they enter literary criticism these facts do damage to both the critics and the artists. The editors do not hold that this anthology maintains an even level of literary excellence. A number of the selec-

17. V. F. Calverton, "The Growth of Negro Literature," in *An Anthology of American Negro Literature,* ed. V. F. Calverton (New York: The Modern Library, 1929), pp. 3–5.

tions have been included as essential to a balanced picture. Literature by Negro authors about Negro experience is a literature in process and like all such literature (including American literature) must be considered as significant, not only because of a body of established masterpieces, but also because of the illumination it sheds upon a social reality. (p. 7)

And, later, in the Introduction to the section entitled "The Novel," the editors elaborate upon this idea by pointing to the relation of revision between *Iola Leroy* and *Clotel,* a relation of the sort central to Calverton's canon, but here defined in most disapproving terms: "There are repetitions of situations from Brown's *Clotel,* something of a forecast of a sort of literary inbreeding which causes Negro writers to be influenced by other Negroes more than should ordinarily be expected" (p. 139). The black canon, for these editors, was that literature which most eloquently refuted white racist stereotypes (p. 5) and which embodied the shared "theme of struggle that is present in so much Negro expression" (p. 6). Theirs, in other words, was a canon that was unified thematically by self-defense against racist literary conventions, and by the expression of what the editors called "strokes of freedom" (p. 6). The formal bond that Calverton had claimed was of no political use for these editors, precisely because they wished to project an integrated canon of American literature. As the editors put it,

> In spite of such unifying bonds as a common rejection of the popular stereotypes and a common "racial" cause, writings by Negroes do not seem to the editors to fall into a unique cultural pattern. Negro writers have adopted the literary traditions that seemed useful for their purposes. They have therefore been influenced by Puritan didacticism, sentimental humanitarianism, local color, regionalism, realism, naturalism, and experimentalism. Phillis Wheatley wrote the same high moralizing verse in the same poetic pattern as her contemporary poets in New England. While Frederick Douglass brought more personal knowledge and bitterness into his antislavery agitation than William Lloyd Garrison and Theodore Parker, he is much closer to them in spirit and in form than to Phillis Wheatley, his predecessor, and Booker T. Washington, his successor. Frances E. W. Harper wrote antislavery poetry in the spirit and pattern of Longfellow and Felicia Hemans; her contemporary, Whitfield, wrote of freedom in the pattern of Byron. And so it goes. Without too great imitativeness, many contemporary Negro writers are closer to O. Henry, Carl Sandburg, Edgar Lee Masters, Edna St. Vincent Millay, Waldo Frank, Ernest Hemingway and John Steinbeck than to each other. The bonds of literary tradition seem to be stronger than race. (pp. 6–7)

So much for a definition of the Afro-American tradition based on formal relationships of revision, text to text.

At the opposite extreme in black canon-formation is the canon defined by Amiri Baraka and Larry Neal in *Black Fire,* published in 1968. This canon, the blackest canon of all, was defined by both formal innovations and by themes: formally, individual selections tended to aspire to the vernacular or to black music, or to performance; theoretically, each selection reinforces the urge toward black liberation, toward "freedom now" with an up-against-the-wall subtext. The hero, the valorized presence, in this volume is the black vernacular: no longer summoned or invoked through familiar and comfortable rubrics such as "The Spirituals" and "The Blues," but *embodied, assumed, presupposed,* in a marvelous act of formal bonding often obscured to some readers by the stridency of the political message the anthology meant to announce. Absent completely was a desire to "prove" our common humanity to white people by demonstrating our power of intellect. No, in *Black Fire,* art and act were one.

III

I have been thinking about these strains in black canon-formation because a group of us are editing still another anthology, which will constitute still another attempt at canon-formation.

W. W. Norton will be publishing the Norton Anthology of Afro-American Literature. The editing of this anthology has been a great dream of mine for a long time. I am very excited about this project. I think that I am most excited about the fact that we will have at our disposal the means to edit an anthology which will define a canon of Afro-American literature for instructors and students at any institution which desires to teach a course in Afro-American literature. Once our anthology is published, no one will ever again be able to use the unavailability of black texts as an excuse not to teach our literature. A well-marketed anthology—particularly a Norton anthology—functions in the academy to *create* a tradition, as well as to define and preserve it. A Norton anthology opens up a literary tradition as simply as opening the cover of a carefully edited and ample book.

I am not unaware of the politics and ironies of canon-formation. The canon that we define will be "our" canon, one possible set of selections among several possible sets of selections. In part to be as eclectic and as democratically "representative" as possible, most other editors of black anthologies have tried to include as many authors and selections (especially excerpts) as possible, in order to preserve and "resurrect" the tradition. I call this the Sears Roebuck approach, the "dream book" of black literature.

We have all benefited from this approach. Indeed, many of our authors have only managed to survive because an enterprising editor was determined to marshall as much evidence as she or he could to show that the black literary tradition existed. While we must be deeply appreciative of that approach and its results, our task will be a different one. Our task will be to bring together the "essential" texts of the canon, the "crucially central" authors, those whom we feel to be indispensable to an understanding of the shape, and shaping, of the tradition. A canon is the essence of the tradition: the connection between the texts of the canon reveals the tradition's inherent, or veiled, logic, its internal rationale.

None of us are naive enough to believe that "the canonical" is self-evident, absolute, or natural. Scholars make canons. Keenly aware of this—and quite frankly, aware of my own biases—I have attempted to bring together as period editors a group of scholar-critics, each of whom combines great expertise in her or his period with her or his own approach to the teaching and analyzing of Afro-American literature. I have attempted, in other words, to bring together scholars whose notions of the black canon might not necessarily agree with my own, or with each other. I have tried to bring together a diverse array of ideological, methodological, and theoretical perspectives, so that we together might produce an anthology which most fully represents the various definitions of what it means to speak of the Afro-American literary tradition, and what it means to *teach* that tradition.

I can say that my own biases toward canon-formation are to stress the formal relationship that obtains among texts in the black tradition—relations of revision, echo, call and response, antiphony, what have you—and to stress the vernacular roots of the tradition, contra Alexander Crummell. Accordingly, let me add that our anthology will include a major innovation in anthology production. Because of the strong oral and vernacular base of so much of our literature, we shall include a cassette tape along with our anthology. This means that each period will include both the printed and spoken text of oral and musical selections of black vernacular culture: sermons, blues, spirituals, R & B, poets reading their own "dialect" poems, speeches, and other performances. Imagine having Bessie Smith and Billie Holiday singing the blues, Langston Hughes reading "The Negro Speaks of Rivers," Sterling Brown reading "Ma Rainey," James Weldon Johnson "The Creation," C. L. Franklin "The Sermon of the Dry Bones," Martin speaking "I Have a Dream," Sonia Sanchez "Talking in Tongues"—the list of possibilities is endless, and exhilarating. So much of our literature seems dead on the page when compared to its performance. Incorporating performance and the black and human voice into our anthology, we will change fundamentally not only the way that our literature is taught but the way in which any literary tradition is even conceived.

Response: *Barbara E. Johnson*

Within the context of a conference explicitly aimed at critical agenda-setting and, hence, at canon making, Gates has attempted to outline a history of previous moments of canon-formation in the Afro-American tradition. Between Alexander Crummell and Greg Tate, between the American Negro Academy and the Swedish Academy, and between *The Negro Caravan, Black Fire,* and the Norton Anthology of Afro-American Literature, the underlying critical and political agendas have been multiple and changing. It is to point toward a new era in Afro-American criticism that Gates has assembled this series of exemplars.

The essay is organized around two fundamental issues: what the black intellectual's stance has been and should be toward white Western culture (in particular, what the black critic's stance should be toward Western literary theory); and how the Afro-American literary and critical tradition has been and should be defined. In addressing the first, Gates describes a variety of stances. For Alexander Crummell, the Western tradition is a sign of empowerment; for Amiri Baraka and Larry Neal, it is an object to be destroyed; for Wole Soyinka, it is a discourse to be deconstructed; for Gates himself, perhaps, it is a source of funds to be diverted for the construction of new Afro-American institutions. In addressing the second issue, Gates describes a series of literary anthologies, ranging from *Les Cenelles,* in which black writers imitate the styles and themes of the French Romantics, through various efforts at heterogeneous resurrection, to anthologies that attempt to define a tradition with its own formal properties and thematic concerns. The culminating item in the series is of course the forthcoming Norton anthology, edited by the indefatigable Gates himself.

At issue most emphatically throughout the paper is the question of education. Education was what was withheld from the slaves; education is the aim of an affordable anthology. But what is interesting about the "scenes of instruction" Gates has assembled is how many of them are indirect or surreptitious. Crummell *overhears* a conversation in which a story is told about Calhoun's requirement that a Negro prove his humanity by learning Greek syntax. Rebecca Cox Jackson *dreams* that a white man teaches her how to read and interpret the word of God. And even Gates himself is instructed by a comment *whispered* to him by a member of the Swedish Academy. These scenes recall the famous passage in

Frederick Douglass's *Narrative* in which Douglass overhears his master teaching his mistress about the dangers of teaching slaves to read and write. Gates follows up these scenes of indirect instruction by quoting Shug's very direct instructions to Celie to "git man off your eyeball." And indeed, the teacher figure in all these scenes, even or especially when the teaching is not intended for the ears which receive it, is a white man. The difficulty is to learn to stop seeing the teacher as a white man, and the white man as a teacher. For who will teach us this?

At this point in Gates's argument, there occurs a highly revealing non sequitur. Immediately following the quotation from Alice Walker, Gates writes: "For non-Western, so-called noncanonical critics, getting the 'man off your eyeball' means using the most sophisticated critical theories and methods available to reappropriate and redefine our own 'colonial' discourses." But this, precisely, doesn't follow.[1] Elsewhere in the essay, Gates indeed argues emphatically for a "vernacular" theory. And here, he goes on to warn against the "Naipaul fallacy" of proving the worth of African literature by showing that it is "the same" as European literature. But what is the function of this particular non sequitur?

I think it indicates what is obvious from the essay as a whole: Gates's present work is driven by an empowering desire to have it both ways, to have his Western theory and his vernacular theory too. And why should anyone *not* have it both ways? Hasn't the Western tradition succeeded precisely by using the logic of having things both ways? By forbidding slaves to get an education, for instance, and then requiring that they prove their humanity by learning Greek syntax. Or, in the following passage from Hume, by setting up a single standard of value and then calling anyone who meets it a "parrot":

I am apt to suspect the negroes, and in general all the other species of men (for there are four or five different kinds) to be naturally inferior to the whites. There never was a civilized nation of any other complexion than white, nor even any individual eminent either in action or speculation. No ingenious manufactures amongst them, no arts, no sciences. . . . Such a uniform and constant difference could not happen, in so many countries and ages, if *nature* had not made an original distinction betwixt these breeds of men. Not to mention our colonies, there are Negro slaves dispersed all over Europe, of which none ever discovered any symptoms of ingenuity. . . . In Jamaica indeed they talk of one negro as a man of parts and learning [Francis Williams, the Cambridge-educated poet who

1. Gates recently pointed out to me that, in seeing a non sequitur here, I am reading "sophisticated" as meaning "Western." A highly revealing misreading. . . .

wrote verse in Latin]; but 'tis likely he is admired for very slender accomplishments, like a parrot, who speaks a few words plainly.[2]

The logic of this passage runs like this: "My thing is the best thing. To be my equal you have to be just like me. If you are like me you are a parrot." This is a no-lose situation for the white man; a no-win situation for the black. Why has it always been the case that "to be equal" has meant "to be like"? All the paradoxes of Western mimesis, of the relation between the imitator, the imitated, and the "thing itself," undergird this conspiracy by the white speaker to have everything both ways.

What Hume (representing here—as he himself intends—Western man as such) fails to consider is the possibility that there could be other value systems, other subject positions that would call upon other activities as signs of value, and would find other names for what Hume calls the "civilized," names that would expose, perhaps, its lining of calculated rapaciousness. Why indeed would one adopt a perspective that is profoundly "dangerous to one's racial self-esteem," as Soyinka puts it? Of what use is a tradition that assigns one an inferior place?

Non sequiturs notwithstanding, Gates is eloquent in his call for an end to the Afro-American critic's indenture to Western cultural paradigms:

We must not succumb, as did Alexander Crummell, to the tragic lure of white power, the mistake of accepting the empowering language of white critical theory as "universal" or as our own language, the mistake of confusing the enabling mask of theory with our own black faces. . . . Now, we must, at last, don the empowering mask of blackness and talk *that* talk, the language of black difference.

Gates demonstrates the complexity of the task by shifting between the words "mask," "face," and "language." The *mask* of theory is contrasted with a black *face,* but then blackness itself becomes a mask, and a language. What is the relation between language and the body? Why have some languages been so successful in their oppression of some bodies? How can one find a language that neither denies the oppression of bodies nor proclaims an essentialized relation *to* bodies? How can the notion of the *mask* help us avoid both the false universalization of linguistic theory and the false essentialism of a simple continuity between bodies and languages?

2. David Hume, "Of National Characters," quoted in Gates's introduction to *"Race," Writing, and Difference* (Chicago: University of Chicago Press, 1985), p. 10 [Gates's bracketed interpolation].

The terms "black" and "white" often imply a relation of mutual exclusion. This binary model is based on two fallacies: the fallacy of positing the existence of pure, unified, and separate traditions, and the fallacy of spatialization. It is as though cultural differences were simply modeled after the spatial or geographical differences that often give rise to them, as if there could really remain such a thing as *cultural* apartheid, once cultures enter into dialogue, or conflict. The image of liminality or the crossroads reinforces the metaphor of separate realms. But spatial models are simply not adequate for cultural and linguistic phenomena. Cultures are not containable within boundaries. Rhetorical figures are not Euclidean. New logical models are needed for describing the task of finding a "vernacular" theory, models that acknowledge the ineradicable trace of Western culture within Afro-American culture (and vice versa) *without* losing the "signifying black difference." Even the word "vernacular" does not name a separate realm: it comes from the Latin "verna," which means "a slave born in his master's home." The vernacular is a difference *within*, not a realm outside. And the "master's home" could not be what it is without all it has stolen from the slave.

Any "vernacular" theory, therefore, cannot be based on a model of mutual exclusion. Black literature and theory must "co-opt" (in Soyinka's words) rather than expel or deny the white man within. Aimé Césaire calls this process "inflection." For as Gates himself implies, it is indeed a linguistic model rather than a geometric model that is more adequate to describe the "signifying black difference" that Gates intends to theorize.

In his plea for a vernacular theory of Afro-American literature, Gates uses the expression "our own" no fewer than nineteen times. In contrast to Woolf's "one's own" or Showalter's "their own," however, the phrase "our own" is an example of what Roman Jakobson calls a "shifter," an expression that takes on different meanings (referents) in different contexts, an expression that *refers to* the instance of its own enunciation. The phrase "our own" is extremely ambiguous. It includes the speaker but cannot be confined to him. Does "we" = "I and you" or "I and them"? When Gates uses the expression "our own," how do the inclusions and exclusions work? The concept of "owning" further complicates the picture.

The ambiguity of "our own" illustrates a highly significant split between the performative and the cognitive dimensions of Gates's language. The shifter indicates that the utterance is interested in proclaiming the fact of its own enunciation. But the information given about the collectivity implied is vague. Does Gates mean all black people (whatever that might mean)? All Afro-Americans? All scholars of Afro-American literature? All black men? All scholars trained in literary theory who are now interested in the black vernacular?

The pronoun "we" has historically proven to be the most empowering and shiftiest shifter of them all. It is through the "we" that discourses of false universality are created. With its cognitive indeterminacy and its performative authority, it is both problematic and unavoidable for discourses of political opposition. For this structure of the stressed subject with an indeterminate predicate may well be the structure necessary for empowerment without essentialism. At the same time, it is an empowerment always in danger of presuming too much. But, then, can there be empowerment without presumption?

To be a subject means to activate the network of discourse from *where one stands*. Discourse is not a circle with one center, but more like a mycelium with many mushrooms. To be a subject also means to take nourishment from more than one source, to construct a new synthesis, a new discursive ragout. In another essay related to the present discussion of canon formation, Gates takes a cue from Hortense Spillers' call for the African-American male to acknowledge the heritage of the *mother,* to hear the voice of the "female within." Gates recounts a Maya-Angelou-like scene in which pudgy four-year-old Skippy Gates is supposed to speak a "piece" in church. At the moment of performance, he forgets his lines, at which point he hears his mother's voice quietly reciting "Jesus was a boy like me, and like him I want to be." Never have the paradoxes of mimesis ("being like") and of the supplementary voice (where do these words come from?) been so well dramatized. With this evocation of the mother's voice (even though here the mother is not speaking "her own" words), Gates movingly reanimates the mother whose death occurred precisely at the moment he would have been on his way to deliver the present paper in the present conference. The fact that the paper to which I am here responding was actually delivered by Hortense Spillers makes the circle of voices all the more poignant.

Speaking of supplementary voices, let me conclude by saying something about the inclusion of a cassette tape with the Norton Anthology of Afro-American Literature. Trained as I am in deconstruction, I have always been suspicious of the privileging of the spoken word as a sign of presence or authenticity. But this attitude clearly cannot account for the *signifying* dimensions (precisely, the inflection) of performance. If Afro-American literature is sometimes, as Gates puts it, "dead on the page," it may be that the dimension it inhabits is not primarily visual or spatial. The West has consistently privileged the visual, as words like "enlightenment" or "revelation" imply. (The words "idea" and "theory" also, in fact, derive from the realm of sight). The New Critical aesthetic that underlies my own sense of poetry (paradox, irony, ambiguity) is also tied to the image of the mute, visible object ("the well-wrought urn"). But I recently came to understand the oral dimension of poetry in a new way. At a conference on Afro-American poetry, I heard two poems delivered orally by their authors: Michael Harper's "Brother John" and June Jordan's "A Short Note to My Very Critical and Well-Beloved Friends and Comrades." Both poems make extensive and effective use of repetition. When I later looked up the printed texts, my eye ran too quickly across the repetitions, catching only the variations, looking for cognitive dissonance. What the performance had done, I realized, was to make me wait. It was a structuring of *time,* not of space. It forced me to take the poem into my experience, not just into my mind. My time was under the poem's control. I think, therefore, that the cassette tape will do more than record the sounds of specific, irreplaceable voices. It will also offer the student—and the teacher—a resistance to the practice of skimming or over-reading, a resistance to the forms of mastery we are required to learn. It will give us all a lesson in letting the other take our time.

Response: *Donald B. Gibson*

I am gratified that Gates, while advancing the cause of the study, teaching, and writing of literature by black authors in his discussion of canon-formation, does not insist on an orthodoxy of critical perspective. The implicit point that he makes when he refers to the diverse "ideological, methodological, and theoretical perspectives" among us is that despite these differences we may move toward a common goal though our modes of transportation may be different and our routes of travel diverse. Some are indeed working very nearly, if not entirely, along the lines articulated by Gates. Others are not. But no matter what course we follow, I cannot imagine that anyone would disagree that an effort "to develop our own criticism" is an extraordinarily worthwhile project. Gates's own recent work, and work by Henderson, Stepto, and Baker (the names that come at once to mind) have gone far in suggesting the possibilities of developing our own criticism. There are many tasks to perform in this vineyard. Let each be about that business.

I believe we have gone a long way toward defining a canon of Afro-American literature, an effort which began, as Gates points out, long ago. I think we might have gone further even than Gates suggests, that a canon exists and it is quite firmly in place and has been for a long time.

When my sixth-grade teacher, Miss Locke, introduced us to black poetry in 1945, she did not have to think hard or long about what poets to bring to us. She brought Phillis Wheatley, Paul Laurence Dunbar, James Weldon Johnson, and Langston Hughes. She, though not an anthologizer or a professional litterateur, had a canon firmly fixed in her consciousness. And so does each of us possess a canon of the mind.

Gates has sought out the first signs of canon making, and had he chosen, he might have pointed to two other anthologies which have had a great impact on the canon, two books published between *The Negro Caravan* in 1940 and *Black Fire* in 1968: *The Poetry of the Negro, 1746–1949,* in 1949, edited by Langston Hughes and Arna Bontemps, and *The Book of Negro Folklore,* in 1959, also edited by Hughes and Bontemps. I seriously doubt that the formation of a criticism of our own will have very much effect on the basic canon, unless we are thinking in very long-range terms. Though Charles Chesnutt's ideas about what literature is and does are quite distant from Gates's I hardly think it possible to conceive of a black literary past without him. Gates's comments on the relation of theory to canon formation are well taken: canons are formed as the result of needs having nothing to do with literature. Yet, the canons we carry around in our minds, already formed, will certainly have as much effect on our sense of the Afro-American literary canon as any theorizing. We are more likely to tailor our theories around the canon than conversely. I am sure that Gates would agree.

Granted a new criticism, a new black criticism, could well enlarge the canon if it provided the means (as post-structuralism sometimes has) to talk about writers whose work seems not to offer problems of reading, about which there seems nothing to say. We would of course hope that any form of discourse about our literature would not simply provide us with something to say (as it seems to me has been the function of critical schemes since the forties). I would hope that we would carry forward the tradition of black writing that has seen it as functional, as having more to do with our social and political well-being than with our need for enjoyment or entertainment. I infer that Gates shares Soyinka's assertion about the relation between politics and literature: "We must utilize the creative and critical tools at hand to stomp racism out. This is our first great task." I believe I understand Gates to be saying that, insisting that the political implications of literature should be at the forefront of our concerns. For, if we believe we can function as literary critics, can choose to be simply literary critics free of political ties and actions, we are sadly mistaken. We are not free enough, to be "just Americans." Gates sounds that political note when he speaks of taking control of our discourse.

We must do nothing to discourage the "up against the wall" subtext as it has appeared from Douglass's fight with Covey as described in the *Autobiography,* through Chesnutt's Josh Green in *The Marrow of Tradition,* through Bigger Thomas, through Malcolm X, up to the spirit manifested in *Black Fire,* however rhetorical that threat might have turned out to be since the sixties.

I would also hope that we would not emerge with a criticism that would do to a great number of black writers what the New Criticism did to Longfellow, Whittier, Lowell, and Holmes. They became, if I may say so in this way, "canon" fodder. The capacity of the kind of criticism that I imagine Gates to be projecting, to deal with the literature of black writers, may well be dependent on the relation of the writer's language to the vernacular. The closer the writer is to the vernacular tradition, the more likely it is that his work will be grist for a black critical mill. This is a problem inherent in our circumstance and situation as Afro-Americans, a problem which I think Gates minimizes when he discusses Soyinka's use of the "master's tongue."

There is an essential difference between our situation and that of Soyinka, who stands in a quite different relation to European culture than we do to American-European culture. Soyinka grew up in his own country, and despite colonialism was not subjected to slavery in an alien land. Soyinka's education undoubtedly implanted within his consciousness European values, but he at least had the support of strong, age-old traditions, traditions not easily suppressed by colonialism, traditions growing at least in native soil, no matter how problematical their daily cultivation. The difference is a perennial and significant one.

Still, a principal fact of bifurcation (double consciousness) exists for both Africans and African-Americans, and, perhaps, it would be well to cure it by virtue of disindenture. But indenture may well come with both postcolonial and civilly righted territory, for even if we create a methodology of our own, we will still plan to come up with something that parallels the master's practice. We carry his assumptions (if we choose to empower him by granting that currently prevailing modes of critical practice belong to him) about what literature is and what we as critics should do. For example, consider the possibility that literary criticism should not be written at all but that it should be a function of unwritten community response or reaction. Consider the possibility that we should not attempt to exist in the same relation to the creative writer as the master in his criticism does. Perhaps we should abandon the assumption that a critic should stand in the relation to literature that the academic critic does. Perhaps aesthetic judgment and "reading" of texts should be left to people other than academicians. My point is that insofar as we have stakes in the academic profession, insofar as we are committed to academic institutions, we are both jailers and jailed. One may end indenture by fulfilling the terms of a contract, just by living out the years. Perhaps our indenture may not be so easily concluded.

One of the reasons that Alexander Crummell accepted Calhoun's definition of who he was had to do with the fact that Crummell's alternatives, given his personality and the times, were scrupulously limited. His chances for possessing his own definition of his identity would have been better had he grown up in surroundings and circumstances more like Soyinka's. Crummell could not possibly have opposed the power implicit in Calhoun's judgment about the requirements necessary to establish Negro humanity unless he had been—as few of us are—a David Walker. Walker would not have gone anywhere, not even across a Boston street, in order to fulfill Calhoun's requirements for admission to the human race. Gates's requirement that Crummell should, ought, might have acted differently is simply ahistorical. Unless we set about to unman all our heroes in order to establish our current perspectives, we must recognize Crummell's honored, black, historically sanctioned place. Must we, should we, ought we denigrate the image of Crummell in order to establish a point that can be established as well by simply admitting that Crummell was no less a captive of his time than we are of ours, than I of mine, than Gates of his?

The issue is not new. Gates might have chosen practically any nineteenth-century black writer or thinker and made the same point (perhaps twentieth-century too). The fundamental issue is the same for practically all black activists and thinkers. (How and whether it is true of all Afro-Americans is an interesting question in itself.)

Frederick Douglass could not conceivably (I think) have recognized an allegiance to the vernacular. He must of necessity have shunned it. One of Douglass's strategies for proving himself not a slave was to prove his high degree of literacy, to prove he was capable of managing the English language at least as well as many whites and better than most. All the basic political values of democratic society are embodied in language; mastering the language means possessing the keys, access, to the center of the dominant culture's political and moral values. Douglass achieved the means of access, as the *Narrative* makes clear, at great price. There was no value in the stock of vernacular; nothing to be achieved by claiming it as valuable in the mid-nineteenth century. One may claim its value now, but only from a very high station. One who has proved his mastery of the master's discourse may then claim the value of the vernacular, for no one doubts the claimant's credentials. Woe be the claimant who is not firmly in control of the language of the dominant culture, for he will not have earned the right to deal in such black-market currency. He will be silenced, not heard.

The closest Douglass comes to identifying with a vernacular tradition is in his critical analysis of slave songs, slave music, in his autobiography.

I did not, when a slave, understand the deep meaning of those rude and apparently incoherent songs. I was myself within the circle; so that I neither saw nor heard as those without might see and hear. They told a tale of woe which was then altogether beyond my feeble comprehension; they were tones loud, long, and deep; they breathed the prayer and complaint of souls boiling over with the bitterest anguish. Every tone was a testimony against slavery, and a prayer to God for deliverance from chains.

The implication of Douglass's utterance is that had he remained within the confines of the vernacular, he would never have been sufficiently distant from that discourse to understand its meaning. In order to understand the meaning of vernacular discourse, he needs to be outside of it. This is so for logical and political reasons. Were the vernacular discourse the dominant mode of linguistic interchange, then it would not be necessary to get outside of it for any reason. Were it the dominant mode, then one could indeed not get outside of it, for it defines, as dominant mode, the limits of the universe of discourse.

The point is that assertion of dominance is not enough. (If "the future is black indeed," then why is it? What will make the future black? It is also interesting that the negative implications of "black future" linger even after the instant recognition of the pun.) The vernacular remains by definition vernacular, by virtue of its relation to something that dominates it. Unless one can supplant the dominant language by, for example, taking over the lexicon, assuming control of linguistic utterance (controlling the press and publication), then one in calling for dominance is likely to be merely rhetorical.

There is nothing wrong with that; rhetorical exercise has its place, if one recognizes that that is what one is about. Douglass could not possibly have related to the vernacular any differently than he did, any differently than Crummell did. It is of significance that Douglass nowhere in his autobiography, except in the passage noted above, even implies a knowledge of a vernacular language. He certainly knew one; he did not acknowledge his knowing, and with good reason for a man of his time.

The same criticism leveled against Crummell might as well be leveled against Du Bois, for he too found difficulty in defining his relation to the vernacular. This is evident in *The Souls of Black Folk* in two ways. First of all, Du Bois finds it necessary in his "Forethought," prefacing the book, to state in a somewhat aslant fashion that he is "bone of the bone and flesh of the flesh of them that live within the veil." It was necessary that he say it, for there was nothing else in his presentation that would have made his racial identity unequivocally clear. Du Bois's language is always standard, educated English (unless he is using Latin or some other language). Secondly, and perhaps more interestingly, is the story told by the epigraphical materials initiating each chapter of *Souls*. There are consistently two epigraphs for each chapter. One is a verse, usually poetry, composed by a white poet, Swinburne, Tennyson, Mrs. Browning, etc.; the other consists of musical notations, and we learn in the final chapter that these notations are phrases from well-known spirituals. We are not told this until the end, but even when the phrases are identified they remain blank ciphers to everyone except those very few who are able to sight-read music. The disparities suggested by the differences between the two kinds of epigraphs are immense. Needless to say, those disparities reflect the distance between Du Bois's own linguistic orientation and the vernacular belonging to the subject of his discourse.

The same condition prevails if we measure distance between the language of the poet and the language of the subject of his interest in this well-known poem.

> O black and unknown bards of long ago,
> How came your lips to touch the sacred fire?
> How, in your darkness, did you come to know
> The power and beauty of the minstrel's lyre?
> Who first from out the still watch, lone and long,
> Feeling the ancient faith of prophets rise
> Within his dark-kept soul, burst into song?

We will say nothing about what these lines indicate about James Weldon Johnson's cultural orientation as reflected in the diction and figures of speech. But the language alone is worlds apart from the language of the spirituals whose character it intends to evoke. I think what Gates has presented to us is extremely valuable, especially given the splendid opportunity offered by the forthcoming Norton anthology to bring theory and practice into meaningful conjunction. My fear is, however, that Gates has not—at least in this context—grappled with the extraordinary complexities underlying the orientation presented here. I am not saying that there are problems too complicated to think about, or that we can do nothing to maintain greater control of our functions as literary critics. I do mean to say that the arena of our concern is a broad one, broader, I think, than here suggested. The issues are laid out in Larry Neal's "Afterword" concluding *Black Fire,* where he struggles face-to-face with the basic issues—historical, cultural, political—broached in Gates's essay. Specifically, he deals with the problem raised by Gates with the Crummell discussion, by reference to Du Bois and the "double consciousness." I believe Neal is being very realistic when he recognizes that the double consciousness is not something that existed long ago but is a present reality and needs to be addressed as such. Neal points to the necessity and desirability (and difficulty) of unifying that consciousness.

Such disunity, it goes without saying, is painful indeed, and how wonderful it would be to free ourselves by virtue of an act of disindenture. But indenture, at least for the moment, may come with the territory.

2

Boundaries: Or Distant Relations and Close Kin

Deborah E. McDowell

I consider it indeed fortuitous to be working on Afro-American women novelists at such a propitious moment in their literary history. The past ten years have produced a veritable watershed of activity, both creative and critical. Charting a new agenda for Afro-American feminist criticism, then, is an alternately heady and intimidating venture, and perhaps a bit premature.

A scant ten years ago, scholars in search of criticism on black women writers faced a huge vacuum that abandoned them to their solitary carrels with only their own thoughts to bounce against each other. Since that time, however, several collections—not all devoted exclusively to literary criticism—and book-length studies have been published in steady succession.[1] Add to these, anthologies placing selections of black women's fiction and poetry in thematic frameworks,[2] countless essays on the subject in literary journals, and more sessions at conferences than either

A version of this essay appeared in *Critical Essays on Toni Morrison*, ed. Nellie McKay (Boston: G. K. Hall), 1988.

1. *Sturdy Black Bridges* (1979), ed. Roseann Pope Bell et al.; *Conditions: Five* (1979), ed. Lorraine Bethel and Barbara Smith; Barbara Christian, *Black Women Novelists: The Development of a Tradition* (1980); *Black Women Writers at Work*, ed. Claudia Tate; *Home Girls: A Black Feminist Anthology* (1983), ed. Barbara Smith; Gloria Wade-Gayles, *No Crystal Stair* (1984); *Conjuring: Black Women Writers and Literary Tradition,* ed. Marjorie Pryse and Hortense Spillers (1985); Barbara Christian, *Black Feminist Criticism* (1985); Susan Willis, *Specifying: Black Women Writing the American Experience* (1986); Hazel Carby, *Reconstructing Womanhood* (1987); Gloria Hull, *Color, Sex, and Poetry* (1987); Nellie McKay, ed., *Critical Essays on Toni Morrison* (1988).

2. See Mary Helen Washington's two anthologies, *Black-Eyed Susans* (Doubleday, 1975) and *Midnight Birds* (Doubleday, 1980), and Erlene Stetson's *Black Sister* (Indiana University Press, 1981).

time or money would permit anyone to attend, and we have, arguably, a small industry.

This work has been written by black women, white men, black men, and white women, which raises the logical and necessary question: *What* is black feminist criticism and *who* does it? Admittedly, any inquiry into a new agenda for Afro-American feminist criticism properly begins with these questions, but we are no closer to answers now than we were ten years ago when Barbara Smith employed the term "black feminist criticism" in her 1977 landmark and still controversial essay "Toward a Black Feminist Criticism."[3] Although it is widely assumed that a black feminist critic is an Afro-American *woman* who brings a feminist perspective to bear on analyses of literature by Afro-American women, anyone familiar with Thadious Davis's work on William Faulkner, Nellie McKay's work on Jean Toomer, Joyce Joyce's work on Richard Wright, to name just three Afro-American women literary scholars, might want to challenge that assumption. Or anyone familiar with Robert Hemenway's biography of Zora Neale Hurston, Barbara Johnson's essays on Hurston, or Henry Gates's edition of Harriet Wilson's *Our Nig,* might want to pose similar challenges.

That we are far from a final definition of black feminist criticism— assuming that that is a desirable goal—should cause no undue concern, for black literary feminists do not comprise a unitary essence, nor is their critical methodology already settled, defined, and conceptually unified. Rather, it is very much in process. And its achievement and promise reside in the process that began with Barbara Smith's astute and timely appeal ten years ago for an approach to literature that would resurrect black writers from oblivion, reveal the subtleties of their writing, and display awareness that the "politics of sex as well as the politics of race and class are crucially interlocking factors in the works of Black women writers" (p. 159).

Smith's appeal for "nonhostile and perceptive analysis" of black women's writings, which fall outside the "'mainstream' of white/male cultural rule," has been answered in some form by many scholars, thus making a full-scale inquiry into the discourse impossible here. I will attempt instead to focus very briefly on selected writings by black feminist critics that point to the broad tendencies and currents, the objectives

---

3. My quotations from this widely reprinted essay are taken from *All the Women Are White, All the Blacks Are Men, But Some of Us Are Brave,* ed. Gloria T. Hull, Patricia Bell-Scott, and Barbara Smith (Old Westbury, N.Y.: The Feminist Press, 1982). Subsequent references to the essay will be indicated parenthetically.

and methodology of the enterprise. Then, through a reading of Toni Morrison's novel *Sula,* a novel that directs Afro-American critics, in general, away from well-worn paths, I will devote the rest of the essay to exploring the directions my own work has taken.

As might be expected, black female identity and "black woman-identification," to quote Lorraine Bethel, have formed the cornerstone and have been/are a rallying point of feminist critics who are black. Appropriately, taking their direction from the literature itself, early black feminist critics focused their energies on what Mary Helen Washington considers "one of the main preoccupations of the black woman writer: the black woman herself." The dominant focus on "the black woman" in black feminist discourse was and still is of vital political necessity; however, as we move toward the future, we need to submit the category "black woman" and similar unexamined unitary concepts to closer scrutiny. "Black womanhood," "black female identity," "black experience" can no longer be viewed as unchanging essences.

Barbara Smith's trenchant assertion that black women's experiences must be comprehended simultaneously in sexual, class, and racial terms is perhaps the single most important principle or emphasis of black feminist criticism, even if it is not always reflected in practice. This principle offers an escape from the critical tendency to homogenize and essentialize black women, for it does not permit us to dissociate the category "black woman" from a varied set of complex social and material realities. Gloria Hull's reading of the Lesbian/poet Angelina Weld Grimke, Hazel Carby's introduction to the recently reprinted edition of Frances Harper's *Iola Leroy,* and Cheryl Wall's recent essay on Nella Larsen are three notable examples of work that views sex, race, and class interactively rather than separately. Let me single out Wall's essay for further comment. She effects a brilliant and sensitive synthesis in her reading of Larsen's subversive use of the tragic mulatto convention, "the only formulation," notes Wall, "historically available to portray educated middle-class black women in fiction."[4]

Early black feminist critics attempted, appropriately, to formulate a methodology that would emerge organically from the work itself. They proceeded with a healthy skepticism about "outside" critical approaches and assumed a healthy separatist and chauvinistic posture. Barbara Smith, for example, recommended that black feminist critics "look first for precedents and insights in interpretation within the works of other

4. "Passing for What? Aspects of Identity in Nella Larsen's Novels," *Black American Literature Forum* 20 (Spring-Summer 1986): 97–111.

black women." She urged us to "write out of [our] own identity and not try to graft the ideas or methodology of white/male literary thought upon the precious materials of black women's art" (p. 164).

Smith's statement implies the common view of black female identity as unitary essence yielding an indigenous critical methodology. As we move toward the 1990s, this unexamined assumption must be submitted to closer scrutiny. Left unexamined, it can result, as it often has, in a basic uniformity of critical posture and approach. Although the diversity of styles, themes, and concerns in black women's writings encourage, if not demand, multiple and interdisciplinary critical approaches, these writers are often collapsed into a unity and examined for the way in which their work reflects the authors' lives, demonstrates "race consciousness," and is rooted in the black experience.[5]

Building on these efforts, we must enter the 1990s recognizing that black women's lives are not uniform. More important, they have not developed in a vacuum, but, rather in a complex social framework that includes interaction with black men, white men, and white women, among diverse social groups and subgroups. And our relationships and loyalties to each group are complex and shifting. It follows, then, that we need not fend off "foreign" methodologies and distance ourselves from different interpretive communities. As black women, we can develop and practice our critical approaches interactively, dialogically, just as we have lived/are living our lives.

As members of a wider discursive fellowship that extends beyond ourselves, we are free to have serious dialogue and interaction with any literary theory or critical methodology that has clear rather than contrived implications for a thoroughgoing consideration of black women writers. Such interaction and dialogue are changing the contours of Afro-American literary history and of Afro-American critical discourse. I shall mention very briefly two of many examples. Joann Braxton applies a gynocritical or gynocentric approach in a recent article that examines Harriet Jacobs' *Incidents in the Life of a Slave Girl* in relation to dominant scholarship on the slave narrative. She argues that, largely because this scholarship has most often treated the narratives of "heroic male slaves" rather than those of their wives or sisters, it is one of the "most skewed in Afro-American literary criticism." She critiques this scholarship for its male bias, its linear logic, its dependence on binary oppositions, and its preoccupation with issues of primacy, authorship, textual unity, comple-

5. Many of the essays in Mari Evans's collection *Black Women Writers: A Critical Introduction* (New York: Anchor Press/Doubleday, 1984) reflect this homogenizing tendency.

tion and length. Braxton calls for alternatives and supplements to the reflexive questions: "Is it first?" "Is it major?" "Is it central?" "Does it conform to established criteria?" She offers one such alternative with her question: "How would the inclusion of women change the shape of the genre?" If we dispense with requirements of length, she adds, the origin of the slave-narrative genre would be pushed back to 1787, two years before Gustavus Vassa's 1789 narrative, with the publication of "Belinda, or the Cruelty of Men Whose Faces Were Like the Moon."[6]

Hortense Spillers usefully complicates literary history all the more and demonstrates how black feminist critics can engage in necessary dialogue with each other. Although Spillers's essay "A Hateful Passion, A Lost Love," does not directly address Barbara Christian's groundbreaking study *Black Women Novelists: The Development of a Tradition*, it offers a departure from Christian's supersessional model of black women's literary history. Spillers urges that we "not . . . acede to the simplifications and mystifications of a strictly historiographical time line." Abandoning linearity, she argues, offers "the greatest freedom of discourse to black people, to black women as critics, teachers, writers, and thinkers."[7]

Similarly, Hazel Carby's essay " 'On the Threshold of Woman's Era': Lynching, Empire, and Sexuality in Black Feminist Theory" is an example of a dialogical critical practice. In her study of race, gender, and patriarchal power in Anne Julia Cooper's essays, Ida B. Wells's journalism, and Pauline Hopkins's novel *Contending Forces*, Carby enters a dialogue with the two academic constituencies with which black feminist critics interact most often: Afro-American cultural analysis and feminist historiography and theory. She notes predictably that the former focuses on "exceptional male intellectual genius"; the latter on "white, middle-class [females] of the metropoles." Refusing to stretch the seams to make either coat fit black women writers, Carby situates her discussion of these writers in the context of the black women's movement of the nineteenth century. She notes, importantly, that her goal is *not* merely to "insert [black] women into the gaps in our cultural history (to compete for intellectual dominance with black men [and white women]) but to shift the object of interpretation . . . to the collective production and interrelation of forms of knowledge among black women intellectuals."[8]

6. "Harriet Jacobs' *Incidents in the Life Of a Slave Girl*," *Massachusetts Review* 27 (Summer 1986): 380–81.
7. "A Hateful Passion, A Lost Love," *Feminist Studies* 9 (1983): 295.
8. " 'On the Threshold of Woman's Era': Lynching, Empire, and Sexuality in Black Feminist Theory," *Critical Inquiry* 12 (Autumn 1985): 263.

Carby's essay clearly shows that black women's writings—if read closely—can generate their own distinctive critical directions. Similarly, Spillers and Braxton demonstrate that the paradigms and critical frameworks and postures that have dominated Afro-American criticism need not be reflexively and habitually employed. Neither of their approaches —whether one would or could classify them as either "foreign" or "domestic"—demands an either/or choice. Rather, they should be seen, most profitably, as dialogically demanding both/and. Such dialogical combinations, formed between close relations *and* distant kin, offer the most humane and cooperative directions for future critical inquiry, and not exclusively for inquiry in which black women are engaged. Toni Morrison's *Sula* encourages the formation of such relations.

II

What shall we call our "self"? Where does it begin? Where does it end? It overflows into everything that belongs to us.

Henry James, *The Portrait of a Lady*

She had clung to Nel as the closest thing to both an other and a self, only to discover that she and Nel were not one and the same thing.

Toni Morrison, *Sula*

If the black feminist's critical *self* is formed in relation to and dialogue with others, what shape might her work take? I would like to suggest one of a myriad of shapes through a reading of *Sula*, a novel that engages and complicates assumptions about and representations of the self.[9] I shall use a small and necessarily selective piece of critical history as initial scaffolding, a piece roughly contemporaneous with the genesis of Afro-American feminist criticism and the publication of *Sula:* the Black Aesthetic movement. Those in the vanguard of the movement, faithful to a paradigm focused almost exclusively on race, loitered at the corner where the psychological "self" and the literary subject meet and often collide. They formulated a discourse that turned on the rhetorical polarities "positive" and "negative," in fulfillment of another part of their mission: to grant racial-image awards. Many demanded that black writers inscribe the "positive" racial self in Afro-American literature. Addison Gayle is a prototypical example. In his 1977 essay "Blueprint for Black Criticism," Gayle appealed specifically for literary characters modeled upon such

---

9. *Sula* (New York: New American Library, 1973). Subsequent references are to this edition and will be indicated parenthetically in the text.

men and women as Sojourner Truth, Harriet Tubman, Martin Delaney, H. Rap Brown, and Fannie Lou Hamer—a kind of Plutarch's *Lives* of the black race. In that they offer images of "heroism, beauty, and courage," Gayle continues, these men and women are "positive" characters, functional "alternatives to the stereotypes of blacks," and thus warriors in the "struggle against American racism."[10]

In the ten years since Gayle issued his blueprint, Afro-American literary criticism has finally seen the beginnings of a paradigm shift, one that has extended the boundaries and altered the terms of its inquiry. Falling in step with recent developments in contemporary critical theory, some critics of Afro-American literature have usefully complicated some of our most common assumptions about the *self*, and about race as a meaningful category in literary study and critical theory.[11] These recent developments have made it difficult, if not impossible, to posit, with any assurance, a "positive" black self, always already unified, coherent, stable, and known.

And yet, despite these important and sophisticated developments, Afro-American critics of Afro-American literature, in both the popular media and academic journals, continue to use the yardstick that measures the "positive" racial self. And perhaps, at no time, has such application been more rigid and determined and judgments more harsh than now, when die-hard critics, reducing contemporary black women writers to a homogenized bloc, have alleged that their portrayal of black male characters is uniformly "negative."

A full inquiry into this debate, which has escaped the pages of literary journals and essay collections, spilling over into the privileged organs of the literary establishment—the *New York Times Review* and the *New York Review of Books*—is not possible here, although it is in urgent need of address. But I shall use Mel Watkins's comments from his June 1986 essay, "Racism, Sexism, and Black Women Writers," published in the *New York Times Book Review* to represent the insistent refrain. Watkins argues that in the great majority of their novels, black women indicate that "sexism is more oppressive than racism." In these works, black males

10. "Blueprint for Black Criticism," *First World* (January–February 1977): 44.

11. See three essays by Henry Louis Gates: "Preface to Blackness: Text and Pretext," in *Afro-American Literature: The Reconstruction of Instruction,* ed. Dexter Fischer and Robert Stepto (New York: MLA, 1979), pp. 44–69; "Criticism in the Jungle," in *Black Literature and Literary Theory,* ed. Henry Gates (New York: Methuen, 1984): 1–24; and "Writing 'Race' and the Difference it Makes," *Critical Inquiry,* 12 (Autumn 1985): 1–20. For critiques of the issue on "'Race', Writing and Difference," in which the last essay appears, see *Critical Inquiry* 13 (Autumn 1986).

are portrayed in an "unflinchingly candid and often negative manner";
almost without exception, they are "thieves, sadists, rapists, and ne'er-
do-wells." In choosing "black men as a target," Watkins continues,
"these writers have set themselves outside a tradition" devoted to "establishing humane, positive images of blacks."[12]

It is useful here to pause and extrapolate the interlocking assumptions
of Watkins's essay most relevant to my concerns. His assumptions are
those that underlie the dominant Afro-American critical paradigm: (1)
the world is neatly divided into black and white; (2) race is the sole
determinant of being and identity, subsuming sexual difference; (3)
identity is preexistent, coherent, and known; and (4) literature has the
power to unify and liberate the race. This paradigm pivots on a set of
oppositions: black/white, positive/negative, self/other.

The overarching preoccupation with "positive" racial representation
has worked in tandem with a static view of the nature of identification in
the act of reading. One result of this arrangement is the insistence on
literary characters who are essentially figurations of myth, akin to Alice
Walker's description, "I am black, beautiful, and strong, and almost
always right."[13] This is the self with which our hypothetical Afro-American critic, desperately seeking flattery, is likely to identify. It is uniformly
"positive" and "good" and defined in contradistinction to its other,
uniformly "negative" and "bad."

Easily recognizable here is the classic condition of "otherness," a
subject permitting a dialogue about and between differences. And, as
feminist theorists consistently and emphatically argue, the opposition of
"self" to "other," and all those oppositions analogous to it, relate hier-
archically, often reproducing the more fundamental opposition between
male and female. Man is self, and woman other.[14] And in this configura-

---

12. "Sexism, Racism, and Black Women Writers," New York Times Book Review, June
1986, p. 36. For similar discussions, see Darryl Pinckney, "Black Victims, Black Villains,"
New York Review of Books 34 (January 29, 1987): 17–20, and Richard Barksdale, "Castra-
tion Symbolism in Recent Black American Fiction," College Language Association Journal
29 (June 1986): 400–413.

13. "The Unglamorous But Worthwhile Duties of the Black Revolutionary Artist, or
of the Black Writer Who Simply Works and Writes," in In Search of Our Mother's Gardens
(New York: Harcourt Brace Jovanovich, 1983), p. 137.

14. Although a whole field of binary oppositions can be viewed as analogous to the
male/female opposition, Cary Nelson rightly cautions against so rigid a reading. He argues
persuasively that when such dualities are considered in cultural and historical context, the
basic male/female opposition breaks down and the qualities associated with each side are
often reversed. See "Envoys of Otherness: Difference and Continuity in Feminist Criticism," in For Alma Mater: Theory and Practice in Feminist Scholarship, ed. Paula Treichler et
al. (Urbana: University of Illinois Press, 1985), pp. 91–118.

tion, as Shoshana Felman puts it eloquently, echoing the dutiful terms of the dominant Afro-American paradigm, woman is "the negative of the positive."[15]

While these observations are commonplace in feminist discourse, their usefulness to students of Afro-American literary history has not been fully interrogated. Preventing such interrogation is an almost exclusive focus on race in Afro-American literary discourse, which is often tantamount to a focus on maleness. The subordination (if not the absolute erasure) of black women in discourses on blackness is well known. The black self has been assumed to be male, historically, of which Gloria Hull, Patricia Bell-Scott, and Barbara Smith are well aware. They do not engage in cheap and idle rhetoric in entitling their landmark anthology *All the Women Are White, All the Blacks Are Men,* for we are all too aware that, with noticeably few exceptions, both in Afro-American critical inquiry and in the Afro-American literary canon,[16] the "face" of race, the "speaking subject," is male.[17]

These limited boundaries are being redrawn, and some of us continue to move the discourse to other territories. The next stage in the development of feminist criticism on Afro-American women writers must lead us beyond the descriptions that keep us locked in opposition and antagonism. Toni Morrison's novel, *Sula* (1973), is rife with liberating possibilities. It frustrates the race- and image-conscious critic at every turn, by transgressing the rhetoric of opposition that excludes women from creative agency. Although the novel teases the reader with various

15. "Women and Madness: The Critical Phallacy," *Diacritics* 5 (Winter 1975): 3.

16. The historical equation of blackness with maleness in discourses on blackness and in the development of the Afro-American literary canon, is an issue calling urgently for examination. For a discussion of how this equation has worked in discourses on slavery, see Deborah Gray White, *Ar'n't I a Woman: Female Slaves in the Plantation South* (New York: Norton, 1985). Gray examines slave women whose experiences are neglected, more often than not, in scholarship on slavery. According to White, the pattern began with the publication of Stanley Elkins's *Slavery, a Problem in American Institutional and Intellectual Life* (Chicago: University of Chicago Press, 1959), in which he posited his controversial "Sambo" thesis of male infantilism and incompetence which historians have since focused their energies on negating. That focus has effectively eclipsed black women from view.

17. See Robert Stepto, *From Behind the Veil: A Study of Afro-American Narrative* (Urbana: University of Illinois Press, 1979), who defines the Afro-American narrative tradition in almost exclusively male terms. See also Henry Gates's preface to the special issue of *Critical Inquiry* (13 [Autumn 1986]) "'Race', Writing, and Difference," in which he describes the beginning of that tradition: the writings of John Gronniosaw, John Marrant, Olaudah Equiano, Ottabah Cugoano, and John Jea, all male. They, he argues, posited both "the individual 'I' of the black author as well as the collective 'I' of the race. Text created author; and black authors, it was hoped, would create or re-create the image of the race in European discourse" (p. 11).

oppositions—good/evil, virgin/whore, self/other—it avoids the false choices they imply and dictate. As Hortense Spillers puts it eloquently, when we read *Sula,* "No Manichean analysis demanding a polarity of interest—black/white, male/female, good/bad [and I might add, positive/negative, self/other]—will do."[18] The narrative insistently blurs and confuses these and other binary oppositions, blurs the boundaries they create, boundaries separating us from others and rendering us "others" to ourselves. *Sula* glories in paradox and ambiguity, beginning with the prologue, which describes the setting, the Bottom, situated spatially in the top. We enter a new world here, a world in which we never get to the "bottom" of things, a world that demands a shift from a dialectical either/or orientation to one that is dialogical or both/and, full of shifts and contradictions, particularly shifting and contradictory conceptions of the self.

The novel questions assumptions about the self of Afro-American literature, opposing historical demands for the representation of a beauideal and offering black women novelists a different set of options. Coming significantly on the heels of the Black Power movement that rendered black women prone or the "queens" of the male warrior—an updated version of a familiar script—the narrative invites the reader to imagine a different script for women that transcends the boundaries of social and linguistic convention.

Finally, *Sula* complicates the process of identification in the reading process, denying the conventional Afro-American critic a reflection of his or her ego ideal.

III

Day and night are mingled in our gazes. . . . If we divide light from night, we give up the lightness of our mixture. . . . We put ourselves into watertight compartments, break ourselves up into parts, cut ourselves in two . . . we are always one and the other, at the same time.

   Luce Irigaray, *This Sex Which Is Not One*

To posit, as *Sula* does, that we are always one and the other at the same time is effectively to challenge a fundamental assumption of Western metaphysics that has operated historically in Afro-American literature and criticism: "the unity of the ego-centered individual self"[19] defined in opposition to an other.

    18. "A Hateful Passion, A Lost Love," *Feminist Studies* 9 (Summer 1983): 296.
    19. Thomas Docherty. *Reading (Absent) Character: Toward a Theory of Characterization in Fiction* (Oxford: Clarendon Press, 1983), p. 265. Subsequent references will be given parenthetically in the text.

Morrison begins by questioning traditional notions of self as they have been translated into narrative. She implicitly criticizes such concepts as "protagonist," "hero," and "major character" by emphatically decentering and deferring the presence of Sula, the title character. Bearing *her* name, the narrative suggests that she is the protagonist, the privileged center, but her presence is constantly deferred. We are first introduced to a caravan of characters: Shadrack, Nel, Helene, Eva, the Deweys, Tar Baby, Hannah, and Plum before we get any sustained treatment of Sula. Economical to begin with, then, the novel is roughly one-third over when Sula is introduced, and it continues almost that long after her death.

Not only does the narrative deny the reader a "central" character, it also denies the whole notion of character as static *essence,* replacing it with the idea of character as *process.*[20] Whereas the former is based on the assumption that the self is knowable, centered, and unified, the latter is based on the assumption that the self is multiple, fluid, relational, and in a perpetual state of becoming. Significantly, Sula, whose eyes are "as steady and clear as rain," is associated throughout with water, fluidity. Her birthmark, which shifts in meaning depending on the viewer's perspective, acts as metaphor for her figurative "selves," her multiple identity. To Nel it is a "stemmed rose"; to her children, a "scary black thing," a "black mark"; to Jude, a "copperhead" and a "rattlesnake"; to Shadrack, a "tadpole." The image of the tadpole reinforces this notion of self as perpetually in process. Sula never achieves completeness of being. She dies in the fetal position, welcoming this "sleep of water," in a passage that clearly suggests she is dying yet aborning (p. 149). Morrison's reconceptualization of character has clear and direct implications for Afro-American literature and critical study, for if the self is perceived as perpetually in process, rather than as a static entity always already formed and known, it is thereby difficult to posit its ideal or "positive" representation.

Appropriate to this conception of character as process, the narrative employs the double, a technique related, as Baruch Hoffman has observed, to the "rupturing of coherence in character."[21] It positions Nel and Sula in adolescence, a state of becoming when they are "unshaped, formless things" (p. 53) "us[ing] each other to grow on," finding "in each other's eyes the intimacy they were looking for" (p. 52). As doubles

20. I am adapting Docherty's distinction between "character as a 'becoming' rather than as an 'essence'." See his *Reading (Absent) Character,* p. 268.

21. *Character in Literature* (Ithaca: Cornell University Press, 1985), p. 79.

Sula and Nel complement and flow into each other, their closeness evoked throughout the narrative in physical metaphors. Sula's return to the Bottom, after a ten-year absence, is, for Nel, "like getting the use of an eye back, having a cataract removed" (p. 95). The two are likened to "two throats and one eye" (p. 147).

But while Sula and Nel are represented as two parts of a self, those parts are distinct; they are complementary, not identical. Although Sula and Nel might share a common vision (suggested by "one eye"), their needs and desires are distinct (they have "two throats").[22] Sula comes to understand the fact of their difference: "She clung to Nel as the closest thing to an other and a self, only to discover that she and Nel were not one and the same thing." The relationship of other to self in this passage, and throughout the narrative, must be seen as "different but connected rather than separate and opposed," to borrow from Carol Gilligan.[23]

Sula's understanding of her relationship to Nel results from self-understanding and self-intimacy, a process that Nel's marriage to Jude interrupts. Like so many women writers, Morrison equates marriage with the death of the female self and imagination. Nel would be the "someone sweet, industrious, and loyal, to shore him up . . . the two of them would make one Jude" (p. 83). After marriage, she freezes into her wifely role, becoming one of the women who had "folded themselves into starched coffins" (p. 122). Her definition of self becomes based on the community's "absolute" moral categories about "good" and "bad" women, categories that result in her separation from and opposition to Sula.

The narrative anticipates that opposition in one of its early descriptions of Nel and Sula. Nel is the color of "wet sandpaper," Sula is "heavy brown" (p. 52), a distinction that can be read as patriarchy's conventional fair lady/ dark/woman, virgin/whore dichotomy, one reflected in Sula's and Nel's separate matrilineages.

Sula's female heritage is an unbroken line of "manloving" women who exist as sexually-desiring subjects rather than as objects of male desire. Her mother, Hannah, "ripple[s] with sex" (p. 42), exasperating the "good" women of the community, who call her "nasty." But that doesn't prevent her from taking her lovers into the pantry for "some touching everyday" (p. 44). In contrast, Nel's is a split heritage. On one side is her grandmother, the whore of the Sundown House and, on the

22. I borrow this point from Judith Kegan Gardiner, "The (US)es of (I)dentity: A Response to Abel on '(E)Merging Identities'," *Signs* 6 (Spring 1981): 439.
23. *In a Different Voice* (Cambridge: Harvard University Press, 1982), p. 147.

other, her great-grandmother, who worshiped the Virgin Mary and counselled Helene "to be constantly on guard for any sign of her mother's wild blood" (p. 17). Nel takes her great-grandmother's counsel to heart, spending her life warding off being "turn[ed] to jelly" and "custard" (p. 22). Jelly and pudding here are metaphors of sexuality characteristic in classic blues lyrics.

Nel's sexuality is not expressed in itself and for her own pleasure, but rather, for the pleasure of her husband and in obedience to a system of ethical judgment and moral virtue, her "only mooring" (p. 139). Because Nel's sexuality is harnessed to and enacted only within the institutions that sanction sexuality for women—marriage and family—she does not own it.[24] It is impossible for her to imagine sex without Jude. After she finds him and Sula in the sex act she describes her thighs—the metaphor for her sexuality—as "empty and dead . . . and it was Sula who had taken the life from them." She concludes that "the both of them . . . left her with no thighs and no heart, just her brain raveling away" (p. 110).

Without Jude, Nel thinks her thighs are useless. Her cause/effect relationship is clear from the plaintive questions she puts to an imaginary God after Jude leaves:

even if I sew up those old pillow cases and rinse down the porch and feed my children and beat the rugs and haul the coal up out of the bin even then nobody. . . . I could be a mule or plow the furrows with my hands if need be or hold these rickety walls up with my back if I knew that somewhere in this world in the pocket of some night I could open my legs to some cowboy lean hips but you are trying to tell me no and O my sweet Jesus, what kind of cross is that? (p. 111)

Sula, on the other hand, "went to bed with men as frequently as she could" (p. 122) and assumed responsibility for her own pleasure. In her first sexual experience with Ajax, significantly, a reenactment of Hannah's sexual rituals in the pantry, Sula "stood wide-legged against the wall and pulled from his track-lean hips all the pleasure her thighs could hold" (p. 125). This is not to suggest that Sula's sexual expression is uncomplicated or unproblematic but rather that, unlike Nel's, it is not attached to anything outside herself, especially not to social definitions of female sexuality and conventions of duty. Although initially she "liked the

24. *In The Bluest Eye* (Washington Square Press, 1970) Morrison is similarly concerned with those women who view sex as a marital duty rather than a source of their own pleasure. Called the Mobile women, they try to rid themselves of the "dreadful funkiness of passion," give their "bod[ies] sparingly and partially," and hope that they will "remain dry between [their] legs" (pp. 68–69).

sootiness of sex," liked "to think of it as wicked" (p. 122), she comes to realize that it was not wicked. Further, apart from bringing her "a special kind of joy," it brought her "misery and the ability to feel deep sorrow" and "a stinging awareness of the endings of things" (pp. 122, 123), a feeling of "her own abiding strength and limitless power" (p. 123). In other words, Sula's sexuality is neither located in the realm of "moral" abstractions nor expressed within the institution of marriage that legitimates sexuality for women. Rather it is in the realm of sensory experience and in the service of the self-exploration that leads to self-intimacy. After sex, Sula enters that "post-coital privateness in which she met herself, welcomed herself, and joined herself in matchless harmony" (p. 123). Unlike Nel, Sula has no ego and therefore does not feel the ego's "compulsion . . . to be consistent with herself" (p. 119). In describing her, Morrison notes that Sula "is experimental with herself [and] perfectly willing to think the unthinkable thing."[25] To Sula, "there was only her own mood and whim," enabling her to explore "that version of herself which she sought to reach out to and touch with an ungloved hand," "to discover it and let others become as intimate with their own selves as she was" (p. 121).

Not only is sexual expression an act of self-exploration, but it is also associated throughout the narrative with creativity, as seen in the long prose poem she creates while making love to Ajax. But, significantly, that creativity is without sufficient outlet within her community. According to Morrison, "If Sula had any sense she'd go somewhere and sing or get into show business," implying that her "strangeness," her "lawlessness" can be sanctioned only in a world like the theater.[26] Because of her community's rigid norms for women, Sula's impulses cannot be absorbed. Without an "art form," her "tremendous curiosity and gift for metaphor" become destructive (p. 121). Without art forms, Sula is the artist become her own work of art.[27] She responds defiantly to Eva's injunction that she make babies to settle herself, "I don't want to make somebody else. I want to make myself" (p. 92).

Because she resists self-exploration, such creativity is closed to Nel. She has no "sparkle or splutter," just a "dull glow" (p. 83). Her imagination has been driven "underground" from years of obeying the norm-

25. "Intimate Things in Place," *Massachusetts Review* (Autumn, 1977): 477.

26. See Bettye J. Parker, "Complexity, Toni Morrison's Women—An Interview Essay," in *Sturdy Black Bridges: Visions of Black Women in Literature,* ed. Roseann P. Bell, Bettye J. Parker, and Beverly Guy-Sheftall (New York: Anchor-Doubleday, 1979), p. 256.

27. For a discussion of this theme in other Morrison novels, see Renita Weems, "'Artists without Art Forms': A Look At One Black Woman's World of Unrevered Black Women," *Conditions: Five* 2 (Autumn 1979): 48–58.

ative female script; she "belonged to the town and all of its ways" (p. 120). The narrative strongly suggests that one cannot belong to the community and preserve the imagination, for the orthodox vocations for women—marriage and motherhood—restrict if not preclude imaginative expression.

Obedience to community also precludes intimacy with self for women. Nel rejects this intimacy, which involves confronting what both Sula and Shadrack have confronted: the unknown parts of themselves. In turning her back on the unknown, Nel fails to grow, to change, or to learn anything about herself until the last page of the novel. She thinks that "hell is change" (p. 108). "One of the last true pedestrians" in the Bottom, Nel walks on the road's shoulder (on its edge, not on the road), "allowing herself to accept rides only when the weather required it" (p. 166).

Nel fits Docherty's description of the type of character who is "fixed and centered upon one locatable ego," blocking "the possibility of authentic response, genuine sentiment." According to this ego-centered schema, "the self can only act in accord with a determined and limited 'characteristic' response" (p. 80). Whereas Sula is an ambiguous character with a repertoire of responses along a continuum and thus cannot be defined as either totally "good" or "bad," Nel's is a limited response: "goodness," "rightness" (as her name "Wright" suggests). As it is classically defined for women, "goodness" is sexual faithfulness, self-abnegation, and the idealization of marriage and motherhood.

After years of nursing the belief that Sula has irreparably wronged her and violated their friendship, Nel goes to visit Sula on her deathbed as any "good woman" would do. "Virtue," "her only mooring," has hidden "from her the true motives for her charity" (p. 139). Their conversation, after years of estrangement, is peppered with references to good and evil, right and wrong. Nel protests, "I was good to you, Sula, why don't that matter?" And Sula responds in her characteristically defiant way: "Being good to somebody is just like being mean to somebody. Risky. You don't get nothing for it." Exasperated because "talking to [Sula] about right and wrong" (pp. 144–45) was impossible, Nel leaves, but not before Sula has the last word. And significantly, that last word takes the form of a question, an uncertainty, not an unambiguous statement of fact or truth:

"How you know?" Sula asked.
"Know what?" Nel still wouldn't look at her.
"About who was good. How you know it was you?"
"What you mean?"
"I mean maybe it wasn't you. Maybe it was me."

In the space of the narrative Nel has another twenty-five years to deflect the contemplation of Sula's question through desperate acts of goodness: visits to "the sick and shut in," the category on the back page of black church bulletins that pulls on the cords of duty. But on one such mission to visit Eva, Nell is confronted with not only the question but Eva's more unsettling suggestion of Nell's guilt in Chicken Little's death as well as her kinship to Sula:

"Tell me how you killed that little boy."
"What? What little boy?"
"The one you threw in the water. . ."
"I didn't throw no little boy in the river. That was Sula."
"You, Sula. What's the difference?"

After years of repression, Nel must own her complicity in Chicken Little's drowning, a complicity that is both sign and symbol of the disowned piece of herself. She recalls the incident in its fullness, remembering "the good feeling she had had when Chicken's hands slipped" (p. 170) and "the tranquillity that follow[ed] [that] . . . joyful stimulation" (p. 170). That remembrance makes space for Nel's psychic reconnection with Sula as friend as well as symbol of that disowned self. Significantly, that reconnection occurs in the cemetery, a metaphor for Nel's buried shadow. The "circles and circles of sorrow" she cries at narrative's end prepare her for what Sula strained to experience throughout her life: the process of mourning and remembering, remembering and mourning that leads to intimacy with self which is all that makes intimacy with others possible.

And the reader must mourn as Nel mourns, must undergo the process of development that Nel undergoes.[28] And as with Nel, that process begins with releasing the static and coherent conception of self and embracing what Sula represents: the self as process and fluid possibility. That embrace enables an altered understanding of the nature of identification in the reading process.

28. *Sula* is an intensely elegiac novel about loss, grieving, and the release of pain. The epigraph signals the concern. "It is sheer good fortune to miss somebody long before they leave you." It implies that leave-taking and loss are inevitable. At the end of the book Shadrack gives over to his grief for Sula, and when he does, he ceases to fill his life with compulsive activity. At Chicken Little's funeral, the women grieve for their own painful childhoods, the "most devastating pain there is" (p. 65). The narrator grieves for a community that has become increasingly atomistic with the passage of time. Barbara Christian also sees these qualities in the novel, reading the epilogue as "a eulogy to the Bottom." See "Community and Nature: The Novels of Toni Morrison," *Journal of Ethnic Studies* 7 (Winter 1980): 64–78.

IV

Recent theories of the act of reading have enriched and complicated—for the good—our understanding of what takes place in the act of reading. They have described the reading process as dialogical, as an interaction between a reader (a "self") and an "other," an interaction in which neither remains the same.[29] In light of this information, we can conceive the act of reading as a process of self-exploration which the narrative strategies of *Sula* compel. What strategies does the narrative employ to generate that process? It deliberately miscues the reader, disappointing the very expectations which the narrative arouses, forcing the reader to shift gears, to change perspective. Though these strategies might well apply to all readers, they have specific implications for Afro-American critics.

Sula threatens readers' assumptions and disappoints their expectations at every turn. It begins by disappointing the reader's expectations of a "realistic" and unified narrative documenting black/white confrontation. The novel's prologue, which describes a community's destruction by white greed and deception, gestures toward documentation and leads the reader to expect familiar black/white tension. But that familiar and expected plot is backgrounded. Foregrounded are the characters whose lives transcend their social circumstances. They laugh, they dance, they sing, and are "mightily preoccupied with earthly things—and each other" (p. 6).

The narrative also retreats from linearity privileged in the realist mode. Though dates entitle its chapters, they relate only indirectly to its central concerns and do not permit the reader to use chronology in order to interpret its events in any cause/effect fashion. In other words, the story's forward movement in time is deliberately nonsequential and without explicit reference to "real" time. The narrative roves lightly over historical events, dates, and details, as seen in the first chapter. Titled "1919," the chapter begins with a reference to World War II, then refers, in quick and paradoxically regressive succession, to National Suicide Day, instituted in 1920, then backwards to Shadrack running across a battlefield in France in World War I.

---

29. Wolfgang Iser, for example, discusses the two "selves" that interact in the reading process: one, the reader's own self or "disposition"; the other, that offered by the text. See *The Act of Reading* (Baltimore: Johns Hopkins University Press, 1978), p. 37. For a thorough overview and synthesis of theories of reading, see Susan R. Suleiman, "Introduction: Varieties of Audience-Oriented Criticism," in *The Reader in the Text*, ed. Susan R. Suleiman and Inge Crosman (Princeton: Princeton University Press, 1980), pp. 3–45.

In addition, the narrative forces us to question our readings, to hold our judgment in check and to continually revise it. Susan Blake is on the mark when she says that "the reader never knows quite what to think" of characters and events in *Sula:* "whether to applaud Eva's self-sacrifice or deplore her tyranny, whether to admire Sula's freedom or condemn her‾ heartlessness."[30] The narrative is neither an apology for Sula's destruction nor an unsympathetic critique of Nel's smug conformity. It does not reduce a complex set of dynamics to a simple opposition or choice between two "pure" alternatives.

Among the strategies Morrison uses to complicate choice and block judgment are the dots within circles (⊙ ⊙ ⊙ ⊙) in the narrative that mark time-breaks and function as stop signs. They compel the reader to pause, think back, evaluate the narrative's events, and formulate new expectations in light of them, expectations that are never quite fulfilled.[31] The Afro-American critic, wanting a world cleansed of uncertainty and contradictions and based on the rhetorical polarities—positive and negative—might ask in frustration, "Can we ever determine the right judgment?" The narrative implies that that answer can only come from within, from exploring all parts of the self. As Nel asks Eva in the scene mentioned earlier, "You think I'm guilty?" Eva whispers, "Who would know that better than you?" (p. 169).

Not only does the narrative disappoint the reader's expectations of correct answers and appropriate judgment, but it also prevents a stable and unified reading of the text, though I have fabricated one here by tracing a dominant thread in the narrative: the relationships and boundaries between self and other. But in exploring this relationship, Morrison deliberately provides echoing passages that threaten to cancel each other out, that thwart the reader's desire for stability and consistency. Recall the passage, "She clung to Nel as the closest thing to both an other and a self: only to discover that she and Nel were not one and the same thing." But the following passage, which falls much later in the narrative, effectively cancels this passage out: Sula learned that "there was no other that you could count on . . . [and] there was no *self* to count on either."

The novel's fragmentary, episodic, elliptical quality helps to thwart textual unity, to prevent a totalized interpretation. An early reviewer described the text as a series of scenes and glimpses, each "writ-

---

30. "Toni Morrison," in *Dictionary of Literary Biography:* vol. 33, *Afro-American Fiction Writers after 1955* (Detroit: Gale, 1984), p. 191.
31. I am indebted here to Jerome Beatty's afterword to *Sula* in *The Norton Introduction to the Short Novel,* 2d. ed., p. 699.

ten . . . from scratch." Since none of them has anything much to do with the ones that preceded them, "we can never piece the glimpses into a coherent picture."[32] Whatever coherence and meaning reside in the narrative, the reader must struggle to create.

The gaps in the text allow for the reader's participation in the creation of meaning in the text. Morrison has commented on the importance of the "affective and participatory relationship between the artist and the audience" and her desire "to have the reader work *with* the author in the construction of the book." She adds, "What is left out is as important as what is there."[33] The reader must fill in the narrative's many gaps: Why is there no funeral for either Plum or Hannah? What happens to Jude? Where *was* Eva during her eighteen-month absence from the Bottom? What really happened to her leg? How does Sula support herself after she returns from her ten-year absence?

The reader's participation in the meaning-making process helps to fill in the gaps in the text as well as to bridge the gaps separating the reader *from* the text. This returns us full circle to the problem posed at the beginning of this essay: the boundary separating some Afro-American readers from any text that opposes a single, unified image of the black self.

As Norman Holland and others have noted, each reader has a vision of the world arising from her/his identity theme. In the act of reading, the reader tries to recreate the text according to that identity theme. As we read, we use the "literary work to symbolize and finally to replicate ourselves,"[34] to reflect ourselves, to affirm ourselves by denying or demeaning the other. But, writing in a different context, Holland usefully suggests that "one of literature's adaptive functions . . . is that it allows us to loosen boundaries between self and not self."[35]

Transgressing that boundary and viewing identity and the self in relation, rather than as coherent, separate, and opposed, permits an analogous view of identification in the reading process. Just as the self is

32. Christopher Lehman-Haupt, review of *Sula* in *New York Times,* 123 (January 7, 1974), p. 29.

33. "Rootedness: The Ancestor as Foundation," in *Black Women Writers: A Critical Evaluation,* ed. Mari Evans (New York: Anchor-Doubleday, 1984), p. 341.

34. "Unity Identity Text Self," PMLA 90 (1975): 816. See also Jean Kennard, "Ourself Behind Ourself: A Theory for Lesbian Readers," in *Gender and Reading,* ed. Elizabeth Flynn and Patrocinio Schweikart (Baltimore: Johns Hopkins University Press, 1986), pp. 63–80.

35. See *Dynamics of Literary Response* (New York: Oxford University Press, 1968), p. 101.

fluid, dynamic, and formed in relation, so is identification a process involving a dialogue between the self and the "otherness" of writers, texts, literary characters, and interpretive communities.

How can a dialogic method of reading serve Afro-American feminist critics, and literary criticism more widely? Borrowing from a recent essay in PMLA, let me suggest that "dialogic reading would not generally reduce others to consistent dialectical counterparts. . . . Nor would it minimize others as rhetorical opponents by attempting to discredit them." Such a model would comprehend that our "self-worlds" can and do impinge on one another, that our meanings and motives are not always present to us, and that "the diversity of critical and theoretical voices is not an issue to be settled or a problem to be resolved but . . . a conversation to be constructed and entered."[36]

Such a model seems even more urgent when we consider that the work of black feminist critics in the 1990s must bear not only on the literature of black women but also on the other "texts" by which that literature is bounded. These "boundary" texts include, as Hortense Spillers has observed, "the various mechanisms of institutional and media life, including conferences, the lecture platform, the television talk show."[37] Although reading these secondary texts is as critical as reading the primary ones, we must be strict with ourselves not to allow reading the former to eclipse the latter.

The last ten years *have* been banner years for black women as writers and critics. In recent months we have seen these "boundary" texts attempt to exile these writers to the peripheries of the Afro-American literary tradition, and to excite them with distorted and pathological charges. These border texts wage war and signify tellingly with metaphors of boundaries, conquests, and conflict. And while it is tempting to join the fight, to read *these* texts, we must forego the temptation and make different, more difficult choices. And we do have choices. We need not inherit the orthodoxy of victimage, inherent in much feminist discourse. As agents, we have a choice of fights, a choice of weapons, a choice of stimuli. More important, we have a choice in how we will expend our energy, energy needed for far more work than all of us— black and white, men and women—can do within the boundaries of our collective lifetimes.

36. Don Bialostosky, "Dialogics as an Art of Discourse in Literary Criticism," PMLA 10 (October 1986): 790.

37. "Cross-currents, Discontinuities: Black Women's Fiction," in *Conjuring: Black Women, Fiction, and Literary Tradition,* ed. Marjorie Pryse and Hortense Spillers, p. 250.

Response: *Hortense J. Spillers*

The only difficulty I have with Deborah McDowell's essay is that I find nothing with which to quarrel in this writing. I am likely not the best choice of *a* respondent to this essay for that reason, because there is a good deal of synonymity of opinion—critical and otherwise—between McDowell and myself. I'm glad.

I would much prefer, then, to trace a handful of *implications* that her reading of Morrison's *Sula* might suggest for all of us in reference to a critical agenda at the turn of the century. In that regard, McDowell and Bernice Johnson Reagon in "Coalition Politics: Turning the Century" express a common posture concerning a black feminist praxis that may well identify the chief avoidance of our entire social exchange, scholarly conferences included. If we accept the configuration of Sula—the subversive figure moving *against* the law, against the expectation—as that fluid, discontinuous, indefinite, heterogeneous property of person that we deny because we feel we must, then quite appropriately, all the terms of *this* discussion and *these* arrangements are thrown in immediate crisis. It is redundant to say "immediate" and "crisis" at once, but I trangress in order to underscore the point: as McDowell asserts, our metaphors of self cannot rest in stasis, but will glory in difference and overflow into everything that belongs to us. If we read McDowell's analysis in Reagon's perspective, then this "embrace" of the "difference within" will generate, quite simply, a different standard of living, or in keeping with the discourse of these sessions, a revised and corrected culture critique: "There is not going to be space to continue as we are or as we were" in "turning the century."[1]

In fully confronting the convergences of differences on our commonly shared cultural practice, we look forward to the dissolving of more than one mystification, as in those pernicious distinctions that certain of our public address maintains—the "academy" and the "vernacular"; the "scholar" and the "folk"; the "ivory tower" and the "real world." Unlike some others, perhaps, I do not believe that what we think, do, and write in the academy has no bearing on our direct relationship to the community—that term we are forever evoking and forever guilty about because we no longer live "there." We have not quite gotten over, or beyond, the particular legacy of the 60s—their achievements (whatever we collectively decide they were); their delu-

---

1. Bernice J. Reagon, in *Home Girls: A Black Feminist Anthology,* ed. Barbara Smith (New York: Kitchen Table, Women of Color Press, 1983), pp. 356–68; 363.

sions (and there were a few); their betrayals (and we do *not* always know "ourselves" and our "mind"); their rehumanation of the African-American person (as we still have yet to carry out the severe mandates of self-love). I am saying that even though certain paradigms of reading, criticism, and theory have shifted and the discursive boundaries have been exploded and reformulated, we have no open way, yet, of "signing" to ourselves (to say nothing of our own "other") that we are, in fact, *arrested* in a *stage of ambivalence*.

And how else could it be, inasmuch as everybody at this conference, to a woman and man, becomes the representative agency of some of the most powerful and complicitous arrangements and institutions in America. Here we sit: On the Philadelphia mainline, the home of Grace Kelly, and the William Penn Foundation, and as we glance through this audience, starting right here with myself, we can evoke the names of institutions that only a short time ago thought of black people in all the terms of "de-niggering" with which we are already familiar. This litany is well known, of course, and I say nothing new in indulging it. But the point is that the issues that McDowell's paper raises open the way to a sort of private and broader inquiry. We might consider this problematic along three lines of stress that we might infer from McDowell's "Self and Other."

(1) The need to develop an "intramural" social and critical practice that indeed comes to fully regard those "differences within" and"between." We are not aloof from that proliferation of gestures of empowerment that fracture an imagined unity of consciousness. (2) The urgency to perceive "community" as an analogue on the shifting subject-position. The "natal community" is a portable space, as movable a feast as oneself. We are in its midst wherever we are. Holding down, as it were, several spaces at once marks the dilemma of African-American culture, of a people, of individual ones of us, and out of it our practice of criticism, teaching, and writing arises. (3) We are called upon, then, to articulate the *spaces* of contradiction.

The specter of *Sula* and its eponymous (anti-?) heroine looms before us with its subversive and discomfiting possibilities.

As McDowell argues, *Sula* holds forth new literary and critical options, not only for the study of texts by Afro-American women, but for Afro-American literary study more generally. The novel certainly helps to set a new agenda for black women's social and narrative possibilities. I would go on to say that the novel and the character also offer figures of ambiguity, of "bad" passions that the heart, the recognition, can no longer afford to deny. If, according to Sonia Sanchez, "we be a *baad* people," then we must come to embrace the full multivocality of meanings and intersections of meaning that the poet's title implies; we do not mean, as an outcome, a radically altered configuration of literary historiography and reading, alone, but, in addition, a radically altered theory of history and culture.

Response: *Michael Awkward*

Deborah McDowell's "Boundaries" ranges over such a wide spectrum that it would be impossible for me to confine my response simply to the question of "black feminist criticism and the 1990s." Certainly, however, my discussions have as their primary impetus my view of both the intellectually liberating and potentially calamitous features of McDowell's project to provide new methods of responding to Afro-American women's texts.

McDowell's discussion suggests the beginnings of a movement of black feminist criticism toward a refreshing—and necessary—new phase which will employ contemporary critical theories of difference and reading to explicate black women's literature. This statement certainly is not inconsistent with views McDowell offered as early as 1980 in her essay "New Directions in Black Feminist Criticism." In that essay McDowell said: "I agree with Annette Kolodny that feminist criticism . . . should salvage what we find useful in past [white male-authored] methodologies, reject what we do not, and, where necessary, move toward 'inventing new methods of analysis.'"[1]

Clearly, McDowell's illuminating reading of Toni Morrison's *Sula* suggests that she has found much that is useful in contemporary critical theory. In particular, her employment of poststructuralist privileging of "otherness" and self-difference provides her with a means of making sense of contemporary Afro-American literature's perhaps most enigmatic and haunting figure. McDowell's discussion of Sula's difference, her failure to conform to what the critic views as traditional Afro-American literary criticism's search for literary representations of the " 'positive' black self, " effectively suggests the appropriateness of her application of poststructuralist critical tools. McDowell writes of *Sula:*

Not only does the narrative deny the reader a "central" character, it also denies the whole notion of character as static *essence,* replacing it with the idea of character as *process.* Whereas the former is based on the assumption that the self is

1. "New Directions for Black Feminist Criticism," in *The New Feminist Criticism,* ed. Elaine Showalter (New York: Pantheon, 1985), p. 193.

knowable, centered, and unified, the latter is based on the assumption that the self is multiple, fluid, relational, and in a perpetual state of becoming.

I do not need to trace here the manifold benefits in McDowell's emphasis on difference in terms of both her explication of the protagonist's personality and her relationship with her "kissin-friend" Nel. In McDowell's able hands, Morrison's novel seems quite clearly made, in several respects, for poststructuralist exegesis. Rather, I want to concentrate my subsequent discussion on what seem to me the potentially injurious consequences for the future of Afro-American feminist criticism of McDowell's essay, particularly the fact that her negative reading of traditional black critical practices is manifested in an apparent rejection of race and culture as necessary guides in the analysis of black literary texts.

For me, the two most troubling aspects of McDowell's arguments are their virtual erasure of race and culture in her reading of *Sula* and the striking difference in her statements here about Afro-American female characters from even her most recently published assertions written before her apparent wholehearted adoption of contemporary critical theory. I want to examine the latter point first, for it suggests, I believe, the problems implicit in McDowell's reading of Morrison's masterpiece, *Sula,* as a locus for a new reading of Afro-American women's novels.

In her recent essay "'The Changing Same': Generational Connections and Black Women Novelists," McDowell writes of the incompatibility between contemporary theories of character and her reading of Afro-American female novelists' traditional depictions of women. She is well aware of the fact that

the current wave of literary/theoretical sophistication calls into question "naive commonsense categories of 'character,' 'protagonist,' or 'hero'" and rejects the "prevalent conception of character in the novel which assumes that "the most successful and 'living' characters are richly delineated autonomous wholes." . . . [D]espite such positions, imag[in]ing the black woman as a "whole" character or "self" has been a consistent preoccupation of black female novelists throughout their literary history. . . . It seems appropriate, therefore, to allow the critical concerns of black women's novels to emerge organically from those texts, rather than to allow current critical fashion to dictate what those concerns should be.[2]

In "Boundaries," however, McDowell offers *Sula,* a text which represents for the critic Toni Morrison's implicit critique of "such concepts as

2. "'The Changing Same': Generational Connections and Black Women Novelists," *New Literary History* 18:2, p. 283.

'protagonist,' 'hero,' and major character', " as a work whose sophisticated reading "helps to reorder the priorities of Afro-American narrative and critical inquiry" by calling into question the very possibility of character and narrative wholeness. For McDowell, Sula/*Sula* is exemplary because of her/its failure to achieve—or strive for—wholeness, because she/it "never achieves completeness of being." Thus, according to McDowell, Sula/*Sula* is an implicit criticism of traditional Afro-American critical inquiry's search for "a 'positive' black self, always already unified, coherent, stable, and known."

Critics such as Addison Gayle and Mel Watkins are certainly fair game for McDowell's perspectives because of their calls for "positive," "good" Afro-American characters. But surely McDowell knows—as her "Changing Same" statement clearly indicates—that "wholeness" *is* viewed as a positive goal in many of Afro-American literature's canonical works, and that, when effectively presented, unity is not represented as "static essence" but as *process.* Such Afro-American female-authored works as Zora Hurston's *Their Eyes Were Watching God,* Paule Marshall's *Praisesong for the Widow,* Morrison's *Song of Solomon,* and, as McDowell herself has argued, Alice Walker's *The Color Purple* all depict the process of an achieved wholeness, and none of them with a naiveté about obstacles to its achievement that McDowell associates with the literature's theoretically unsophisticated critics. If poststructuralist readings of *Sula* serve as potential models for a new, better, black feminist criticism, to which other texts—according to McDowell's own "Changing Same" reading of Afro-American women characters—can a privileged fragmentation be applied? Wholeness in Afro-American women's novels can best be viewed, I think, not as a sign of static black selves or narrative self-difference but as authorial exploration of the possibilities of black unity in a historically divisive and racist setting.

My second question concerns whether Afro-American adoption of the type of interactive, dialogical relationships with other critical schools that McDowell calls for requires the virtual erasure of the significance of racial and cultural differences in discussions of black texts. McDowell's minimization of the significance of race/culture is glaringly manifested in her otherwise remarkable analysis of what I call the "broken boundaries" of *Sula's* nominally linear narrative structure and in her discussions of reading. Certainly she is correct when she states: "The narrative also retreats from linearity privileged in the realist mode. Though dates entitle its chapters, they relate only indirectly to its central concerns and do not permit the reader to use chronology in order to interpret its events in any cause/effect fashion. In other words, the story's forward movement in time is deliberately nonsequential and without explicit reference to "real" time.

McDowell attributes the text's nonlinearity not to its author's structural exploration, in a traditionally linear Western expressive system, of what black cultural scholars have commonly suggested are black conceptions of time but, rather, for want of a better phrase, to *Sula*'s postmodernist impulses. Much of the novel's cultural specificity is lost in such a critical manuever; it fails to view Morrison's revisionist acts as being of a kind with Afro-American adaptations of such Western expressive and cultural forms as religion and language. In "Characteristics of Negro Expression," Hurston says of such revisionary impulses: "while [the Afro-American] lives and moves in the midst of a white civilisation, everything that he touches is re-interpreted for his own use."[3] I believe that the Afro-American critic ought to be committed to exploring the blackness of black texts; at the very least s/he should be able, even during the process of the most energetically poststructuralist rhetorical flight, to acknowledge that there is black expressive cultural precedence for technical experimentation such as Morrison's. I do not believe that critical theory is inherently resistant to such insights, but it needs to be "re-interpreted," appropriated, blackened or *denigrated,* if you will, for use in the analysis of the blackness of Afro-American texts by critics more interested than McDowell is in "Boundaries" in such exploration.

Without such appropriation or *denigration,* the Afro-American "post-structuralist" will find him/herself almost by necessity virtually erasing the blackness out of Afro-American authorial utterance. When McDowell, for example, cites Morrison's discussion of the "participatory relationship between the artist and the audience," she is strategically selective about what she includes—and excludes—from the novelist's quite important statement about her aesthetics. She includes the novelist's assertion that the reader's role is essential because "What is left out [of the text] is as important as what is there." The reader, then, serves as a co-author in Morrison's texts, filling in gaps Morrison intentionally leaves to allow her/his participation.

What McDowell leaves out of this passage, however, is the self-consciously *denigrative* nature of Morrison's aesthetics. Morrison is speaking in parts of the passage the critic fails to quote of connections between her work and what she calls "Black art." Morrison says:

3. "Characteristics of Negro Expression," in *Negro: An Anthology,* ed. Nancy Cunard (1934; London: Negro Universities Press, 1969), p. 28.

There are things that I try to incorporate into my fiction that are directly and deliberately related to what I regard as the major characteristics of Black art. . . . One of which is the ability to be both print and oral literature: to combine those two aspects so that the stories can be read in silence, of course, but one should be able to hear them as well. It [the Afro-American novel] should try deliberately to make you stand up and make you feel something profoundly in the same way that a Black preacher requires his congregation to speak, to join him in the sermon, . . . to stand up and to weep and to cry and to accede to or change and to modify—to expand on the sermon that is being delivered. In the same way that a musician's music is enhanced when there is a response from the audience. Now in a book, which closes, after all—it's of some importance to me to try to make that connection—to try to make that happen also. And, having at my disposal only the letters of the alphabet and some punctuation, I have to provide the places and spaces so that the reader can participate. Because it is the affective and participatory relationship between the artist or the speaker and the audience that is of primary importance, as it is in these other art forms that I have described.[4]

Clearly there are connections between Afro-American call and response and contemporary views of the reader's role in the construction of textual meaning, but just as clear is the fact that Morrison's words and intent are being decontextualized, misread, if one does not at least mention that she is self-consciously placing her work in the expressive tradition of her people that dates back hundreds, perhaps thousands, of years. Surely the commendable desire for critical dialogue does not necessitate that we bracket cultural difference in an attempt to make our textual interpretations and the black works that spawn them indistinguishable from other texts in the Western literary tradition. Surely black feminist criticism in the 1990s must not attempt, as does one of Morrison's debilitatingly divided characters (in the Du Boisian sense where self-difference is equated not with liberation but with war), to "get rid of the funkiness"[5] of black female literary voices who proudly display, in some of the most provocative novels in Afro-American literary history, their black difference.

4. "Rootedness: The Ancestor as Foundation," In *Black Women Writers (1950–1980)*, ed. Mari Evans (New York: Doubleday, 1984), pp. 341–42.
5. *The Bluest Eye* (New York: Washington Square Press, 1970), p. 68.

3

Toward a Poetics of
Afro-American Autobiography

William L. Andrews

Since the mid-1960s, students of Afro-American autobiography have enjoyed increasing success in attracting the attention of the larger scholarly community to their critical enterprise. Before *Many Thousand Gone,* Charles Nichols's ground-breaking celebration of the slave narratives in 1963, black American autobiography had received only one book-length study, the sociological reading done by Rebecca Chalmers Barton in *Witnesses for Freedom* (1948). But once the public began to read the wealth of black autobiographies spawned by the upheavals of the 1960s, it didn't take long for scholars to start rediscovering black autobiography, first in reviews, then in critical essays, and eventually in ambitious attempts to define a tradition of Afro-American first-person writing. In 1974 two books, Stephen Butterfield's *Black Autobiography in America* and Sidonie Smith's *Where I'm Bound: Patterns of Slavery and Freedom in Black American Autobiography,* proposed rationales, historical frameworks, and evaluative principles for the interpretation of the Afro-American autobiographical tradition as a whole. Since then, however, no one has felt confident enough to try to put the history of black American autobiography between covers. Instead, the focus of literary scholarship has centered on the notable subgenre of the slave narrative. This has yielded two substantial volumes of essays and two literary histories, along with a plethora of articles. I can think of no other genre of Afro-American literature whose earliest history has been more extensively studied than autobiography. The significance of this fact is something I want to return to later when I talk about agendas, past and future, for black autobiography studies. But first, I want to pay tribute to the collective scholarly success achieved by researchers and critics of this genre.

The great achievement of critics of Afro-American autobiography since the 1960s has been to recover, interpret, and publicize the value of Afro-American autobiography to both the black and the larger white American communities of readers. The study of black autobiography has had a salutary effect on the black community's sense of its own literary resources and on the white literate community's sense of the importance of those resources. We have seen the study of black autobiography prove its utility to sociologists (such as Barton), anthropologists (such as Barbara Babcock-Abrahams), linguists (such as William Labov), social historians (such as John Blassingame and George Rawick), and literary historians (such as Frances Foster and myself).[1] After having been confined almost exclusively to black male autobiographies, the field is now opening up to the study of black women's autobiographies. Nevertheless, with some notable exceptions, critics, whether male or female, have treated Afro-American autobiography more as a document than as a monument, to use Panofsky's neat distinction between works that are viewed as a means and those viewed as an end. These autobiographical works have been viewed as a commentary on something extrinsic rather than as statements of something intrinsic to themselves.[2]

We have been moving away from a primarily documentary approach to Afro-American autobiography. We need not today argue that black personal narratives are relevant to the study of multiple humanistic disci-

1. See Rebecca Chalmers Barton, *Witnesses for Freedom* (1948; rpt., Oakdale, N.Y.: Dowling College Press, 1976); Barbara Babcock-Abrahams, "'A Tolerated Margin of Mess': The Trickster and His Tales Reconsidered," *Journal of the Folklore Institute* 11, no. 1 (1974): 147–86; William Labov, *Language in the Inner City* (Philadelphia: University of Pennsylvania Press, 1972); John W. Blassingame, *The Slave Community* (New York: Oxford University Press, 1972); George P. Rawick, ed., *The American Slave: A Composite Autobiography,* 19 vols. (Westport, Conn.: Greenwood, 1972); Frances Smith Foster, *Witnessing Slavery* (Westport: Greenwood, 1979); William L. Andrews, *To Tell a Free Story* (Urbana: University of Illinois Press, 1986).

2. A few of the exceptional treatments of Afro-American autobiography are Robert Stepto's work on the slave narrative and *Up From Slavery* in his *From Behind the Veil* (Urbana: University of Illinois Press, 1979); Houston A. Baker and John Sekora, "Written Off: Narratives, Master Texts, and Afro-American Writing," *Studies in Black American Literature* 1 (1983): 43–62; R. Baxter Miller, "'For a Moment I Wondered': Theory and Symbolic Form in the Autobiographies of Langston Hughes," *Langston Hughes Review* 3 (Fall 1984): 1–6; Sondra O'Neale, "Reconstruction of the Composite Self: New Images of Black Women in Maya Angelou's Continuing Autobiography," in Mari Evans, ed., *Black Women Writers (1950–1980)* (New York: Anchor, 1984), pp. 25–36; Henry Louis Gates, Jr., "James Gronniosaw and the Trope of the Talking Book," *Southern Review* 22 (April 1986): 252–72. Panofsky's distinction is found in his *Meaning in the Visual Arts* (1955).

plines. The question at the moment is whether we are ready to assert that the study of black autobiography can be *its own* discipline. It is one thing to say that this genre can tell us a great deal about black history or black psychology or black speech or black gender roles or black cultural traditions, not to mention white literary traditions. But it is quite another to say that black American autobiography can tell us a great deal about autobiography per se, autobiography as a *form* of oral and written expression, regardless of who wrote it or when it was written. Are we ready to claim that Afro-American autobiography is important to study for its own sake, as part of the discipline of reading and writing about literature?

If the answer to these questions is yes, then we need to start thinking seriously about a poetics of Afro-American autobiography. We need to start asking as many questions about the formal dimensions of this genre as we have posed about its thematic dimensions. I believe we have arrived at a place in our development as critics where we can recognize that the multifarious forms of storytelling in Afro-American literature profoundly signify—as well as signify on—the great themes of black narrative, both autobiographical and fictional, in this country. If this is true, then to study form in black autobiography need not mean a slighting, but rather a heightening, of the sociopolitical import of this genre. After all, as Fredric Jameson has convincingly argued, all texts can be read as having an "*ideology of form*." To study seriously the form of a text, then, does not mean disregarding history or acceding to the notion that extrinsic to form there is "some inertly social 'content'" (to use Jameson's derisive phrase) that the author labors to re-present in the text. Even the most narrowly political *explication de texte*, Jameson stresses, should construe "purely formal patterns as a symbolic enactment of the social within the formal and the aesthetic."[3] The problem with too much of the criticism that has been written on black autobiography is that it pays too little attention to the social, historical, or ideological significance of the forms of black narrating that have evolved since the mid-eighteenth century. To put it simply, we have read too many black autobiographies as works, not as texts.

What we need primarily from a poetics of Afro-American autobiography, it seems to me, are suggestive ways of thinking and rethinking the relationships of theme and form. We must resist any tendency to place form and theme in a binary opposition that valorizes one at the

---

3. Fredric Jameson, *The Political Unconscious* (Ithaca, N.Y.: Cornell University Press, 1981), pp. 76–77.

expense of the other. An agenda for the criticism of Afro-American autobiography in the 1990s ought to raise two questions simultaneously: "What does it mean?" and "How does it work?" These questions should be simultaneously posed in order always to explore or analyze black autobiography as a symbolic act that is both constative— i.e., that refers to something extrinsic—and performative—i.e., that enacts something by its very existence as a text. I believe our present critical moment is especially propitious to give credence and currency to the issue of a poetics of Afro-American autobiography. Theoretical interest in cultural criticism empowers us to claim the genre as a legitimate and necessary sphere for critical and theoretical debate. If we do not make such a claim and attempt to establish some ground rules for a poetics of Afro-American autobiography, who else will? And if someone outside the community of Afro-Americanists undertakes the project, will we like the result?

The poetics of Afro-American autobiography that I am proposing needs to be informed by a revised conception of the history of this genre. We have inherited from the 1960s a peculiar version of black American literary history, the parameters of which are implied in today's de facto canon of Afro-American autobiography. If the number of paperback editions and critical essays are indicative of canonical status, Afro-American autobiography has five canonical texts: Douglass's 1845 *Narrative,* Washington's *Up From Slavery,* Wright's *Black Boy, The Autobiography of Malcolm X,* and Maya Angelou's *I Know Why the Caged Bird Sings.* One reason these works have become canonical, I believe, is that they all have been compared and interpreted as major evolutions of the slave narrative, a tradition epitomized by Douglass's 1845 *Narrative,* which is certainly *the* central text in Afro-American autobiography studies today.

To say that the roots, if not the soul, of Afro-American autobiography are to be found in the slave narrative is to utter a truism, of course. But like all critical truisms, this one needs careful reconsideration. If we take a close look at what people call "the slave narrative," we discover that a particular kind of slave narrative has assumed a position of privilege in the literary history of Afro-American autobiography. When critics of autobiography talk about the slave narrative, what they refer to, invariably, are the antebellum slave narratives. The autobiographies that ex-slaves wrote after emancipation have been almost entirely ignored or condescendingly dismissed from serious scholarly consideration by literary historians. This despite the fact that the slave narrative continued to dominate Afro-American autobiography for seventy years, from the end of the Civil War until well into the Depression. Of this massive corpus of

postbellum slave narratives, only the oral accounts that the WPA collected in the 1930s have been studied, and these almost entirely by
historians.[4]

I call attention to this large lacuna in the literary history of black
American autobiography as it is currently conceived because this matter
bears directly on the issue of creating a poetics of Afro-American autobiography. It is very difficult to develop a viable set of principles for the
study of a genre if one proceeds from a skewed sense of the history of that
genre. Yet our autobiography criticism has been operating with a sense
of Afro-American literary history that is dangerously distorted. Our
problem arises partly because no one has done the type of scholarship
that would fill the gap in our awareness of what was happening to black
American autobiography from 1865 through the 1920s.

Our problem is a function, to a significant degree, of the politics of
literary interpretation in the 1960s and early 1970s. During that era,
white reviewers, critics, and academics first began to read black autobiography, forced to do so by the personal narratives of revolutionaries
such as Malcolm X, Eldridge Cleaver, George Jackson, and Angela
Davis. It was easy to see that the most widely read black autobiography
up to the 1960s—Washington's postbellum slave narrative, *Up from
Slavery*—did not foreground adequately the apocalyptic tone or revolutionary message of a *Soul on Ice* or a *Soledad Brother*. Not surprisingly,
during the 1960s *Up from Slavery* gradually lost its once privileged status
and was supplanted by Douglass's 1845 *Narrative,* a work that seemed to
accord much better with the experience and rhetoric of the most popular
black autobiographers of the 1960s. Douglass soon became the most
celebrated black autobiographer before Malcolm, and his *Narrative*
became the epitome of and model for the slave narrative in most early
studies of black autobiography, especially in Stephen Butterfield's influential book.

Taking Douglass's 1845 *Narrative* as the master text in the history of
Afro-American autobiography, Butterfield fashioned a chronicle of
black American autobiography that highlights writers whose lives and
styles seemed to echo Douglass's. Those who did not fit this mold were
generally ignored by Butterfield, although sometimes writers who di-
verged from Douglass were treated didactically as examples of how black

4. But see, as a notable exception, John Edgar Wideman's "Charles Chesnutt and the
WPA Narratives: The Oral and Literate Roots of Afro-American Literature," in Charles T.
Davis and Henry Louis Gates, Jr., eds., *The Slave's Narrative* (New York: Oxford Univer-
sity Press, 1985), pp. 59–78.

autobiographers could write about the wrong things in the wrong ways. Explicit in Butterfield's work is an ideological test for the inclusion of a black autobiography in his canon, a test based primarily on thematic, not formal, criteria—on what the autobiographies were written about, not on how they were written. Autobiographies that recount what Butterfield believed to be the paradigmatic black experience in America received careful and generally celebratory study. Blacks who did not lead exemplary—and I mean this in both senses of the word—lives he generally ignored. Thus Booker T. Washington, whom many have called the most influential black autobiographer between 1900 and 1960, receives little more than a couple of brief mentions in *Black Autobiography in America,* and they stress how *un*representative Washington's thinking was in comparison to that of his black contemporaries in autobiography. Washington's autobiography does not conform to a tradition of black autobiography that Butterfield defines as central by virtue of the prominence within it of "the identity crisis, the alienation, the restless movement," and a particular set of "views on education, knowledge, and resistance" (p. 155). Unfortunately, Butterfield seems to have reached this conclusion about the tradition without considering the more fundamental canon-formation question of how any historian of black autobiography should define representativeness in the genre and what significance he or she should assign to unrepresentative expression.

Unlike Butterfield, Sidonie Smith in *Where I'm Bound* could find room in the major tradition of black American autobiography for a text as apparently atypical as *Up from Slavery.* In fact, Smith devotes an entire chapter to *Up from Slavery.* She also outlines a considerable body of black first-person writing in the Washingtonian mode and acknowledges that the black "middle-class success stories" that Butterfield dismisses from his study are neither apolitical nor insignificant. This does not mean, however, that Smith was comfortable with the mode of Washington's self-presentation, particularly with the way in which he aligned his sense of success with the standards of the dominant socioeconomic order of his day. Is this not indicative, Smith wonders, of Washington's "rejection of his black identity and heritage," even of a pathetically masked "self-hatred"? How else can one explain a black autobiography that seems to endorse the norms of a racist socioeconomic order in such a "literal, unironic, unreflective" (p. 43) manner?

The problems that *Up from Slavery* presented for Sidonie Smith and Stephen Butterfield point up several theoretical issues that must be taken up before a useful poetics of Afro-American autobiography can be created. If Washington's autobiography is marginal to Butterfield's concept

of the black autobiographical tradition but central to Smith's, is the issue
a matter of which critic is right? Or do we need first to decide the
function of the presumably marginal and presumably central in any
attempt to reconstruct the dynamics of the history of Afro-American
autobiography? Thus far critics have theorized about the function of
black autobiography as marginal to white autobiography, leaving the
knottier problem of defining the same parameters *within* black autobiography for today's scholars. The response to Washington's modes of
self-presentation in *Black Autobiography in America* and *Where I'm Bound*
also reminds us of the highly vexed problem of how to define selfhood in
this tradition. Butterfield in particular, and Smith to a lesser degree,
seem to have reflected too little on the danger of reading history backwards—in Washington's case, of judging his model of selfhood as
dubious because it did not conform to models of selfhood that had been
authorized by black autobiographers of the 1960s and early 1970s.

The more fundamental question is, how *is* selfhood signified in the
Afro-American autobiographical tradition? Is selfhood a fairly static ideal in this tradition, as Butterfield suggests by his insistence on measuring
twentieth-century black self-awareness by a standard set in a handful of
antebellum slave narratives? Or is selfhood a dynamic notion, constituted as Smith suggests by an evolving appreciation among black
autobiographers of the complex meaning of freedom and slavery in
successive periods of history and by the degree to which an individual
autobiographer seeks and finds "liberation through the creative act of
writing autobiography itself" (p. x). It seems to me that Smith's approach to the problem of selfhood in this tradition is more reliable than
Butterfield's; undoubtedly the majority of critics working in this field
have leaned much more in her direction than in Butterfield's when trying
to assess the significance of self in black autobiography. Yet we still lack a
body of theoretical criticism that offers a means of thinking systemat-
ically about the rhetoric of selfhood in black autobiography, or indeed,
whether a term like "the self" is of any particular use anymore in discussing texts in this field.

If we are to have a new agenda for black autobiography criticism in the
1990s, we must give credit to the old agendas of the 1960s and 1970s
while recognizing too where we're bound by them. We cannot read the
history of Afro-American autobiography as though it validates a certain
model of black selfhood or approved notions of black experience without
acknowledging our own motives in desiring such validation. We cannot
deem a single black autobiography as representative of class or sexual
groups (as Smith does when she makes Angelou's autobiography the

text of "black womanhood") without acknowledging both the advantages and disadvantages of assigning a text representative status. If we wish to identify the black autobiographical tradition as "revolutionary," we must become politically sophisticated enough as critics to recognize that "revolutionary narratives" were not just written before 1865 and after 1960. If we take Bakhtin's version of literary history seriously, we should see that all narrative forms since the rise of the novel have been undergoing repeated revolutions, or "novelization." The novel is not only an inherently revolutionary genre but also one that ceaselessly novelizes, i.e., revolutionizes, the form and content of other narrative types—such as autobiography—closely allied to it. Under the influence of "novelization," traditions and generic standards of narrative form undergo constant revision. Nothing from the past remains wholly privileged; the novel forces all narrative forms into "a living contact with unfinished, still-evolving contemporary reality (the open-ended present)."[5]

My reading of black American autobiography from the nineteenth century suggests that the slave narrative underwent the kind of novelization that Bakhtin describes. There were revolutions in Afro-American autobiography between 1865 and 1920 of which we have little awareness because of the narrowness of our notions of what constitutes revolution in the literary history of black narrative.

I do not have time to make a genuine argument here about the ways in which we might rethink what we mean by "revolutionary narratives." I can only say that my study of the slave narrative has convinced me that between 1865 and 1930 some of the defining parameters of Afro-American autobiography—such as the image of slavery and the idea of heroic selfhood—underwent subtle but extremely significant revision. In my mind, these revisions amount to a striking evolution, if not a revolution, in the history of black autobiography, especially in the depiction of slavery. If I am right, then the study of the total history of the slave narrative can teach us more than we presently know about how the changing demands of the present have always compelled the revision of the past in black American autobiography.

What if we apply this axiomatic principle of autobiography study to the slave narrative? What if we read enough slave narratives to cause us to discover that the image of slavery, along with the metaphor of black selfhood, undergoes revision as the nineteenth century evolves? I am not

5. M. M. Bakhtin, *The Dialogic Imagination,* ed. Michael Holquist, trans. Caryl Emerson and Michael Holquist (Austin: University of Texas Press, 1981), p. 7.

speaking here about a wholesale face-lift; I am talking about many subtle (but significant) reshapings of the features of slavery and concomitant reassessments of the meaning of black selfhood both before and after slavery. What should we make of this revising of the image of slavery, especially if the postbellum ex-slaves did not portray slavery as harshly as their antebellum predecessors?

When critics and historians of black autobiography have addressed this question, they have posited the image of slavery in antebellum black autobiography as an orthodoxy. Here is what one recent literary historian has written about the postbellum slave narrative:

From the Reconstruction period on, a number of autobiographical writings of exslaves were published. These works, however, did not dwell upon the horrors of their writers' past conditions of servitude but were instead cheerleading exercises to urge continued opportunities for integration of blacks into American society or to depict black contributions to the Horatio Alger tradition. Their [these ex-slave narrators'] descriptions of slavery were mild and offered as "historical" evidence only.[6]

It is not difficult to see in this statement a critical bias in favor of a certain type of slave narrative—one that dwells upon "the horrors of their writers' past conditions of servitude" rather than one that highlights how far the ex-slave has come in his or her pursuit of the American Dream. It is not hard to draw invidious implications from this bias— namely, that the postbellum slave narrative was written by people who were so obsessed by bourgeois social-climbing that they could not or would not tell the whole truth about the ugly realities of their past. The trouble with such conclusions is that they substitute black bourgeoisie bashing—a prime-time sport in the 1960s—for serious research into the significance of middle-class status to ex-slaves in the late nineteenth and early twentieth centuries.

At present we know too little about the ideological implications of the postbellum slave narrative and other works of the middle period in the history of black American autobiography from the end of the Civil War to the onset of the Depression. A reading of even a few of the better-known texts of this era will reveal autobiographers who proudly regarded themselves as middle-class, a status that they aspired to in defiance of what they saw as American racism's program of keeping black people mired in poverty and powerlessness. The identification of these

6. Frances Smith Foster, *Witnessing Slavery* (Westport, Conn.: Greenwood, 1979), 150.

autobiographers with many of the institutions and myths of the American mainstream seems clearly at variance with the anti-institutional, romantic individualism of the antebellum fugitive-slave narrator. There can be little doubt, then, that mid-course in the history of black American autobiography some important paradigm shifts occurred. The question is, whether to call such shifts ideological reversal, a deviation *from* the paradigm into a kind of historical byway or dead end in the tradition—or to read them as indicative of a revision *of* the paradigm, literally, a looking back again at the assumptions on which fundamental parameters of the tradition, such as the concepts of selfhood, freedom, and slavery, had been based. No critic should dismiss such revising of the past as merely "revisionistic," i.e., merely reactionary, without first considering why it may have been necessary and strategic for black autobiographers to retool the black past in order to address the exigencies of the present. Failure to consider this issue has restricted our access to two neglected traditions in Afro-American autobiography: (1) most of the autobiographies published during what Charles Chesnutt called the post-bellum-pre-Harlem era, and (2) the origins of middle-class black autobiography in the United States.

A poetics of Afro-American autobiography must take into account the inevitable revision of traditions that has occurred in the past and that continues to occur today. Let me suggest that revising the past does not necessarily mean a deviation from historical truth. Revision can itself be indicative *of* a historical truth, not the truth embedded in something believed to be past but the truth emerging in something the autobiographer faces in the present.[7] It may be that the history of Afro-American autobiography has evolved through a rhythm of revisionary renewals of certain powerful myths and images of the past in response to the changing realities of the present. In any case, the dynamic principle that I see in the history of Afro-American autobiography is the *revising*, not the canonizing, of traditions, and even texts.

Booker T. Washington was not the first slave narrator to revise the image of slavery to suit his rhetorical needs and his historical circumstances. When William Wells Brown, whose justly famous slave narrative is impeccably antisouthern, wrote the fulsome *My Southern Home* in 1881, he played havoc not only with a literary tradition but also with his own authority as a charter member of the heroic fugitive school of Afro-

7. An example of this approach is Timothy Dow Adams, " 'I Do Believe Him Though I Know He Lies': Lying as Genre and Metaphor in Richard Wright's *Black Boy*," *Prose Studies* 8 (September 1985): 172–85.

American autobiography. Maybe this is why no one writes about Brown's postbellum slave narrative—it often contradicts what Brown wrote in 1846 about himself and slavery, and we don't know what to make of such self-contradiction. Yet J. Saunders Redding said in *To Make a Poet Black* that *My Southern Home* is unquestionably Brown's best book. Did Redding know things about Afro-American literary history that we need to relearn?

The first major principle of the poetics of Afro-American autobiography, then, is the recognition that revision often, though not always, signifies formal renewal where black autobiography is concerned. The study of the revising and renewal of traditions in Afro-American autobiography may yield at least two benefits. We may begin to uncover forces that underly this dynamic so that we can write more sophisticated histories of the evolution of Afro-American autobiography. Second, we may begin to revise our own canon of Afro-American autobiography, or perhaps to develop alternative canons.

To bring these two possibilities closer to reality, we need to remember that more than one critic has called autobiography the most democratic of literary genres. We need a suitably democratic criticism. In other words, we need to take an inclusive approach to the study of Afro-American autobiography. To do this is to put in abeyance our normal expectations about what should and should not happen in a text or between a text and its reader. Feminist scholarship in Afro-American autobiography has done much to challenge and change assumptions we have followed in reconstructing the history and traditions of this genre. Jean Fagan Yellin's edition of *Incidents in the Life of a Slave Girl* has had a major impact on the way the entire antebellum slave narrative tradition is conceived. No doubt Joann Braxton's new history of black women's autobiography, with its emphasis on a muted "tradition within a tradition," will initiate even more broad-scale reassessments of the canon of Afro-American autobiography.[8] Now that we have the Schomburg Library of Nineteenth-Century Black Women Writers, of which Henry Louis Gates, Jr., is the general editor, the task of revaluation of the past in black autobiography will be much easier and hence much more pressing for critics to take up.

As we gain a more complete picture of the traditions in black American autobiography, the need grows for new histories of Afro-American autobiography. Hayden White's essay "The Value of Narrativity in the

8. Braxton's *Autobiography by Black American Women: A Tradition within a Tradition* is forthcoming from Temple University Press.

Representation of Reality" makes a convincing argument about the authority and moral imperative that narrative invests in any set of elements that it structures.[9] Taking White's contention seriously, I believe that the best way to legitimize and empower the study of Afro-American autobiography as a literary discipline is to create narrative histories of this genre. This is a challenging task, especially given the many theoretical problems that writing literary history presents today. But we must not be content with recovering the pieces of Afro-American autobiography; we must reconstitute the puzzle and interpret its significance in our own allegories of reading, for better or for worse. Thus I look forward to the work of people such as Nellie McKay, whose projected study of black women's autobiography from 1920 to 1970 will give us another chapter in the genre history I hope to see written by many hands in the 1990s.

A further principle of the poetics of Afro-American autobiography that I wish to discuss is the most fundamental one, the sine qua non, it seems to me, for critics who wish to understand not only what black autobiography means but how it works on both the synchronic and diachronic planes. If there is an overarching or underlying motif in Afro-American autobiography, I believe it is the phenomenon that I have elsewhere labeled "free storytelling." My definition and explanation reads: "The history of Afro-American autobiography is one of increasingly free storytelling, signaled in the ways black narratives address their readers and reconstruct personal history, ways often at variance with literary conventions and social proprieties of discourse."[10] My reading of the history of black American autobiography is far from complete, having concentrated primarily on two eras, from 1760 to 1865 and from 1865 to 1930. But from my work, I see no reason not to affirm my conviction that freedom is not just the theme but the *sign* of Afro-American autobiography. To realize this is to open one's eyes to the formal, stylistic, and rhetorical richness of black narrative tradition.

Black people have written autobiographies for many reasons, but one of the most pervasive is the desire to demonstrate one's freedom in and through oral or written storytelling. Some writers are better at this than others, of course. What I am interested in here is the revolutionary implication of free storytelling for the evaluation of texts as well as for understanding of traditions in Afro-American autobiography. If the

9. Hayden White, "The Value of Narrativity in the Representation of Reality," *Critical Inquiry* 7 (1980): 5–28.
10. *To Tell a Free Story*, p. xi.

1960s and 1970s were a time to applaud "revolutionary narratives" on the basis of ideological content, can the 1980s and 1990s become the time to appreciate what is revolutionary in the formal evolution of black narratives?

If the burden of black autobiography in America is to *tell* freedom, not just tell *about* freedom, then what I hope we will see in the 1990s is a criticism that helps us to recognize free storytelling in its many manifestations throughout the history of this genre. There can be no single definition of this principle of freedom in our poetics of Afro-American autobiography. Telling freedom can involve demonstrating one's liberation from any outworn or restrictive form of thinking or writing. To discover whether, or the extent to which, this is true, we will need a more sophisticated critical vocabulary than the one I have been using here. It is heartening to see such a vocabulary being developed and used by critics like Houston Baker, Henry Louis Gates, Jr., and Hortense Spillers, not just in application to autobiography but also to all storytelling forms in black American literature.

In *Blues, Ideology, and Afro-American Literature,* Baker homes in on "blues moments" in Afro-American discourse when the "trained" voice translates into metaphorical and formal terms the "unrestrained mobility and unlimited freedom" of the railroad, the focal and aural symbol of black vernacular expression in this country. To read and hear the blues in this extended fashion is to suggest that freedom plays through Afro-American narrative in ways hitherto unimagined. When Gates calls signifyin(g) "the trope of tropes" in Afro-American literature and goes on to show that its essence is to revise, reverse, or otherwise make free with sign, signified, and indeed, the person who plays the role of the signifier, he grounds the idea of free storytelling in another cultural setting and provides a systematic way of tracing its operation in a text. When Spillers says that " 'tradition' for the black women's writing community is a matrix of literary *discontinuities*"; when she argues that black women writers "engage no allegiance to a hierarchy of dynastic meanings," but rather revise each other's stories without regard for the priorities or influences that literary history might like to impose, then she is calling attention to the historical dimensions of free storytelling in the black female narrative. When black women make free with tradition to the point of seeming to contradict all that "tradition" has been privileged to mean in academic discourse, then it is time, Spillers reminds us, to reexamine what we think tradition is. As we do this, I think we will begin to understand the freedom that black women autobiographers have sought, or that has claimed them willy-nilly, in their participation in the revisionary renewals of Afro-American autobiography.[11]

I conclude my remarks acutely aware that I have not acknowledged all those critics whose work I admire and from whom I have learned much about Afro-American autobiography. Had I done this, however, my footnotes would have become longer than my text. Criticism, like literature (to paraphrase Langston Hughes), is "a big sea full of many fish." In the spirit of Hughes I've cast my net, not to show off a catch, but rather to display the net and how it might be cast.

Response: *Sandra Pouchet Paquet*

Professor Andrews raises key issues in his proposed agenda for the study of Afro-American autobiography in the 1990s. His call for a poetics of Afro-American autobiography touches core themes surrounding the nature of Afro-American literature as a whole. He seeks to establish a careful distinction between a poetics of Afro-American autobiography per se and a poetics of Afro-American literature.

It is the Afro-American in the subject title that is ascendant in the discussion that follows. In my opinion, the confluence of racial and national consciousness that gives Afro-American culture its distinctive character overarches questions of ideology, canon-formation, literary history, and the search for definitive tropes and signs.[1] I will address some of these issues and also suggest some analogous concerns in West Indian literature about autobiography as a literary mode.

To begin with a commonplace, a comprehensive theory of Afro-American autobiography is extraordinarily complex. It includes letters, journals, diaries, and oral histories as well as formal autobiographies. Not only do critical issues differ among these forms of autobiography, but there are additional critical questions about the interrelationship between these forms in Afro-American autobiography. There are also

11. See Houston A. Baker, Jr., *Blues, Ideology, and Afro-American Literature* (Chicago: University of Chicago Press, 1984); Henry L. Gates, Jr., "The 'Blackness of Blackness': A Critique of the Sign and the Signifying Monkey," *Critical Inquiry* 9 (June 1983): 685–723; and Hortense Spillers, "Cross-Currents, Discontinuities: Black Women's Fiction," in Marjorie Pryse and Hortense J. Spillers, eds., *Conjuring: Black Women, Fiction, and Literary Tradition* (Bloomington: Indiana University Press, 1985), pp. 249–61.

1. Elizabeth W. Bruss writes in *Autobiographical Acts* (Baltimore: Johns Hopkins University Press, 1976): "Autobiography thus acquires its meaning by participating in symbolic systems making up literature and culture" (p. 6).

questions of cultural context which are of central importance when the
genre is identified as distinctively Afro-American. The idea of a culturally
distinct Afro-American literary tradition identifies a creative effort that
begins with the oral traditions of our African ancestors who first re-
corded their epic experience as slaves in the New World. The idea of
Afro-American autobiography as opposed to American autobiography,
or simply autobiography, postulates a continuation of that creative effort
and a functional responsibility to the ethos of an evolving Afro-American
community.

The idea of Afro-American autobiography assumes that the Afro-
American experience is an organizing concern in the autobiographical
forms under scrutiny. It follows, therefore, that a poetics of Afro-American autobiography will examine the generic preoccupation of autobiography with the individual self in the context of the epic experience of
African-Americans. As critics of an evolving Afro-American literary tradition, we go to Afro-American autobiography with expectations that it
will reflect the epic experience of the group. Autobiography written by
African-Americans may not always serve this function, or may do so with
varying degrees of intensity, or in ways that we do not recognize. However, an important measure of aesthetic value remains the specific context
supplied by the epic experience of African-Americans in the New World.
A poetics of Afro-American autobiography should evaluate the balance
between the self-expressive, generic function and other functional aspects of autobiography in this context.[2]

William Andrews's search for the *sign* of the genre is a case in point. In
a poetics of Afro-American autobiography this search is circumscribed
by questions of cultural allegiance. The sign of the genre must reflect the
values of both the genre and an Afro-American cultural context. Thus,
however useful it may be as a descriptive term, "free storytelling" is too
culturally neutral to serve the same function as "signifying monkey" or
"blues" as an interpretive trope.[3] What is even more to the point in
constructing a poetics of Afro-American autobiography is that all three
terms have currency as *signs* descriptive of pervasive cultural values rather
than of a specific genre or artistic form.

The role of ideology in identifying the symbolic systems that make up
Afro-American literature and culture, and in identifying/naming texts

2. Ibid, pp. 10–11.
3. See Henry Louis Gates, Jr., "The 'Blackness of Blackness': A Critique of the Sign
and the Signifying Monkey," in *Black Literature and Literary Theory*, ed. Gates (New York
and London: Methuen, 1984), pp. 285–321; and Houston A. Baker, Jr., *Blues, Ideology,
and Afro-American Literature* (Chicago: University of Chicago Press, 1984).

that are perceived to be in dialogue with those symbolic systems can be a troubling one, as William Andrews points out.[4] As critics and literary historians, we are interpreters rather than creators of such symbolic systems. But while we question a canon that serves short-lived political ends, we understand that ideology is always with us in canon-formation. In *Blues, Ideology, and Afro-American Literature,* Houston A. Baker, Jr., maintains that "the 'art object' as well as its value are selective constructions of the critic's tropes and models."[5] In fact, every culture has ideological underpinnings, though they are often perceived in religious rather than political terms.[6]

A poetics of Afro-American autobiography must be framed in dialogue with the ideological underpinnings of Afro-American culture as they are revealed through the creative genius of African-Americans. Such an ideological test in canon-formation is inescapable as a criterion of aesthetic value, and it ought not to be confused with the edicts of a popular political movement. It is the epic stature of certain key texts, in form or theme—or, to quote Hortense Spillers, "their total and dynamic situatedness"[7]—rather than the narrow political bias of the 1960s, that gives the antebellum slave narratives their privileged position in Afro-American autobiography and credits Frederick Douglass's 1845 *Narrative* as a master text. After all, our canon has a place for Harriet Brent Jacobs's *Incidents in the Life of a Slave Girl,* as well as Douglass's 1845 *Narrative* and Booker T. Washington's *Up From Slavery,* despite the different functional values of these texts within an expansive cultural matrix.

Ideally, canon-formation identifies core texts of a developing literary tradition. It is open-ended. A literary tradition, as Hortense Spillers observes in "Cross-Currents, Discontinuities: Black Women's Fiction," is "a matrix of literary *discontinuities* that partially articulate various periods of consciousness in the history of an African-American people."[8] A

4. In "The 'Blackness of Blackness'," Gates proposes "a theory of formal revision; it is topological; it is often characterized by pastiche; and, most crucially, it turns on repetition of formal structures and their difference" (pp. 285–86).

5. Baker, *Blues,* p. 10.

6. See Derek Walcott's "The Muse of History" in *Is Massa Day Dead?*, ed. Orde Coombs (New York: Anchor Books, 1974), pp. 1–27: "It returns us to Eliot's pronouncement, that a culture cannot exist without a religion, and to other pronouncements irradiating that idea, that an epic poetry cannot exist without a religion" (p. 11).

7. Hortense J. Spillers, "Cross-Currents, Discontinuities: Black Women's Fiction," in *Conjuring: Black Women, Fiction, and Literary Tradition,* ed. Marjorie Pryse and Hortense J. Spillers (Bloomington: Indiana University Press, 1985), p. 258.

8. Spillers, "Cross-Currents," p. 251.

literary tradition establishes itself in a generational cycle of renewal and rebirth. It is always in process and, therefore, incomplete. If an evolving literary tradition is open-ended, in an unfolding pattern of assimilation and transformation, then it is the task of critics to keep a poetics of Afro-American autobiography responsive to the expressive variety of African-American creative genius. Recent developments in Afro-American women's writing remind us that writers are continually opening up new ways of organizing experience and shaping new metaphors for the collective Afro-American experience. Such developments must make critics sensitive to the reality that canons are fluid. Our angle of vision changes, not only with race, class, and gender, but also with the dynamics of any given historical moment.

The call for new literary histories of Afro-American autobiography directly addresses the inequities of canon-formation grounded in literary history. The feminist charge of male dominance of both the history and poetics of autobiography is well founded.[9] Charges of patriarchal exclusion remind us that, historically, literary history has served the bias of critics and literary historians alike. Literary history is by its very nature self-serving and, in this respect, can menace the living tradition it attempts to serve.

A poetics that is grounded exclusively in literary history is bound by the allegiance that informs it. Literary history, writes Hortense Spillers, is committed "to a hierarchy of dynastic meanings that unfolds in linear succession and according to our customary sense of 'influence'."[10] It seeks to clarify the ancestral vision and to codify it in selected metaphors of past generations. In reality, literary history fosters veneration of the ancestral genius rather than dialogue; it nourishes imitation rather than assimilation. Here, the theme of ancestry that is everywhere an issue in Afro-American literature and criticism reveals its repressive as well as its nurturing aspects. A poetics of Afro-American autobiography grounded exclusively in literary history is continually in danger of defeating the living tradition it serves. A true poetics of Afro-American autobiography will reflect the broader context furnished by an evolving Afro-American literary and cultural tradition as well as the specific context furnished by a new inclusive literary history. Indeed, the writing of Afro-American literary histories is at best myth-making, and ought to be subject to the same fundamentals of assimilation and renewal that pertain to Afro-

9. Sidonie Smith, *A Poetics of Women's Autobiography* (Bloomington and Indianapolis: Indiana University Press, 1987), especially pp. 12–16.
10. Spillers, "Cross-Currents," p. 258.

American literature as a whole. This would give the writing of such literary histories status as the partial recall of the race, and limit its authority over the literary and cultural traditions it serves.

The critical issues surrounding a poetics of Afro-American auto-biography are also important to core texts of West Indian auto-biography. It is true that West Indian autobiography as a genre appears to have no comparable depth of history, no status in West Indian liter-ature that compares with the paradigmatic quality of Afro-American autobiography in relation to Afro-American literature as a whole .*The Life of Olaudah Equiano, or Gustavus Vassa the African. Written by Himself* (1789) is still unclaimed as a literary ancestor in the English-speaking Caribbean. *The History of Mary Prince* (1831) and *The Wonderful Adven-tures of Mrs. Seacole in Many Lands* (1857) are largely ignored by West Indian critics and literary historians. Certainly, Equiano's rejection of the West Indian landscape appears to be at cross-purposes with the develop-ment of national literatures and the growth of national consciousness in the West Indies in this century. But the critical issues surrounding these works are still to be defined from a West Indian point of view. In fact, autobiography as a substantive component in West Indian literature is a recent development. Its emergence has been tentative and its boundaries blurred by an overlay of fiction and, more recently, of poetry.

In two key works, George Lamming's *In the Castle of My Skin* (1953) and Derek Walcott's *Another Life* (1973), the autobiographical imper-ative is largely subsumed in the discourses of fiction and poetry. In C. L. R. James's *Beyond the Boundary* (1963), autobiography is a frame-work for cultural assessment and intellectual history. However, these three works distill a central argument about the story of the self being representative of more than individual experience. They are celebrations of community rather than of the rugged individualism of some black Horatio Alger, middle-class entrepreneur, or politician. In each case, the individual predicament of the writer as autobiographical subject dis-solves into the collective predicament of a representative island community.

This use of autobiography for a purpose that is collective rather than individual is an aesthetic value that links these West Indian works to Afro-American autobiographical modes. However, in each of these texts there is a conscious repression of the autobiographical self that is atypical of core texts in Afro-American autobiography. In Lamming's auto-biographical novel *In the Castle of My Skin,* the narrative is split into two autonomous voices. Self-representation is muted and elusive as Lam-ming subordinates sections of autobiography to a dominant omniscient narrative.[11] On a visit to the University of Pennsylvania in November 1987, Derek Walcott explained that in *Another Life* he abandoned autobiography to elegy and intellectual history. Similarly, C. L. R. James prefaces *Beyond the Boundary* with an announcement that the text is not autobiography but cultural history within the framework of autobiography.[12]

In its fledgling status, West Indian autobiography appears grounded in issues of West Indian selfhood. It is dominated by an ideology of racial and national consciousness. Thus the canon currently enshrines *Another Life* rather than Edgar Mittelholzer's *A Swarthy Boy* (1963), and recognizes Claude McKay's unfinished account of his childhood and youth in Jamaica, *My Green Hills of Jamaica* (posthumous, 1979), rather than *A Long Way from Home* (1937). In the emerging West Indian autobiographical canon, self-inquiry is self-imaging and self-evaluation, but it is also cultural assessment. It is a way of laying claim to a landscape that is at once geographical, historical, and cultural.

Despite the differences, there are important correspondences and parallels between Afro-American autobiography and its West Indian counterpart. Both have their genesis in the epic struggle of African slaves to name their vision and experience of the New World. Both record the epic struggle to create a language and cultural forms that express the transformation of self endemic to slavery, and the double inheritance of a transplanted and transformed African culture and a dominant, hostile European culture. Like their Afro-American counterparts, core texts of West Indian autobiography record their communities' struggle to survive and renew the terms of that struggle for future generations. In these texts, self-knowledge is defined in terms of a broader inquiry about American or Caribbean culture, history, and identity. Significantly, it is the authors of these autobiographical texts, rather than critics and literary historians, who first invoke their respective cultures as the context in which the search for self-knowledge is embedded. Thus, it becomes impossible to separate the autobiographical text from the cultural tradition out of which it springs, without violating the integrity of the text.

One inference to be drawn here is that Afro-American literature is as much a national literature as any of the regional literatures of the modern Caribbean. The Martiniquan poet and novelist Edouard Glissant writes: "One may speak of a national literature, in the modern sense of the term,

11. See George Lamming's remarkable Introduction to the Schocken edition of *In the Castle of My Skin* (New York: 1983).

12. C. L. R. James, *Beyond the Boundary* (London: Hutchinson, 1963).

only in the instance where a community, faced with a threat to its collective survival, endeavors through the creative use of the spoken and written word to express the very reason for its existence."[13] In this respect then, a culturally distinct Afro-American literature is not determined exclusively by race or color but by fidelity to the moral and cultural imperative of its primal beginnings in slavery and apartheid. To abandon this primal hierarchy of value is the beginning of another tradition.

Its origins in slavery and apartheid have given Afro-American literature a compulsive thematics that poses a general condition for Afro-American writing. In the modern Caribbean, the cultural ethos is different; slavery and apartheid have given way to what Wilson Harris of Guyana calls the "ground of accommodation," and "the art of creative coexistence."[14] But the relationship between text and culture is essentially the same for the literatures of both worlds. A poetics of Afro-American autobiography, like a poetics of West Indian autobiography, is necessarily embedded in broader cultural issues of collective survival, or it loses its cultural validity.

Response: *Geneviève Fabre*

I would like to respond first as a French person who belongs to that wider scholarly community whose attention has been drawn to the wealth of slave narratives recently made available to an ever-expanding readership, as well as to the equally impressive amount of scholarship that has been directed toward the study of Afro-American autobiography, offering a great variety of viewpoints and perspectives. My remarks will focus on slave narratives.

It seems to me that our own interest in this body of work has, in a more modest way, followed the same stages that Andrews notes in his essay. We in France first approached those texts as important documents and testimonies, highlighting important aspects of plantation life that we knew little about, aspects that had not been fully analyzed and dealt with in history books. At a time when French historians were reflecting upon their discipline,[1] calling for the end of global history and trying to define

13. Edouard Glissant, "Literature and the Nation in Martinique," *Caliban* 4, no. 1, p. 3.

14. Wilson Harris, "History, Fable and Myth in the Caribbean and Guianas," *Caribbean Quarterly* 16, no. 2, p. 8.

1. J. LeGoff and P. Nora, *Faire de l'histoire*, 3 vols. (Paris: Gallimard, 1974). Paul Veyne, *Comment on écrit l'histoire* (Paris: Le Seuil, 1971). Collective, *L'Histoire et ses méthodes* (Paris: Gallimard, 1961). Ph. Ariès, *Le temps de l'histoire* (Paris: Plon, 1954). M. de Certeau, *L'Absent de l'histoire* (Paris: Mame, 1973).

new approaches, new problems, slave narratives appeared as important new objects and microhistories. It was most important for us to realize that so many narratives had been written or collected, important to have access to them. We felt the slave's point of view had not been sufficiently documented or seriously taken into account.

Conversely, the need to contextualize was also of course emphasized. Our students were anxious to read books about slavery in order to reconstruct the framework in which each text could be read and to grasp its significance in antebellum America. The job was to understand the historical, political, and cultural conditions of the emergence of these texts, the forces with or against which they worked, their modes of distribution, the readership that they were trying to reach, their relationship with the abolitionist movement and with other antislavery writings. All this, we thought, would help us analyze the structures and inner strategies of the texts and the true nature of the autobiographical act. We were concerned to identify the narrators, their roles both as members of the black community of slaves or freemen and as mediators between the black and the white worlds, between the world created by the text (*le monde du texte*) and that of the reader.[2]

There were many other questions we wished to address: the origin and development of the genre, its successive transformations throughout the eighteenth and nineteenth centuries, the ways it differed from other literary forms—romance or picaresque—and from other autobiographies, or the perhaps unique tradition it had created, a tradition where self-definition, examination, discovery, and salvation could not be pursued with the same means as in "white" autobiography. In the slave's text collective identity was more important than the individual self; narrators constantly wavered between conventions and cultural imperatives they found inadequate for their task and the necessity to invent new tools, create speech acts for a better understanding of that basic yet perplexing reality, "the white man's power to enslave the black man."[3] Writing, for the slave narrator, became an act of empowerment, a way of struggling to take control of one's existence through the command of the word.

Other problems came up: that of literacy in its correlation to political rights, also as an achievement the slaves were striving for. Literacy became a goal which could secure fragments of freedom in a world that violently suppressed all knowledge and expression. There was the prob-

2. P. Ricoeur, *Le Temps raconté* (Paris: Le Seuil, 1985).
3. F. Douglass, *Narrative of the Life of Frederick Douglass* (New York: Anchor, 1973), chap. 6, p. 36.

lem of the revisions of the "black image in the white mind" as well as the revision of prevalent myths and common allegations (that slaves had no mind, no memory, no history . . .), ideological lies and assumptions. We were also interested in the narrative form through which slaves articulated their experience, their impulses and ideals, in what Paul Ricoeur calls the "narrated time,"[4] in dramatizations, in the various presentations and metaphors of the self, in self-authentication but also in the figurations of collective life and consciousness.

We, therefore, experimented with various *degrés de lecture*, from the literal to the more hidden meanings, and approached the texts from several perspectives: as primary source material documenting aspects of the sociocultural and intellectual history of Afro-Americans, as vital cultural forms, partly derived from orality, which created a new tradition in modes of thinking as well as in modes of writing. We saw the texts as imaginative, reflexive, and symbolic enactments, as creative responses to a specific experience and historical situation which had perhaps been instrumental in changing the course of history.

Two sets of scholarly works came to be of great importance to us. One came from an international, although mostly French, community of scholars;[5] the other was most directly related to the study of black autobiography.

Social scientists and historians were asserting the importance of autobiography and life stories as highly valuable material in their disciplines. They were also examining cultural, methodological, and theoretical problems this study raised. The emphasis here was mainly on the relation between culture and identity, the individual self and the collectivity. In essays that came out in *Cahiers Internationaux de Sociologie* (1980), autobiographical data were defined by Nicole Gagnon and Françoise Morin as expressions of identity and treated as "ethnotexts." Some of these approaches proved fruitful to the study of black autobiography inasmuch as slave narratives made claims to an identity that had long been denied or made invisible and were affirming the authority and legitimacy of the newly raised distinctive voice. The writing of a narrative was a

4. Ricoeur, *Le Temps raconté*.
5. P. Joutard, *Ces voix qui nous viennent du passé* (Paris: Hachette, 1983). F. Zonabend, *La Mémoire longue* (Paris: PUF, 1980). F. Ferraroti, *Histoire et histoire de vie*. A. Leroi-Gourhan, *La Mémoire et ses rythmes* (Paris: Albin Michel, 1965). M. Serres, *Hermès ou la communication* (Paris: Minuit, 1968). J. Vansina, *De la tradition orale* (Paris: Tervuren, 1961). F. Braudel, *Ecrits sur l'histoire* (Paris: 1969). B. Verhaegen, *Introduction à l'histoire immédiate* (Belgium, Ducolot, 1974). M. Foucault, *Archéologie du savoir* (Paris: Gallimard, 1968).

baptism, a way of claiming a spiritual birthright, an initiation rite into a world of freedom whose full implications had to be construed: freedom of the slave, freedom of the narrator. The writing act was also a way of expressing the silent, unknown souls of a whole community of being, a way of forging a collective identity against odds and presumptions.

Simultaneously, a French scholar was offering new insights into autobiography. Philippe Lejeune[6] examined the principles which govern the genre, the conventions operating in it, the special, implicit and explicit, contract established with the reader, the rhetorical presence or absence of a narrator-subject in genuine, disguised, or faked autobiographies, the uncertain margin between biography, autobiography, and fictional narrative. Through his analysis of a wide spectrum of "autobiographical" texts, Lejeune invited us to look at aspects and issues we had overlooked and to replace them in the specific context of the slave narrative.

The second set of works came from scholarship bearing more directly on Afro-Americans; from the research, first, of black historians (like John Blassingame, in *Slave Testimony*) with their impulse to revise former historiography, drawing attention to the problem of reliability, representativeness, veracity, credibility, and, second, of literary historians or critics who presented black autobiography as having a key place in Afro-American letters. Books or essays on black autobiography have been instrumental in helping us pose a richer and more diversified problematic, in perfecting our tools of analysis and in understanding what the blueprints for a black poetics could be. They were also serving two objectives: to include autobiography in the canonical texts of Afro-American literature, and to show how slave narratves have been the Ur-texts, creating a tradition important enough to be a constant literary and cultural reference for writers and scholars.

William Andrews's work brings together many of the questions which different studies have raised; it also breaks new ground by developing these inquiries and investigations and revealing new implications. It takes a strong stand against certain assumptions—such as James Olney's (in *The Slave's Narrative,* ed. Doris and Bates, pp. 143–75)—that most narrators remain "slaves to a prescribed conventional and imposed form" or "captive to the abolitionist intentions" and could not be free creators, and that their works do not qualify as either autobiography or literature. Since I do not think Andrews's essay in its concise form does justice to all

6. Philippe Lejeune, *Le pacte autobiographique* (Paris: Gallimard, 1975).

his analysis in *To Tell a Free Story,* I shall make several references to that book, which I consider a major work in the field.

In the first part of his argument Andrews reclaims black autobiography for literary criticism and asserts the need to rescue it from social scientists and from the multiple uses it has been put to in humanistic disciplines. This claim has been made repeatedly and can be extended to different genres (theatre, novel, etc.), and I find echoes of the same preoccupation among Hispanic and other "ethnic" writers who call for their own literary space within the American scene.

Scholars in Afro-American studies have had a leading role, encouraging scholars in other fields; Asian-American, Hispanic, Amerindian literatures are now being interpreted for their own specific readership as well as for a broader audience. The same regrets and fears are being expressed: that those literatures receive subliterary minority status and are appraised mostly for their historical, sociological, and documentary value. The same demands are made for highly sophisticated literary analysis. I also detect among other ethnic groups some envy toward the scholarship achieved by black academics as well as toward the scope of Afro-American literary works to which this scholarship has been applied: the effort devoted to retrieve texts from oblivion; the attention given to little-known works, to reediting forgotten texts, to the unearthing of unpublished manuscripts, to the whole output of women writers; the will to extend the field to be explored beyond a few canonical texts.

Each generation of critics, Andrews claims, has its own politics of literary interpretation and preferences, its favorite texts, its privileged references. We certainly have to reflect upon the reasons for such choices. We have definitely moved away from the 1960s and 1970s; fashions have changed but there is a trend toward more *inclusiveness*. This principle should perhaps be further discussed, since it is tempered by the necessity of being discriminative, of defining the achievement of one work compared to that of another. One can be wary about value judgments, but if they must be made, what are to be the criteria of excellence? Who is to set them? And to what end?

We are now faced by a plurality of techniques in literary criticism, which may be quite puzzling and overwhelming—techniques often borrowed from other disciplines (linguistics, semiotics, psychoanalysis, cultural or interpretive anthropology . . .) A choice has to be made here, too, and I wonder what determines the preference: the critic's attraction to one school, or the special quality of the texts that call for a particular approach? Or can any technique be applied to any work and be equally brilliant and convincing whatever the text under consideration? We have reached a point where the quality of a work seems to be attested to or measured by the degree of sophistication that can be applied to its study: the more elaborate the criticism, the greater the work.

One is tempted to argue for a diversified and analytical approach that would arise from the object examined, not one that can be artificially fastened on from outside. Some of these naive questions may be relevant to the forging of a black poetics, and we may ask: which is ultimately served most by a brilliant, highly sophisticated analysis—the text, its writer, the reader or the critic, the theory used? How much does the reader, the "common reader," benefit from it? Does the scholarly examination of a text, the current growing conceptualization of black literature enhance or spoil the *plaisir de la lecture,* stimulate or jeopardize the basic relation to the Afro-American reader or the broader community of readers? Is there an ongoing dialogue and interaction between reader, writer, narrator, and critic, and also, as Ricoeur says, between *le monde du texte* and *le monde du lecteur,* and can new theories be induced from these interactions?

Artist, audience, and aesthetic form are part of a larger collective experience which their mutual participation contributes to create. When Andrews says, "If we do not make such a claim . . . who else will?" who is *we?* Close examination of black autobiography shows how indebted new, evolving black poetics can be to that literary "vernacular" form, how it can help define Afro-American cultural uniqueness and difference, define the claims and commitments, the new premises which have to be distinct from the ones set by the mainstream literary establishment.

Concerning the second principle outlined by Andrews, that of *free* storytelling, I was most interested by the analysis in his book of the ways that Afro-American narrators broke free from certain imposed, widely accepted conventions, how they were able to manipulate and subvert them, "separating the conventions, norms and patterns of discourse of an existing genre from its standard context." Not only do narrators reconstruct their lives but they also reconstruct "a set of conditions in which the reader will find it appropriate to reexamine the concept of identity and personal value."

Black autobiography forces us to reconsider "determinants of personhood in white America." Andrews shows how oratory and rhetorical devices and stances orient the reader's response, force attention to certain facts, and attempt to communicate the paradoxes of black experience in the United States. Narrators were very much aware of the bias of the average reader, who often embodied official white moral standards, and this reader—fictive or implied—is always addressed directly or indirectly in the text. Andrews insists on the fact that autobiography also incorporates into the narrative texture forms of discourse that extend beyond a rhetorical relationship between narrator and reader and dramatize the sociolinguistic reality with and against which all black speech-action contended for authority. With the help of various speech-act theories Andrews examines the different dimensions of speech. Truth-telling, as he demonstrates, is a central issue in a genre that is supposed to make more ostensible truth claims. But, forced to adapt itself to a perverse social system and communication situation set by white culture, Afro-American autobiography fictionalized itself: the narrators, who want to tell the truth but not the whole truth that could not easily be believed, fictionalize their true story.

In telling a *free* story, black autobiography establishes a new poetics in autobiographical writing, different from the mainstream American tradition, with its self-devised conventions that are often deviations from the norm. Some black autobiographers stood at a critical moment in Afro-American cultural and intellectual history. Some slave narratives became provocative and challenging acts of empowerment forcing revisions and reconsideration of old presuppositions, disrupting the rules of mental and literary discourse and current patterns of thought, revealing new narrative possibilities. They fashioned new images of freedom, a freedom that concerned not only the slave's life and physical survival but also his role and introduction in the American Republic and on the literary scene. It is this political, mental, and literary freedom, this image of the narrator as a free mind and free artist, that prevails and has been handed down to several generations of Afro-American writers who have found in slave narratives their literary and spiritual models; as the French historian Pierre Nora would say, they found their *lieux de mémoire*.[7]

It is on this notion of *loci of memory* that I would like to conclude. Authors of slave narratives were the first creators, shapers, and organizers of a collective memory and historical consciousness; they wove complex webs of significance between place and time (the plantation, the "peculiar institution," and postrevolutionary, pre–Civil War America), past and present, enslavement and freedom (slaveholding South, free blacks, abolitionist and antislavery forces in North and South). They pointed to the problematic existence of freedom—in a country which could simultaneously support and condemn slavery and has not yet paid its dues to the sons and daughters of its former slaves. They also pointed to the importance of literacy, a literacy that was always denied and had to be fought for and that became one of the secret keys to freedom. Freedom

7. P. Nora, *Les lieux de mémoire* (Paris: Gallimard, 1985).

and literacy, inscribed as they are in the will, imagination, and art of the narratives, in the formulations of their impulses, motives, and ideals, are their *lieux de mémoire*. The narratives must not be forgotten; they are being revisited, read, and reinterpreted. They have become chosen and cherished objects of memory, depositories of experience, of knowledge, and of the secrets of the present. They can help explain aspects of Afro-American life. The attention they are constantly receiving and which incessantly reveals new meanings and symbolic ramifications, testifies to this "will to remember," to the "spiritual strivings" and endeavors of the forebears who paved the way for future generations.

Just as slave narrators tried to create out of their experience a memory they could transmit, and strove to find a language that could best express it, their readers and critics are inventing many rituals (and this gathering of scholars for our present conference is definitely one of them) which may turn these early writings into *lieux de mémoire, lieux* that are materially, functionally, and symbolically alive and forever present, that have become crucial components of the literary and historical heritage, and that can stimulate the understanding and the collective imagination, generating new creative acts.

I would like to venture a last remark on the organization of this conference. I am struck by the absence of any discussion of drama, theater, and dramatic criticism. Is it because these artistic forms are not to be included in the canon and are not considered fundamental in the elaboration of a black poetics? Yet it seems to me that dramatic forms— to be found in the black church and in music as well as on the street corner, in verbal interactions and linguistic practices, as in various ritualizations of everyday life—constitute an essential aspect of Afro-American cultural expression and have contributed to the emergence of a distinctive and rich tradition and genre: the theater. One may wonder— considering the indifference of critics, the dearth of critical analytical tools for that precise expressive form, the difficulties encountered in producing and publishing plays—what will happen to the theatrical arts. How is one to interpret the silence of critics? Is it an immediate consequence of the present silence of playwrights and can it contribute to prolonging it? Is it because theater is definitely out of fashion and out of the field of examination of critical analysis? Or is it considered a substandard form relegated to the world of entertainment? If critics, writers, and the reader-audience have to come together to evolve the new poetics, we are prompted to ask the question: Where are all these partners? Has drama been wiped out of Afro-American cultural life and letters, or is it simply absent from the academic debate?

4

The First-Person in
Afro-American Fiction

Richard Yarborough

In examining the current state of the black novel in the United States, one is struck both by the degree to which our conception of the Afro-American fictive tradition has evolved over the past decade or so and also by the amount of work—in particular, "literary archaeology"—yet to be done if progress is to continue. For example, although the explosion of interest in Afro-American literature in the 1960s and early 1970s resulted in the production of a large number of bibliographies, catalogs of library holdings, and reprints of journals and periodicals in microform, scholars in the field still frequently lack the necessary research tools. One important case is Walter Schatz's *Directory of Afro-American Resources* (1970), which, while remaining invaluable, is seriously out of date. Likewise, bibliographies of Afro-American fiction published as recently as the late seventies already demand revision.

We are also in desperate need of carefully prepared editions of major texts, more interviews with literary figures—both old and young—and bibliographical studies of so-called "minor" authors. *Give Us Each Day,* Gloria T. Hull's edition of Alice Dunbar-Nelson's diary (Norton); Harriet Jacobs's *Incidents in the Life of a Slave Girl* (Harvard), edited by Jean Fagan Yellin; John McCluskey's *The City of Refuge: The Collected Stories of Rudolph Fisher* (Missouri); and Frances Smith Foster's forthcoming collection of the works of Frances E. W. Harper (Feminist Press) should serve as models for similar projects in the future. In addition, greater efforts must be made to track down and preserve the papers of Afro-American writers. Progress in these areas depends not only upon strong support from academic and research institutions and from publishers, but also upon the dedication of new critics and librarians to tote the burden carried by earlier generations. Who will follow in the footsteps of scholars like E. J. Josey, Ann Shockley, Ernest Kaiser, Rayford Logan, and Dorothy Porter? Are we producing individuals who will take on the crucial (and yet somewhat unglamorous) tasks that must be done?

On the positive side, several efforts to preserve and nurture Afro-American fiction deserve mention. One example is the housing of Charles Blockson's extensive book collection at Temple University several years ago. Another is the long-awaited microfiche publication by Chadwyck-Healey of the massive amount of primary material gathered as a direct result of the Black Periodical Literature Project, directed by Henry Louis Gates and Anthony Appiah. Then there is the CAABL Project headed by Maryemma Graham at the University of Mississippi, an especially intriguing attempt to apply computer technology to the analysis of Afro-American fiction.

In a related area, we have seen the appearance in recent years of several major biographies of black writers: examples include works by Arnold Rampersad, on Langston Hughes, by John Hope Franklin, on George Washington Williams, and by Nellie McKay, on Jean Toomer. Moreover, we can look forward to other studies like that of Nella Larsen by Thadious Davis. Yet, for each such biography that appears, there remain numerous others still to be written.

It is difficult to overstate the crucial role these biographical and bibliographical works have played in the development not only of Afro-American letters generally, but also of scholarship produced in the field. In turn, the growth in both the amount and sophistication of this scholarship has brought about a perceptible shift in the status of Afro-American texts in the American canon. We now find not just Richard Wright and Ralph Ellison taught outside of Afro-American literature courses, but also Zora Neale Hurston, Frederick Douglass, and Alice Walker. This new visibility of black American writers is especially evident in the increasing numbers of women's literature courses.

As the status of Afro-American literature within dominant American educational institutions has evolved, there has been talk of the need to establish an Afro-American canon. Although canonization may well result from the institutionalization of any body of artistic production, we should keep in mind that this process necessarily entails an exclusionary component. Consequently, the definition of the criteria to be used to determine which texts will be privileged must not only be informed by a realistic awareness of the complex political forces which come into play in such enterprises but also be developed in the context of our best sense of the history of the field. The requisite political awareness to which I refer can only result from each scholar's coming to terms with the ideological implications of his or her commitment to the literature, to the profession, to the institutions within which he or she works. The second condition—the "best sense" of the history of Afro-American fiction—cannot be met without the literary archaeological work that I have been discussing.

My point here is this: Although the apparently inevitable process of canonization is shaped by many forces—economic, political, and otherwise—over which, to be frank, most scholars have little control, what we can and should effect is the preparation of the ground upon which the canon is to be constructed. That is, we cannot be content merely to scrape the topsoil off buried—and because unseen, unheard—fictional texts by black American authors. We must continually attempt to resuscitate these materials through careful interpretation and judicious contextualization so that the stifled voices ring clearly once more. Given the many extraliterary factors that help to determine which texts survive and which do not, it is likely that the revivification of lost or neglected black fiction will have to be an ongoing and frustratingly repetitious task.

For example, two years ago, I provided an afterword for a new reprint edition of William Attaway's *Blood on the Forge*. The novel first appeared in 1941 and was deemed a commercial disappointment by the publisher, who had hoped to latch the book onto the coattails of Richard Wright's best-selling *Native Son* (1940). In 1953, Attaway's book was released as a paperback; and if we take the lurid appeal on the cover as any indication, it was directed toward a mass readership accustomed to an unchallenging diet of sensationalistic pulp fiction. (The cover of this edition depicts a tan-skinned, buxom woman of indeterminate ethnicity glancing in the direction of a young black man playing a guitar; through the window behind him, we see the fiery sky over a mill. The caption above this scene teases, "Her Body Was Fire—Her Heart Was Steel.") In 1970, *Blood on the Forge* was launched into the literary marketplace once more as part of the Collier African and Afro-American Novel series. Finally, in 1987 the Monthly Review Press reprinted the novel again. Does the relatively poor sales record of Attaway's book to this point indicate that it is simply finding its own level, that it does not merit the attention necessary to keep it in print? Not at all. Rather, I would vehemently argue that here, once again, we see the disconcerting degree to which factors other than the literary quality of a black text come into play in determining its fate.

The case of *Blood on the Forge* is instructive in additional ways as well, for gathering information on its creator brought me face to face with some of the research problems mentioned above. I soon discovered, for example, that there was some question regarding Attaway's exact date of birth. Then, after several months on the project, I learned from a scholar in North Carolina (who had received the information from the singer Harry Belafonte) that Attaway was currently living in Los Angeles, only ten miles or so from my office at UCLA. When I called to arrange an interview or to see if Attaway himself would be interested in providing a preface to his novel, I was told that he had died but a few months earlier. One can only speculate as to what a rich source of information Attaway might have proven.[1]

Finally, the peculiar history of *Blood on the Forge* reveals the dismaying rapidity with which black novels continue to go out of print. Only twenty years since the end of the sixties, it is already necessary to salvage the work of important writers of that era whose fiction has fallen by the wayside. Examples include books by William Demby, Robert Deane Pharr, and William Melvin Kelley. Not to place the recovery of such texts high on our scholarly agenda is to participate in canonization by default: If the texts are not in print, they will not be bought or taught. My most recent experience with this problem grew out of my plans to offer a graduate seminar in 1987 on Alice Walker and Ishmael Reed, neither of whom could, by any stretch of the imagination, be considered a marginal or unimportant talent. When I attempted to discover why *Flight to Canada* was the only one of Reed's novels not listed in *Books in Print* as available in paperback, Avon informed me that they were dropping all of his titles. My phone call to Reed himself confirmed this. As a result, I ended up teaching a seminar on Alice Walker and leading off with the work of Toomer, Larsen, and Hurston. The canonical implications of the choices with which I was presented should be obvious.

This situation is hardly new. And although my experience with Reed's novels demonstrates that there remains much room for improvement, a number of compensating positive developments have taken place recently. Most importantly, within the past several years, we have seen the following novels reprinted in affordable paperback editions: *Mojo Hand* by Jane Phillips; *The Man Who Cried I Am* by John A. Williams; *Corregidora* and *Eva's Man* by Gayl Jones; *Home to Harlem* by Claude McKay; *Kindred* by Octavia Butler; Nella Larsen's *Passing* and *Quicksand; South Street* by David Bradley; *Youngblood* by John O. Killens; Richard Wright's *Lawd Today; Runner Mack* by Barry Beckham; *The Lynchers* by John E. Wideman; *The Flagellants* by Carlene H. Polite;

---

1. Another tragic aspect of this project involved Attaway's sister, Ruth, a successful New York actress. In an attempt to locate Attaway's papers, I contacted her just as *Blood on the Forge* was entering production. She was, however, reluctant to let anyone see her brother's material. Within months of the book's publication in 1987, I learned that Ruth Attaway had died in an apartment fire.

Raymond Andrews's *Appalachee Red* and *Rosiebelle Lee Wildcat Tennessee;* and *This Child's Gonna Live* by Sarah Wright. (In fact, some of Reed's books are beginning to reappear as well.) Particularly noteworthy is the valuable service performed by small publishers and university presses that not only help to keep older titles in print but have also begun to provide outlets for new works by established authors deemed commercial risks by larger companies. For example, in addition to reissuing *If He Hollers Let Him Go* by Chester Himes and *The Man Who Cried I Am* by John A. Williams, Thunder's Mouth Press has brought out new fiction like Williams's *Jacob's Ladder* and Cyrus Colter's *A Chocolate Soldier*. This encouraging trend will likely continue. Already underway are such ambitious projects as Howard University Press's Library of Contemporary Literature, Beacon's Black Women Writers Series, and Northeastern University Press's Library of Black Literature. Worthy of special mention here is the recent publication of Oxford's thirty-volume Schomburg Library of Nineteenth-Century Black Women Writers set. And then we have the more modest but hardly less significant release of *Blacks,* a collection of much of Gwendolyn Brooks's past work (including *Maud Martha*), by her own David Publishing Company in Chicago.

Contemporary Afro-American fiction is affected not only by many of the aforementioned difficulties but also by some of the same factors that have made revising the entire American literary canon such a desperately needed enterprise. That is, in constructing a canon of black fiction, we should take care that we do not ignore the contemporary artists. Like most authors currently on the scene in this country, many of today's Afro-American fiction writers have gone underreviewed and thus underread. This last problem, in turn, raises two other issues that I can only acknowledge here. The first is the degree to which, with rare exceptions, the black periodical press has forsaken the nurturing role it has filled since the days of *Anglo-African, New National Era, Voice of the Negro, Colored American, Crisis, Opportunity, Negro Story, Challenge, Negro Digest, Black World,* and *Third World*. Such publications supported Afro-American writers not only by offering a stage for new works but also by insuring that the fiction produced did not go without comment. Alain Locke's annual "Year in Negro Literature" feature in *Opportunity* and Ernest Kaiser's idiosyncratic but utterly remarkable annotated lists of black books in *Freedomways* are but two examples. A second, related topic is the way in which the contemporary critic committed to Afro-American fiction defines his or her role vis-à-vis today's writers. That is, if new black authors are left to negotiate the mainstream American literary marketplace as their only route to finding a sensitive, supportive readership, many of them will be in serious trouble. And their condition is not unrelated to the state of the field of Afro-American letters generally.

These are complex and thorny problems, and I would presume to offer only a few possible strategies for dealing with them constructively. To paraphrase one of my more imaginative undergraduates who was describing the peculiar plight of Paul Laurence Dunbar, the black writer in the United States is likely to have difficulty dealing with "Marse Public" for quite some time. One way in which critics of Afro-American fiction might play a mediating role in this uneasy relationship is to find occasions to share their own work with a popular audience. This might include such activities as reviewing new works of black fiction for publications aimed at the general reader, presenting public lectures on Afro-American literature when the opportunity arises, and working with local reading groups. High school and college teachers can play an especially influential role by incorporating new texts into their courses. Such activities are time-consuming and almost never rewarded by those who render judgment on our scholarly worth and even our professional survival. These commitments can, however, make a considerable difference in the life of a given text and in the health and growth of an entire literary tradition and ultimately are their own reward.

A consideration of the burgeoning scholarship on Afro-American literature—specifically, on black autobiography—brings me to my primary topic: the use of first-person point of view in Afro-American fiction. One important result of this recent criticism has been the extent to which it has alerted us to the complex sculpting of the self in black autobiographies, whether by Julia Foote, Richard Wright, or Maya Angelou. That is, we now bring to black autobiographies critical strategies some would have thought to be reserved for the study of fiction. In fact, one can even argue that conventional constructions of the Afro-American fictive canon have begun to be abandoned for a more important genealogical tracing of the Afro-American prose narrative tradition that begins with Gustavus Vassa, runs through Frederick Douglass, Harriet Jacobs, Booker T. Washington, James Weldon Johnson, and Ralph Ellison, and concludes with Toni Morrison, David Bradley, and Alice Walker. The merit of this formulation, however, is less interesting to me than the question it raises about authorial choices: Why have so few Afro-American fiction writers before the mid-twentieth century used the first-person point of view?

Since I initially began working on early Afro-American fiction, I have been struck by the scarcity of novels and stories presented from the first-person perspective. This fact is even more intriguing given the degree to which autobiographical writings have played such a dominant role in the Afro-American literary tradition. In offering some speculations about this peculiar aspect of the history of black narrative strategy, I first want to go back to the roots of Afro-American fiction in the antebellum period.

Scholars of black autobiographies have noted how thoroughly such texts have been shaped by the authors' quite understandable obsession with self-authentication—especially during the battle to destroy slavery, an institution grounded on the claim that blacks constitute, in nearly every important way, an inferior race. As a result, most Afro-American writers dedicated themselves to convincing a white readership that blacks were not only human but fully endowed with the traits and abilities necessary for them to meet or surpass the standards used to adjudge acceptability into the white, bourgeois American mainstream. And this goal, in turn, entailed establishing, as William Andrews puts it, "that the black narrator was, despite all prejudice and propaganda, a *truth-teller*" (emphasis mine).[2]

Given the abiding concern of early black writers with establishing the credibility of their literary voices and thus of their views of reality, fiction as a mode of self-expression must have generated some extremely ambivalent feelings. That is, why use *fiction* as a weapon in the battle to gain a hearing for the *true* version of the Afro-American experience? Furthermore, could black writers even *afford* to create a fictionalized "self"? For many authors, the self-justifying (and often therefore race-justifying) urge must have been so powerful that the very thought of using the first-person point of view (a mode of expression that blacks literally had to fight for) to create an openly fabricated voice must have appeared so irrelevant as to seem downright perverse—if it occurred to them at all. Thus, it is hardly surprising that white authors produced fictionalized first-person "black" narratives before their Afro-American counterparts attempted to do so. *The Slave; or Memoirs of Archy Moore* (1836; revised and reissued in 1852 as *The White Slave; or, Memoirs of a Fugitive*), by a white journalist named Richard Hildreth, and *Autobiography of a Female Slave* (1857) by Mattie Griffiths, a white former slaveholder from Kentucky, are the best-known examples.

Ironically, in their attempts to tell their true stories in auto-biographical form, black authors frequently utilized strategies drawn

2. William Andrews, *To Tell a Free Story: The First Century of Afro-American Autobiography, 1760–1865* (Urbana: University of Illinois, 1986), p. 1.

from fiction—especially the sentimental romance—to appeal more effectively to the emotions of their readers. And just as we see fictionalizing
tactics in Afro-American autobiography, the autobiographical urge finds
its way into black fiction. However, we generally have to look for clues
other than the first-person pronoun, for the self-shaping process manifests itself in covert, indirect ways; ambivalently endorsed, it is often
ambiguously expressed. I would further argue that the black author's
"self" intrudes into this early fiction in a glancing fashion—through the
veiled, most likely unconscious projection into the text of some of his or
her deeper fears, desires, concerns, and dreams.

This tendency is, of course, true of a great deal of fiction, regardless of
factors like race, gender, and class. I am here merely offering the possibility that the avoidance of the first-person point of view in most Afro-
American fiction before World War II suggests a complex attitude toward issues of identity and self-disclosure on the part of the writers. In
some cases, it may have even represented a form of self-alienation. That
is, the act of seriously committing him- or herself to the creation of a
fictional first-person voice entails for an author a plumbing of his or her
own psychic depths—a process that must have been exceedingly painful
for black artists who had to expend a considerable amount of energy in
simply keeping their more dangerous and unruly emotions under tight
rein lest they lose the audience they were trying to reach.

At this point, it would be useful to examine the fiction of William
Wells Brown, who is currently considered the first Afro-American novelist. Brown presents a most fascinating case, for he was especially casual in
maintaining generic distinctions in his prose. Accordingly, when we read
his autobiographical writings and then the various versions of his novel,
Clotel, we notice some revealing parallels and some telling disjunctions.
The first involves one of his central concerns—the marginal social status
of light-skinned black slaves. In his autobiography, he notes how his own
near-white complexion alienated him from both blacks and whites.
However, when Brown carries this theme over into *Clotel* (first published in 1853), he focuses exclusively upon the plight of near-white
female slaves—especially Clotel, who suffers greatly at the hands of a new
owner who cuts her long, flowing hair and makes her work in the broil-
ing sun in an attempt to darken her complexion.

In the first edition of the novel, we do have a light-skinned, blue-eyed,
black male, George Green. Yet, he experiences none of the treatment
accorded Clotel. In fact, far from being the stereotypically pitiful tragic
mulatto, Green is presented as a surviving member of Nat Turner's band
of rebel slaves. And when Brown does use this heroic figure to dramatize

aspects of his own experience, he chooses an incident that highlights just how far he and his protagonist have progressed beyond their original exploited and unenlightened slave condition. Toward the end of *Clotel,* we see George Green reading a copy of Roscoe's *Leo X;* in the biographical sketch that prefaces *Clotel* (and that is, oddly enough, presented from the third-person perspective), a section of Brown's diary is quoted in which he mentions (in the first-person) reading the same text.[3]

Finally, there is the slave character Pompey, whose job is to disguise the ages of his master's other slaves before their sale in order to increase their prices. "Of real Negro blood," Pompey proudly boasts of himself, "Dis nigger is no countefit; he is de genewine artekil."[4] (His physical features—large eyes and lips, woolly hair, and beautiful, white teeth— evidently exemplify what Brown means by "real" here.) Interestingly enough, Pompey's job in *Clotel* is one that Brown himself filled before his escape and that he describes in his autobiography.[5] Clearly, Pompey represents the black man in a degrading role that Brown knew firsthand from his own time in captivity. By the time *Clotel* was published in 1853, however, Brown was a free man and a prominent figure in the abolition movement. Most importantly, he was no longer a recently escaped slave, dedicated to telling the true story of his oppression; rather, having already produced a popular autobiography, he was now a literary artist in control of his own fictional narrative. Eagerly taking advantage of the capacity of fiction to reshape reality, he portrays Pompey in stereotypical terms that he would never have applied to himself. (In fact, Brown frequently commented upon his own mixed-blood heritage.) Doing so distances him from a particularly distasteful aspect of his past while still permitting him to reveal to his white readers a curious side of the "peculiar institution."

Something similar informs his treatment of Clotel and George. On the one hand, Brown doubtless found it easier to dramatize the anguish he experienced because of his skin color by presenting the sympathy-evoking victimization of beautiful, innocent, near-white slave women than to do so through his male heroic figures—especially give his commitment to the sentimental literary conventions of the time and to the

3. William Wells Brown, *Clotel; or, The President's Daughter* (1853; reprint, New York: Citadel, 1969), p. 233; "Narrative of the Life and Escape of William Wells Brown," in *Clotel,* p. 53.

4. Brown, *Clotel,* p. 70.

5. See "Narrative," in *Clotel,* pp. 20–21; William Wells Brown, *Narrative of William Wells Brown, a Fugitive Slave,* in *Puttin' On Ole Massa,* ed. Gilbert Osofsky (New York: Harper and Row, Harper Torchbooks, 1969), pp. 192–93.

predominantly white female audience he had in mind. On the other hand, not only does he incorporate one of the more praiseworthy incidents from his own life into his depiction of the courageous, noble George but he explicitly locates this character in a militant black heroic tradition that Brown himself could not personally claim. I would trace these tendencies back to his fascination (obsession might not be too strong a term) with black male heroism, especially in its more violent manifestations. Here, however, I merely want to stress the degree to which Brown uses fiction to revise, in a sense, his own life-story. Doing so from the first-person point of view would have been extraordinarily difficult, given both the implied distinctions Brown sensed (however vaguely) between fiction and autobiography and also the pressing political motivations behind his decision to use the novel not as an apologia, as a carefully orchestrated presentation of self, but as a political weapon designed to strike broadly and melodramatically at the system of slavery.

A glance at another early novel, Harriet Wilson's *Our Nig; or, Sketches from the Life of a Free Black* (1859), manifests this ambivalent narrative posture in a strikingly different fashion. Apparently composed under stressful conditions imposed by both poor health and economic pressure, Wilson's novel evinces less control than much of Brown's work. However, Wilson's failure—through lack of time, craft, or desire—to resolve the issue of perspective affords us a revealing look at the problem I have been discussing and explains the occasional breakdown in point of view in the book. That is, in writing a narrative evidently based largely on her own life, Wilson conflates fiction, fictional autobiography, and autobiography. We find evidence of this tendency in her inconsistent pronoun usage, which occurs at the moments of greatest tension. And I would further argue that these moments do not take place at the emotional peaks of the narrative but rather at points where we are literally on the border between the fictional and nonfictional realms—that is, in the chapter headings. For example, the title of chapter 1 is "Mag Smith, My Mother"; that of chapter 2, "My Father's Death"; that of chapter 3, "A New Home for Me." Yet the heroine throughout the text proper is presented in the third person.[6]

Let me summarize briefly: I am contending that the scarcity of first-person fictional narratives by blacks before the turn of the century is at least indirectly related to the dominance of autobiographies (that is, "true" first-person narratives) in Afro-American writing. On the one

6. Harriet Wilson, *Our Nig; or, Sketches from the Life of a Free Black* (1859; reprint, New York: Random House, 1983).

hand, fiction would have appeared to accord the author a great deal more freedom from representational restraints than did autobiography. On the other hand, however, although the early black writer found this freedom quite useful in shaping the image of the Afro-American, he or she was largely uninterested in taking full advantage of the unique capacity of the first-person fictional narrative to facilitate the creation of not just a fabricated world, but a completely fabricated self. Black authors ultimately must have sensed that the more representational expectations the white reader brought to their fiction, the greater the chance of their texts actually affecting that reader's conception of (and thus treatment of) blacks.

Moreover, given both the audience envisioned by most early Afro-American fiction writers and the priority placed on convincing this readership that many blacks were at least no different from whites and perhaps somewhat superior in moral terms, these authors may have sensed that adopting the first-person perspective in their novels and short stories would negate the power of the authorial voice to evaluate and explain the frequently victimized fictional characters. This perspective would also preclude easy moral generalizations, and most nineteenth-century black writers were far more interested in breaking racial conflict down to it simplest ethical components than they were in rendering the Afro-American experience with a degree of complexity that the average white reader could not readily digest. After all, although these authors may have often responded to the cultural and psychological aspects of race, class, and gender with mixed feelings, their public stances on racism were hardly ambivalent. Finally, many Afro-American writers apparently needed to preserve the distance provided by the third-person perspective—by, in other words, the clear (and safe) distinction between the controlling authorial voice and that of the controlled character.

If these are some of the reasons for the lack of first-person fictional narratives in early black literature in the United States, then the question remains: Why do such texts begin to appear toward the end of the nineteenth century? I would offer three possible explanations.

First, there was the general literary trend toward psychological realism and impressionism around the turn of the century. From this standpoint, W. E. B. Du Bois's powerful articulation of the complex psychological dynamics of the Afro-American experience in *The Souls of Black Folk* (1903) constitutes one of the single most important steps in the evolving conceptualization of the black self and in the changing presentation of that self in narrative form. This movement toward impressionism encouraged writers to turn away from the use of race as primarily a signification of external, material conditions (in some works, skin color even seems to fall into this category) and toward the idea of race as marked primarily by distinctive traits, values, and, most important, perspectives.

Second, black authors around the turn of the century possessed radically different backgrounds from those of their immediate predecessors. One of the more significant developments was the degree to which the younger black fiction writers had relatively high levels of formal education and therefore a firmer grounding in contemporary literary models. This generational shift is partially responsible for a related factor: a somewhat greater security underlying these artists' sense of self-definition, which, in turn, can liberate the creative imagination and thereby permit an increased ability to "play" with narrative voice.

Third, there was the growing attempt on the part of predominantly middle-class black writers to capture in their fiction the black folk-voice and, occasionally, the manipulative strategies informing black folk-expression. Ironically, some Afro-American authors may have perceived the overwhelming success of white dialect and folk artists as the permission they needed to incorporate into their own work aspects of their collective black past that their class allegiances discouraged them from acknowledging. (It is also interesting to consider the use of the first-person in Afro-American poetry as well, especially in the dialect verse produced by black writers around the turn of the century. Dunbar, for instance, was able to adopt a first-person black folk-voice in his poetry, but not in his fiction.)

I would hasten to add that these factors would not have brought an overnight shift in narrative tactics. In the last decades of the nineteenth century, we continue to find numerous Afro-American novels which manifest the given writer's attempt to distance the authorial voice from the black character. This avoidance can derive not only from compulsive self-effacement but also from a conscious tactical decision. An instance of the latter occurs in the novel *Appointed* (1894) by Walter Stowers and William Anderson. The black protagonist of the book, John Saunders, is a well-trained, intelligent, politically aware, and underemployed young man—just like each of the coauthors. And when Saunders expresses his frustration at the prejudice he encounters, we are hearing the complaints of Stowers and Anderson. Yet, they choose not to focus most of their attention upon this realistically depicted figure who so obviously embodies many of their own values and concerns. Rather, in a desperate attempt to appeal to a potentially sympathetic white audience, Stowers and

Anderson relegate Saunders to a supporting role and, in fact, kill him off well before the close of the novel. Other examples are not difficult to find.

At this point, I want to look briefly at several key transitional texts— Charles Chesnutt's *The Conjure Woman* (1899), Sutton E. Griggs's *Imperium in Imperio* (1899), and James Weldon Johnson's *The Auto-biography of an Ex-Colored Man* (1912). In the case of Chesnutt's conjure sketches, the use of a first-person narrator does not constitute the adoption of an identifiably "black" voice. In fact, the strategy informing these stories works most efficiently if the reader presumes a white narrator. Thus, Chesnutt is consciously playing off of an assumption underlying a great deal of the earlier fiction by blacks: that there is really no such thing as a racially neutral narrator; that in American literary culture, the shaping narrative voice, unless defined otherwise, is presumed to be white (and usually male). Hopeful that the white reader would identify with the controlling or empowered consciousness in the text and thereby eventually come to share the author's views on the issues raised in the fiction, many black authors would just as soon have had their narrative voice appear "colorless"—that is, white. Chesnutt's genius lay in his ability to perceive and to exploit the manipulative potential of this strategy. Ironically, however, in order to entrap the white reader, Chesnutt chooses to distance the first-person narrative voice as far as possible from a black perspective. "Baxter Procrustes" exemplifies Chesnutt's adoption of this "colorless" voice in a story that has nothing to do with race. (A minor work that falls into this same category is Edward A. Johnson's *Light Ahead for the Negro* [1904]. Modeled after Edward Bellamy's influential utopian novel *Looking Backward,* Johnson's book is another early instance of the use of the first-person perspective in black fiction. However, not only is his narrator, Gilbert Twitchell, identified as white but the black characters in the text are few and far between.)

Sutton E. Griggs's *Imperium in Imperio* represents a second turn-of-the-century attempt to exploit the effects of shifts in point of view on the verisimilitude of the fictional text. The novel opens with a preface in which the author claims that he is merely presenting to the reader material given him by Berl Trout, a former member of the nationalist black organization called "Imperium in Imperio." Immediately following the introductory remarks is "Berl Trout's Dying Declaration," a first-person apologia addressed directly to the reader. Then, in the last chapter we receive Trout's summation of the entire affair, again from his first-person point of view. Griggs must have felt that this elaborate, somewhat unwieldy scaffolding would authenticate the veracity of Trout and therefore the reality of the situations described in the text. More important, however, is the degree to which Griggs's manipulation of perspective here permits him to maintain his distance from a highly charged ideological conflict that he viewed with deep ambivalence.

James Weldon Johnson's *The Autobiography of an Ex-Colored Man* represents the first sophisticated structural exploration of the generic fluidity underlying much of Afro-American autobiographical writing (fictional and nonfictional) and the first successful attempt to exploit this generic fluidity as an apt representation of the psychological tensions (the "double consciousness," Du Bois would say) inherent in the black experience. A key aspect of Johnson's revolutionary approach was his ability to maintain his distance from the unnamed narrator, and a dramatic sign of his ability to commit himself to the fictional consciousness he was attempting to create was his decision to publish the book anonymously. There are occasions where the mask slips—for example, in the more didactic sections of the novel, where Johnson uses the narrator to discuss the great cultural gifts that blacks have given America. However, such minor missteps do not lessen the importance of Johnson's achievement.

In the 1920s, 1930s, and 1940s we encounter the gradually increasing adoption of the first-person point of view in Afro-American fiction. Relevant titles include "Fern" and other stories in Jean Toomer's *Cane,* Zora Neale Hurston's hybrid text *Mules and Men,* Langston Hughes's Simple sketches, and much of Chester Himes's work, including *If He Hollers Let Him Go* and stories like the marvelous "Cotton Gonna Kill Me Yet." Then, after World War II, we find a sudden explosion of first-person fiction by Afro-American writers. These books come to mind: *Invisible Man* by Ralph Ellison, *Cast the First Stone* by Chester Himes, *Giovanni's Room* by James Baldwin, *The Messenger* by Charles Wright, *Ladies of the Rachmaninoff Eyes* by Henry Van Dyke, *Blueschild Baby* by George Cain, *Daddy Was a Number Runner* by Louise Meriwether, *All-Night Visitors* by Clarence Major, *Train Whistle Guitar* by Albert Murray, *The Soul Murder Case* and *SRO* by Robert Deane Pharr, *Snakes* and *Sitting Pretty* by Al Young, stories by Toni Cade Bambara and James Alan McPherson, *The Bluest Eye* by Toni Morrison, *Eva's Man* by Gayl Jones, *Kindred* by Octavia Butler, *The Color Purple* by Alice Walker, *Oxherding Tale* by Charles Johnson, *The Chaneysville Incident* by David Bradley, *Sarah Phillips* by Andrea Lee, Rosa Guy's *A Measure of Time,* and Ernest Gaines's *Of Love and Dust, The Autobiography of Miss Jane Pittman, Bloodline,* and *A Gathering of Old Men.* This list could be even longer.

What is particularly fascinating about many of these texts is the degree to which the factors that discouraged early Afro-American writers from using the first-person point of view appear to be precisely the reasons why modern black authors adopt it. That is, more recent writers have seemed especially interested in dramatizing the tension between perception and reality, between the exposition of self and the masking of self. The most important battleground of racial conflict is now seen to lie within the individual, and an understanding of that conflict entails a complex vivisection of identity itself. It is no coincidence that several of the books mentioned above appear to be modeled after slave narratives. The best examples are *Oxherding Tale* by Charles Johnson, *The Autobiography of Miss Jane Pittman* by Ernest Gaines, *The Chaneysville Incident* by David Bradley, and perhaps *Kindred* by Octavia Butler.

My main goal in this consideration of narrative perspective is not to arrive at an all-encompassing formulation designed to cover every case. Rather, I want to offer a slightly different way to view black fiction, especially that published before the Harlem Renaissance. Even with the later, better-known texts, however, the angle of vision I have attempted to lay out here can help to focus attention upon structural characteristics of Afro-American fiction that do not receive enough analysis.

At its most speculative, this approach also leads to some fascinating conjectures regarding texts that in some ways cry out for a shift in perspective. Nella Larsen's *Passing* (1929) is one example. This probing examination of the pressure brought to bear on Irene Redfield's life by the daring and foolhardy behavior of her naive friend Clare Kendry has often reminded me of an influential novel published only four years earlier—Fitzgerald's *The Great Gatsby* (1925). One wonders if it occurred to Larsen to immerse us more deeply into the mind of her heroine by allowing her to tell her own story, as Fitzgerald does with Nick Carraway. (Later applications of this narrative technique in black fiction include Morrison's use of Claudia in *The Bluest Eye* and Gaines's use of Jim Kelly in *Of Love and Dust.*) Likewise, might Hughes's *Not Without Laughter* have more directly anticipated Albert Murray's *Train Whistle Guitar* if it had been told from the young protagonist's point of view?

And what of Hurston's *Their Eyes Were Watching God,* a novel that at least twice veers close to fusing the authorial voice with that of the main character, Janie, who is presented from the third-person perspective? The first instance occurs at the outset of the text, where one is struck by the lack of distance between the language of the black folk-characters and that of the authorial voice. Then, at the end of chapter 1, as we ready ourselves to hear Janie tell her story to Phoebe, we turn the page and see not "I," but rather "Janie" at the beginning of chapter 2.[7]

This approach might enable us to grapple more effectively with other structurally problematic texts as well. Why, for example, does Morrison feel it necessary to break out of the limitations of Claudia's perspective in *The Bluest Eye?* And might Walker's innovative adaptation of the epistolary form in *The Color Purple* represent her attempt to have her cake and eat it, too? On the one hand, her strategy permits her to present the reader with two first-person narrators, Celie and Nettie, without violating the internal logic of the novel. On the other hand, the epistolary form itself implies the existence of a distanced, controlling third consciousness—that of the author who is ordering the texts within the text. What would Walker have lost had she chosen to restrict herself to Celie's perspective? Is it possible that, like many earlier Afro-American authors, Walker was at some level loathe to risk her reader's presuming an identification between herself, the empowered author, and Celie, the victimized protagonist?

I will bring such speculations to a close with two cautious predictions. The first is that as we become more familiar with the fiction published by blacks in early Afro-American periodicals, we will be more likely to encounter the use of the first-person point of view. My assumption here is that addressing a primarily black audience may have lessened somewhat the anxiety of self-dramatization otherwise experienced by Afro-American fiction writers before World War II. My second forecast is that the production of autobiographies by black writers will become increasingly rare. Exceptions like *Brothers and Keepers* by John Wideman will certainly appear. But we have only to consider the distance between Maya Angelou's *I Know Why the Caged Bird Sings* and Andrea Lee's *Russian Journal* to sense that something has changed. The younger black authors today (especially the males) possess, I would argue, a radically different sense of mission than did their immediately preceding generation. Many of the women do as well; but it is more likely that some black female writers will, for quite understandable ideological reasons, continue to accept the role of group spokesperson or even that of artistic

7. For further treatments of this issue, see the chapter by Henry Louis Gates, Jr., on "Zora Neale Hurston and the Speakerly Text" in his *The Signifying Monkey: A Theory of Afro-American Literary Criticism* (New York: Oxford University Press, 1988); Robert B. Stepto, *From Behind the Veil: A Study of Afro-American Narrative* (Urbana: University of Illinois Press, 1979), pp. 164–67; and Mary Helen Washington, *Invented Lives: Narratives of Black Woman, 1860–1960* (Garden City, N.Y.: Anchor Press/Doubleday, 1987), pp. 237–54.

heroine, both of which would encourage the literary presentation of the given author's experience as exemplary.

Like the condition of blacks in this country generally, Afro-American fiction in the 1990s faces both daunting challenges and unique opportunities. In the final analysis, we can only guess what stories black writers will tell as they express the diverse strivings of Afro-Americans in the last decade of this century. Scholars in the field have an obligation to attend to the artistic manifestation of these strivings with both seriousness and humility and to find in the critical enterprise not just the rewards that literature offers all readers but also the satisfaction awaiting those who choose to bear witness and who, by doing so, both abet and, in a minor way, partake in the creative act itself.

Response: *Robert B. Stepto*

I

Richard Yarborough begins his essay with a call for more Afro-Americanist "literary archaeology," and while some might consider this a conservative, business-as-usual activity not entirely suited for an agenda for the 1990s, I do not think that anyone would argue that such activities should be put off or abandoned. Clearly, there is a need to update bibliographies and directories, to create new literary dictionaries (let us praise here Trudier Harris, Thadious Davis, et al. for their recent efforts), to collect, to edit, to interview, and so on.

In responding to Yarborough's question, "Are we producing individuals who will take on the crucial (and yet somewhat unglamorous) tasks that must be done?" I would say, "yes and no," though if pressed, I would have to answer, "no." "Yes" comes to mind because, in this era of GPOP fellowships, CIC fellowships, and Compton fellowships, our graduate schools are developing more Afro-Americanists in literature than ever before, and the number, of course, increases significantly when one necessarily adds in those nonminority graduate student Afro-Americanists who are not eligible for the above-mentioned fellowships but who are "coming along" nonetheless. At Yale, for example, by my unofficial count, nine Ph.D.'s have been granted to Afro-Americanists in literature since 1975, and that is a very conservative figure since it does not include the young scholars who wrote non-Afro-Americanist dissertations but who have still contributed to the Afro-Americanist field

(Kimberly Benston obviously fits in this category, but so do or will
Barbara Bowen and Anthony Barthelmay).

Yet I must say "no" as well, and rather emphatically, since it seems
clear that most younger scholars join older scholars in treating literary
archeology as something others do, or as something they might do—
especially after they have done some "real" work. This attitude or perspective is easy to castigate, but we should not: younger scholars are
merely responding as we did to what the academy seems to value most.
And so it seems necessary to blame for this situation not the younger
scholar but the expectations of graduate education and, also, what is
usually expected of junior faculty working their way up through the
ranks.

Regarding the former, I think it lamentable that the writing of critical
and/or theoretical essays is frequently the sole means of completing
Afro-Americanist graduate seminars, and steadfastly the preferred means
of completing the requirements for Afro-Americanist master's theses and
doctoral dissertations. There are many archaeological projects requiring
both dogged primary research and sensitive literary analysis that draw
upon a student's accumulated learning (how else, for example, does one
write a cogent annotation?), and which frankly may be more important
in the long run to the student and to the academy at large than yet
another discussion of, say, Richard Wright, James Baldwin, or—to mention a newer cottage industry—Zora Neale Hurston. Moreover, many
archaeological projects constitute a proper and often missing prelimi-
nary or intermediate step to the writing of a sophisticated, fully informed
discussion. In other words, I can clearly envision situations in which
completing an archaeological project at the M.A. level is the *best*
preparation for writing critical or theoretical dissertations shortly there-
after. The developing graduate student has much to gain from this: a
better dissertation should occur, partly because the student has been
intimate with key primary materials ever since the early stages of his or
her graduate education, and the student is in a much better position to
achieve a "leg up" in the profession since, if all has gone well, he or she
will have both an important dissertation and a needed research tool
worthy of publication.

Regarding what is expected of junior faculty, I have to say at once that
this is an area in which change will be more difficult. Yet change should
be worked for nonetheless. My concern, in the area of literary archaeology, is that while critical or annotated editions of medieval,
Renaissance, or even Victorian texts readily bring promotions when
properly done, the thoughtful, comparably researched Afro-American

edition may not—because it is deemed, shall we say, so "different," or, as a journal editor said of my first article, "so special." (The article was published elsewhere.) And so I worry, not without cause, about young Afro-Americanists abandoning archaeological projects, sometimes forever, because there are few reasons to be confident about how such a project will be received in even the present academy. One reason to continue to work for the eradication of cultural xenophobia from departments of literary study is so that Afro-American "recovery" projects may be seen as comparable to other such projects, when that is the case.

Professor Yarborough calls also for the missing literary biographies, and this is an area in which we have to expect that work will be done. After all, there is far more evidence that literary biographers prosper professionally (consider here, William Andrews, Michel Fabre, Robert Hemenway, Nellie McKay, Arnold Rampersad—a mere sampling, of course) in comparison to dedicated literary archaeologists. But whether we are producing the scholars who will undertake this work is quite difficult to remark upon, partly because younger scholars usually are not encouraged to work on literary biographies early in their careers (not at the dissertation level, certainly), and partly because the present view of what constitutes the cutting edge of literary study either does not accommodate literary biography or relegates it to one of many back burners. Herein we reenact a now familiar dilemma confronting the literary Afro-Americanist: shall we complete "old" projects and run the risk of being seen as "stuck" in old habits and modes of inquiry, or shall we strike out and not just join but challenge those colleagues positioned at the edge of the new? The most obvious answer to this point is that while younger scholars may prudently choose not to run the risk cited above, established scholars need not submit to that restriction. In other words, in my view, the extent to which Afro-Americanist literary biography will prosper in the next decade is predicated almost exclusively upon whether senior people will take advantage of the opportunity before them to complete *any kind* of good work—this being an opportunity younger scholars have in theory but often not in fact.

II

Let me take up directly Yarborough's question, "Why have so few Afro-American fiction writers before the mid-twentieth century used the first-person point of view?" While I do not think it is precisely a matter, as Yarborough suggests, of the "openly fabricated voice" seeming "irrelevant" or "downright perverse," I do agree with his assessments stressing the authorial anxieties which may be reasonably associated with first-person narration. However, I think he needs to consider not just the inner feelings of the would-be writer but also the peculiar antebellum pressures in writing for American audiences, especially the so-called friendly or supportive audiences comprised mainly of abolitionists. Here, I am reminded of James Olney's useful remarks in his slave-narrative discussion regarding the "conventions of slave-narrative writing established by [the] triangular relationship of narrator, audience, and sponsors."[1] Most pertinent is Olney's observation that the slave narrator is in "an irresolvably tight bind" in that he or she is "debarred from use of a memory that would make anything of his narrative beyond or other than the purely, merely episodic, and . . . denied access . . . to the configurational dimension of narrative."[2] With this in mind, it seems reasonable to argue that many antebellum black writers may well have considered the writing of first-person narrative, given its near synonymity for them with "slave narrative," to be a stifling, debilitating, deliberating activity—and to be as well an activity that *sustained* the "bind" the slave narrator often was in, instead of dismantling it so that new relationships could be founded between black authors and American audiences.

And so we should not be surprised that third-person narrative was attempted, for at the least third-person narratives can at once create for audiences (requiring them) illusions of objectivity and create as well for authors outlets for stifled memory: as Yarborough himself points out, with reference to Brown's *Clotel*, characters can become versions of the authorial self precisely because they are versions of personal memory. Third-person narrative fiction was a new freedom, or was potentially so, because many selves could be guardedly remembered or offered as fantasized projections. (Consider here, as I have discussed elsewhere, the personal usefulness to Frederick Douglass of writing a fiction, "The Heroic Slave," in which the telling of another former slave's swashbuckling escape to freedom doubles as a revision of Douglass's own, more modest, adventure.)[3]

In pursuing Yarborough's question, we should not forget the models before the early Afro-American fiction writer that made third-person narrative more attractive than first-person narrative. First, many early

1. James Olney, "'I Was Born:' Slave Narratives, Their Status as Autobiography and as Literature," in Charles T. Davis and Henry Louis Gates, Jr., eds., *The Slave's Narrative* New York: Oxford University Press, 1985), p. 154.

2. Ibid., p. 150.

3. Robert B. Stepto, "Storytelling in Early Afro-American Fiction: Frederick Douglass's *The Heroic Slave*," *Georgia Review* 36 (Summer 1982): 355–68.

fictions were fictive accounts of actual events, or of a series of events—the aforementioned "The Heroic Slave," for example, "stories" the *Creole* slave revolt, led by Madison Washington, in 1841. This grounding of fiction in historical event in itself led some authors, logically if not creatively, to adopt a third-person historiographical or reportorial mode of discourse. Second, I would observe that reportage and storytelling often share common ground, and that third-person narrative is often pursued in nineteenth-century Afro-American texts precisely because of the perceived opportunity to commingle or even confuse reportage and storytelling; certainly this is the case with William Wells Brown, whom Yarborough discusses in other ways. Let it be clear that in referring here to storytelling I do not have in mind at all a certain kind of modern or contemporary storytelling in which may figure an individualized, possibly idiosyncratic, narrator whose storytelling is almost inevitably, at some point, an autobiographical act. (Normal Mailer's antics in *Armies of the Night* come first to mind.) I am thinking exclusively of the older, more vernacular models for what is in effect a self-effacing narration, models discerned in storytelling generally and more particularly in, say, the traditional ballad. In these models, what is clear is that third-person narrative strategies are pursued in great part because they are communal strategies—community creating and community enhancing. I would therefore argue that third-person narration was additionally attractive to the early Afro-American fictionist because it offered the opportunity to *resemble* the storyteller or balladeer in communal context, and to appear less, thereby, like a writing author expatriated to another culture. By contemporary standards, it appears that this opportunity was squandered. But I do not think it is merely charitable to say that few black writers knew where to begin to take advantage of this opportunity, given the degree to which few antebellum Americans of any race had a notion of how to marry literate and vernacular culture in written art.

As for *written* models for third-person narration, I would cite in particular the King James Bible—often the first book Afro-Americans read or had "read in," partly because it was at times a primer for reading—and Harriet Beecher Stowe's *Uncle Tom's Cabin*, a novel that instigated much of the Afro-American fiction of the 1850s, whether in response to Stowe or more simply in an effort to profit from the market Stowe's novel almost singularly had created. Given the impact of *Uncle Tom's Cabin*, and the fact that it was a literary sensation precisely at the time Brown was completing *Clotel*, I am a little surprised that Yarborough does not bring Stowe into his discussion of Brown. The obvious point of entry for this, it seems to me, is where Yarborough thoughtfully considers the fictive presentation of Brown's selves (or at least, two of his selves) in the characters of the light-skinned, militant George Green, and the dark-skinned, collusionist-in-slavery's-system, Pompey. While some complicated autobiographical acts are evidently afoot here, so too, I think, are writerly activities designed both to echo and to revise Stowe's light and dark, militant and meek, Negro heroes, George Harris (is it a mere coincidence that both Green and Harris share the given name of George?) and Uncle Tom.

More could be made of how Brown's Pompey revises Stowe's Tom, but even in its undeveloped state my point about the ties between Brown and Stowe should remind us that any agenda for Afro-Americanist literary criticism in the next decade should include a call for more comparative Americanist discussion. Some of us have turned away from this work, possibly because it seemed to Americanize or "bleach" the black texts considered, or possibly because such acts of criticism seemed to promote consensus and/or accommodation. I have no doubt that some members of this conference might wish to question this agenda item exactly for these reasons. They might add that what this agenda is all about is the consolidation of power, and that a call for comparative scholarship creates, however unintentionally, possibilities for power sharing, or worse, power dissipation. But I make the call nonetheless, if for no other reason than the sincere belief that the work of the future includes the tasks to which Afro-Americanists who are Americanists are attracted.

III

Yarborough raises many more provocative questions, and I would like to respond to one more, this one from his essay's last pages. There he asks of Alice Walker's *The Color Purple:* "Is it possible that, like many earlier Afro-American authors, Walker was at some level loathe to risk her reader's presuming an identification between herself, the empowered author, and Celie, the victimized protagonist?" I think the answer is "yes," but would add that, at this point in her career, Walker probably is as resigned as are other Afro-American writers to the inevitability that *some* American readers (and non-American ones, too) are going to read all black fictions as either autobiographies or "social science fictions" (Albert Murray's term) or both. What is impressive, as Yarborough reminds us, is that Walker makes no overt, conventional effort to enter the text as the "empowered author"; there is no machinery cranking out statements like, "Once I, a college graduate and proven writer, gained Celie's confidence, she told me her story and shared with me the letters she and Nettie had so passionately and needfully written." Why there is no such distancing strategy in *The Color Purple* is a question I have taken up before, but since those remarks have appeared in print only recently and only in Europe, I feel free to repeat some of them here, while advancing fresh comments as well.[4]

In brief, my current view is that while Walker was "loathe to risk her reader's presuming an identification between herself. . . and Celie," she was even more loathe to risk the possibility that, if she appeared in the text as Celie's author, amanuensis, sponsor, or confidante, readers would see the unmistakable affinity between her authorial acts and those of countless intruding "friends" from a more "literate" culture—friends white and black. In other words, for Walker, it is better to be confused with Celie than to be readily associated, through certain narrative conventions, with the likes of patronizing abolitionists, talented-tenth types, and liberal friends of the darker races.

"Patronizing" is a key word here, for unquestionably Walker's decision not to appear as an intruding, manipulative narrator is in part one not to resemble through narrative conventions most of the *men* (and some of the women) who previously have "introduced" to the reading public a "black talent." And just as Walker doesn't want to appear, basically, like a man (or like some women) from "another culture," she also has no desire to thrust that culture—a *competing* culture, since intruding voices are competing voices—into her text. While the history of *The Color Purple* as a cultural event has largely been one of empowered readers discovering Celie (and her world), and while the act of reading Celie has involved on some level inviting her into the empowered culture (can there be any doubt that if there *were* a Celie, she would be "doing" the talk shows and hiring an agent? Is there doubt that the Spielberg film wasn't the next best thing that could be arranged?), the novel itself works in another direction. Closure and comedy come not with removal to another territory (probably a "male resolution"; certainly, one received by many as such—think here at the very least of Twain's Huck and Wright's *Black Boy*) but with *reunion* on Celie's porch. Yarborough is right to wonder if Walker's narrative strategies "represent her attempt to have her cake and eat it, too." Reunion cuts in many different directions: it keeps Celie's world intact, and enhances that world, too, partly by repeopling it, but it also marks the end (as goal, as conclusion) of Celie's

4. Robert B. Stepto, "After the 1960s: The Boom in Afro-American Fiction," in Malcolm Bradbury and Sigmund Ro, eds., *Contemporary American Fiction*, Stratford-upon-Avon Series (London: Edward Arnold, 1986), pp. 89–104.

literary authorship. The author who lives on—who keeps on writing—is not Celie but Walker, and it is in this elliptical way that Walker enters the text, has the last word, and stakes claim to any future word.

Response: *Eleanor W. Traylor*

James Weldon Johnson knew his reader so well that he played his rag anonymously. *The Autobiography of An Ex-Colored Man* (1912) is not only the first ragtime composition played in American fiction, it is, also, the first cross-examination of the "I" traditionalized by the heroic narratives of self-emancipated slaves. The syncopation of the rag split the atom of the narrative self in *The Autobiography*, exposing the anguished duel between an ego and an id. And the maestro's mediation, though hardly heard as a riff, much less as a bang, modernized the narrative "I" of Afro-American fiction. Johnson's fear was justified. Readers read an autobiography, not a fiction. And even after the stunning successes which follow *The Autobiography of an Ex-Colored Man*—the caroling of *Cane,* the gospel of *Go Tell It on the Mountain,* the jam of *Invisible Man,* the solo of *The Bluest Eye*—the identity of the first-person maestro/ narrator of Afro-American fiction is still beguiled by the biographical lover. But the third-person narrator has also won what Richard Wright has called "the pre-conscious assumptions" of devotees (p. 46). Wright also knew his readers. And, perhaps, not so ironically after all, spoke trenchantly on the subject of the "autonomy of craft." Addressing the "Court of American Public Opinion," Wright reminds us that "the limitations of the craft [of writing] constitute some of its greatest virtues"; and that "a vulgarized simplicity constitutes the greatest danger in tracing the reciprocal interplay between the writer and his environment" (p. 47).

The medley of these reflections is what Richard Yarborough's study of "black narrative strategies" wakes to resonance. And to his strategic question "Why have so few Afro-American fiction writers before the mid-twentieth century used the first-person point of view?" his own answers are cogent.[1] However, before and after mid-century, in both

---

1. Namely, that those writers were "largely uninterested in taking full advantage of the unique capacity of the first-person fictional narrative to facilitate the creation of . . . a fabricated world [or] a completely fabricated self"; they deferred to a middle-class audience; they desired the power of the authorial voice to evaluate and explain the frequently victimized fictional characters; and finally they wished to preserve the distance provided by the third-person perspective.

mimetic and expository voice, the Afro-American writer has opened up the panoramic vista where we may clearly observe some characteristic strategies of point-of-view in Afro-American fiction. Let us pause for a moment and enjoy the view.

Returning to what is by now, perhaps, a very familiar place, we arrive at a village. In this place, we hear a discourse on point-of-view. A speaker is talking about *looking*. He is a stranger in the village, but is he? The villagers think so. They *look* at him that way. He *looks* at them, studying amazement. Both the villagers and the speaker look at something else. The speaker discourses on what they may see and on what, in fact, he sees. What it is that the villagers and the speaker see *speaks*. The speaker, the stranger, the storefront preacher from Harlem, a writer who has come to the village to work, looks at what he identifies as a speaking subject. He says: "The Cathedral at Chartres . . . *says* something to the people of this village which it cannot *say* to me; but it is important to understand that this cathedral *says* something to me which it cannot *say* to them" (Baldwin, pp. 88–89, my emphasis). If the cathedral is a speaking text, then the question already here posed is not "Is there a text?" as Stanley Fish more recently has put it, but which one? "Perhaps," continues the speaker, "they [the villagers] are struck by the power of the spires and the glory of the stained glass windows. . . . I am terrified by the slippery bottomless well to be found in the crypt down which heretics were hurled to death, and by the obscene inescapable gargoyles strutting out of the stone seeming to say that God and the devil can never be divorced." But the speaker grants the view of the villagers. "After all," he says, "they have known God longer than I have known him and in a *different* way " (Baldwin, p. 89, my emphasis). Gazing at one text, examining its "spheres of existence" (a phrase I borrow most gratefully from that other seer, C. L. R. James, echoing Eliot), the speaker's language becomes heuristic as it calls out other texts. A canonical examination begins:

For this village, even were it incomparably more remote and incredibly more primitive, is the West, the West onto which I have been so strangely grafted. These people cannot be, from the point of view of power, strangers anywhere in the world . . . even if they do not know it. The most illiterate among them is related, in a way that I am not, to Dante, Shakespeare, Michelangelo, Aeschylus, Da Vinci, Rembrandt, and Racine; the cathedral at Chartres says something to them which it cannot say to me. . . . Out of their hymns and dances come Beethoven and Bach. Go back a few centuries and they are in their full glory—but I am in Africa watching the conquerors arrive. (Baldwin, p. 83)

Here the looker, the writer, becomes also a reader. He reads the text of Chartres backward and forward, recalling other texts; thereby, he becomes mediator of his own reading as he hands that reading over to other readers as a way of looking.

Moving to another site, perhaps one less travelled, we arrive in a city. We hear another discourse on point of view. In an essay entitled "City Limits, Village Values: Concepts of the Neighborhood in Black Fiction," another writer reads a text. Toni Morrison recalls Baldwin's "Stranger in the Village":

When James Baldwin looked at Chartres, he was doing more than reflecting on the schizophrenia of Western civilization. He was responding to what is universally believed to be the best and the most magnificent features of pre-industrial life from the singular position of a Black writer. His is an extraordinary observation for many reasons, one of which is that it brings up the question of how a dispossessed people, a disenfranchised people, a people without orthodox power *views* the cities that it inhabits but does not have a claim to. (p. 35, my emphasis)

For Morrison, Chartres reads "city," what Houston Baker would, doubtless, call the big *C.* Morrison's essay, a discourse on point of view, also reads as a discourse on *difference* and, as Henry Louis Gates, Jr., has put it, "the difference it makes." In her words:

In spite of their historical labor and enterprise—(the Black-owned oyster houses of Wall Street, the Black stone masons of Manhattan, the iron workers of New Orleans) the affection of Black writers for the city (whenever displayed) seems to be for the village within it—the neighborhoods and the population of those neighborhoods. The city itself was "a crypt down which heretics were hurled." (p. 37)

Examining, also, "spheres of existence," the speaker begins a discourse on views of the city, observing:

Mainstream writers are appalled by the urban. "Viewing 'progress' with alarm" has the frequency of a cliché. And there is a similar hostility among Black writers as well. Yet the assumptions of white writers are markedly different from Black ones. Although the anti-urbanism of white writers from Melville to Dos Passos and Hemingway to Cheever is couched in terms of blight, automation, and Babbitry, it nevertheless seems to originate not from any intrinsic hatred of the idea of a city, over life in and with nature, but from a wholehearted acceptance of the mandates of individualism, which, presumably, cities curtail. (Morrison, p. 36)

Now the speaker reads two texts, Baldwin's "Stranger in the Village" and Henry Adams's *Mont-Saint-Michel and Chartres,* a line of which has served as twin epigraph of her essay: "We come to Chartres . . . for the cathedral that fills our ideal." And reading two texts, she summons a library. A canonical examination begins:

From Huck Finn to the disengaged intellectual, from Paul Bunyan to Jay Gatsby, "society" is seen as a diminishing of freedom—corrupting. In [mainstream] writings, a commitment to a social cause is doomed to failure (inevitably and rightly doomed in their point of view) because such commitments curtail individual freedom and dehumanize issues and people. (p. 36)

It is important to note the speaker's gloss where she defines "society" to mean "masses" and "dehumanize" to suggest "taking away a character's singularity." She continues,

We live, after all, in a country where three Italian immigrants were jailed in the same decade: one, Al Capone, a greedy pursuer of individual freedom, was a folk hero; two others, Sacco and Vanzetti, who put society above personal comfort, deserved execution according to the wisdom of the time. The country, on the other hand, represents to these mainstream writers the possibility of personal freedom, nobility, privacy, and purity. (p. 36)

The discourse of this reading-writing speaker, before whom we pause at such length, is important here not only in the vital sense of "intertextuality" that Professor Robert Stepto has clarified, but insofar as it helps us address the question of fictional choice regarding point of view. What this speaker is getting at is this:

Hemingway's "earth that abideth forever" is a holiday excursion—not a way of life where the character actually lives. It is an opportunity to be heroically alone, to transcend society and define one's single private self. Although Gatsby's dream is, according to Carraway, unadaptable to Eastern [urban] life, and although Hemingway's people are busy excluding society and living by private codes of self-discipline, endurance and stubborn individualism, none is seen as having fulfilled lives in the natural environment. . . . The delicious, regenerative qualities of nature are outside even Gopher Prairie, which is described as being as lethal . . . as New York City. Perhaps the anti-urbanism [of mainstream writers] is not anti-urban at all, but anti-social. (Morrison, p. 36)

The difference for the speaker is this:

When Black artists write, whether they profess love of urban life as Langston Hughes did, or despise it as Baldwin does, whether they are awed by the city or terrified of it. . . . The general hostility to the city is not the result of the disappearance of grandeur or the absence of freedom. And the idealization of the country is not pastoral delight in things being right with God. Writer after writer after writer concedes explicitly or implicitly that the ancestor is the matrix of his yearning. The city is wholesome, loved when such an ancestor is on the scene. . . . The country is beautiful, healing because—more often than not, such an ancestor is there. (Morrison, pp. 37–39)

From such an excursion, we may return to Professor Yarborough's question of fictional choice: "Why have so few Afro-American fiction writers before the mid-twentieth century used the first-person point of view?" And returning to the question, we also, as he wisely does, return "to the roots of Afro-American fiction in the antebellum period." But now we might add one more suggestion which may enhance his own. Professor Yarborough has observed that William Wells Brown, one of the earliest Afro-American novelists, "presents a most fascinating case, for he was especially casual in maintaining generic distinctions in his prose. Accordingly, when we read his autobiographical writings and then the various versions of his novel, *Clotel,* we notice some revealing parallels and some telling disjunctions." The disjunctions toward which Professor Yarborough points are interesting. Yet equally interesting is the possibility of conjunction. For as early as *Clotel* (1853), so-called third-person narratives of Afro-American novelists seem to employ what Robert Scholes has called "multiple narrators" (p. 262). We may immediately concede the question of greater or lesser degrees of sophistication. And while many of those novels imply, as Yarborough has noticed, an authorial presence such as Brown's in *Clotel,* yet that presence seems to manifest itself as a plurality looking from several points of vantage. For example, in *Clotel,* we may read Georgiana, Pompey, Currer, the daughters, the preacher, Whittier, Carter, Shakespeare—all the epigraphic voices—as narrators. The multiple in the third-person voice seems to open a fourth narrating space—the reader's—who can, is, encouraged to retell the story.

Narratives employing this multiple-narrative strategy before 1950— among these Langston Hughes's *Not Without Laughter* (1930), Zora Neale Hurston's *Jonah's Gourd Vine* (1934), Ann Petry's *The Street* (1946)—seem to realize their existence in an interrogative mode. No "monolithic . . . acute eye . . . objective observer of the uniformity among diverse phenomenon, i.e. the positivistic scientist or . . . the behaviorist psychoanalyst—the detective" (Spanos, p. 150) answers the questions which these novels raise. The reader occupies that space. Clotel, for example, raises a chorus of questions: Who is her father? Who is her mother? What is white? What is black? What is mulatto? Is there a human being in this place? The contemporary popular lyric of Bill Withers resounds the mode and tone:

Uh who is he? and
Uh who is she? and
Uh [what is they] to me.

It is true that the first-person narrator may raise these questions as the ex-colored man certainly does. But the singular reporter cannot mine the lode which the third-person multiple narrator seeks. For that narration summons a silent subject who, otherwise, will not speak. The summoning requires a ritual involving what Robert Bellah calls a community of memory (p. 152). Often it is a rite of reclamation and, simultaneously, a rite of disengagement that we witness and may engage. Upon the enactment of the rite, a silent history becomes a resonant myth (memory). "It was a question of his ancestry," says one narrator of *Not Without Laughter*. As in *Clotel*, the multiple narrators chorus testimony which helps the reader to reengage the overarching question of the novel: Who is her father? Whoever the father is, he will not remain "trapped" in history, for, by the novel's rite, he is unmasked in the realm of myth.

For the contemporary writer, "the worst thing that can happen in a city [or in a village] is when the ancestor becomes merely a parent or an adult and thereby is seen as a betrayer—one who has abandoned his or her traditional role of advisor with a strong commitment to the past" (Morrison, p. 41). This observation leads us to consider, by its lights, a novel such as *Sally Hemings* by Barbara Chase-Riboud. In the Afterword and Acknowledgments, we are told:

My last acknowledgment is to a nineteenth-century novel, *Clotel, or the President's Daughter,* published in England in 1853 by William Wells Brown, a runaway slave, considered the father of the Afro-American novel. Although I read the original version only after I wrote this book, I was touched to the quick by the recognition of cadences, themes, wellsprings of feeling that are the roots of Afro-American writing. That the theme of this novel, the first black novel published outside the United States, is the same and was written by an ex-patriate in the true sense of the word, only brings the circle full round. (p. 370)

In a novel which employs historical document as "narrator," the major narrating voice seems to read her own text, *Sally Hemings,* and the text of its ancestry, *Clotel*. When her silent subject, Sally Hemings, is by ritual conduced to speak, that subject displaces *nothing:*

You have nothing to say?
Nothing.
Nothing?
Nothing.

with *something* quite startling:

> *Lord, keep me from sinking down*
> I *repeated* over and again into that silence.
>   (p. 347, my emphasis).

In the unmasking of *Sally Hemings,* history (silence) is displaced in the discovery of heritage (a plenitude of voices).

And heritage is the subject of "The Stranger in the Village." For Baldwin, echoing Joyce, worries that "people are trapped in history and history is trapped in them" (p. 81). The desire of the multiple narrators of so-called "third-person" Afro-American narrative is liberation. Its narrative strategies engage us in the powerful act of re-creation. Such a re-creation, through memory, affirms "the power of culture to appropriate and shape the world" (Reilly, p. 27), allowing us to claim our heritage and "repeat into the silence" our own regenerative identity.

Works Cited

Baker, Houston A., Jr. "Discovering America: Generational Shifts, Afro-American Literary Criticism, and the Study of Expressive Culture." In *Blues, Ideology, and Afro-American Literature*. Chicago: University of Chicago Press, 1984. Pp. 64–112.

Baldwin, James. "Stranger in the Village." In *Notes of A Native Son*. Reprinted in *The Price of the Ticket: Collected Nonfiction, 1948–1985*. New York: St. Martin's Press, 1985. Pp. 79–90.

Bellah, Robert, et al. *Habits of the Heart*. New York: Harper, 1985.

Chase-Riboud, Barbara. *Sally Hemings*. New York: Viking, 1979.

Gates, Henry Louis, Jr., ed. *"Race," Writing, and Difference*. Chicago: University of Chicago Press, 1985. Pp. 1–20.

Morrison, Toni. "City Limits, Village Values: Concepts of the Neighborhood in Black Fiction." In *Literature and the Urban Experience*. Michael C. Jaye and Ann Chalmers Watts, eds. New Brunswick: Rutgers University Press, 1981. Pp. 35–43.

Reilly, John M. "Thinking History in *The Man Who Cried I Am*." *Black American Literary Forum* 21, 1–2 (Spring-Summer 1987): 26–42.

Scholes, Robert, and Robert Kellog. *The Nature of Narrative*. New York: Oxford University Press, 1966.

Spanos, William V. "The Detective and the Boundary: Some Notes on the Postmodern Literary Imagination." *Boundary* 2 (Fall 1972): 147–68.

Stepto, Robert B. *From Behind the Veil: A Study of Afro-American Narrative*. Urbana: University of Illinois Press, 1979.

Wright, Richard. "Blueprint for Negro Writers." In *Richard Wright Reader*. Ellen Wright and Michel Fabre, eds. New York: Harper, 1978.

5

There Is No More Beautiful Way:
Theory and the Poetics of Afro-American
Women's Writing

Houston A. Baker, Jr.

I

A theory is an explanation. Successful theories offer global description
and predictive adequacy. Their goal is an order of understanding different from intuitive knowledge, common sense, or appreciation. They
begin where such modes of thought end, or at least where they fail to
address questions that require for their answers more than enumeration,
cataloguing, impressionistic summaries, selected lists, or nonce critical
formulations.

Proposed responses to the question "What is Afro-American literature?" might include anthologies, literary histories, bibliographies,
survey courses, or reading lists. These responses—as useful as they might
be—are not theory. For theory is occupied preeminently with assumptions, presuppositions, and principles of production rather than with the
orderly handling of material products represented by anthologies and
survey courses. Theory's relentless tendency is to go beyond the tangible
in search of a *metalevel* of explanation. A concern for metalevels, rather
than tangible products, is also a founding condition of Afro-American
intellectual history.

Africans uprooted from ancestral soil, stripped of material culture,
and victimized by brutal contact with various European nations were
compelled not only to maintain their cultural heritage at a *meta* (as
opposed to a material) level, but also to apprehend the operative metaphysics of various alien cultures.

The primacy of nonmaterial transactions in the African's initial negotiations of the New World led to a privileging of the roles and figures of

medicine men, griots, conjurers, priests, or priestesses.[1] This emphasis on spiritual leadership (and leadings of the spirit) was embodied in at least one form as the founding institution of Afro-American group life—the church, which in its very name sometimes bodies forth the spiritual syncretism of its founding: "African Methodist Episcopal."

The generative conditions of African life in the New World that privilege spiritual negotiation also make autobiography the premiere genre of Afro-American discourse. Bereft of material, geographical, or political inscriptions of a state and a common mind, New World Africans were compelled to seek a personal, spiritual assurance of worth. Their quest was analogous to Puritan religious meditations in the mainland British colonies of North America such as Jonathan Edwards's *Personal Narrative*.[2] For, like their Puritan fellows in deracination and sometimes forced immigration, Africans were compelled to verify a self's being-in-the-world. They were forced to construct and inscribe unique person-hood in what appeared to be a blank and uncertain environment. Afro-American intellectual history, therefore, is keenly theoretical because it pays a compulsory attention both to metalevels of cultural negotiation and to autobiographical inscription. Our intellectual history privileges the unseen and the intangibly personal. The trajectory of this history is from what might be called the workings of a distinctively syncretic spirit to autobiographical incorporation or expressive embodiment of such spirit-work. Two images suggest themselves as illustrations of this trajectory.

One image is the frontispiece of Phillis Wheatley's *Poems on Various Subjects Religious and Moral* (1773).[3] Clad in servant's clothing, the young and distinctively African-featured poet Phillis holds pen in hand and looks meditatively ahead, concentrating on something that remains invisible for viewers of her portrait. But the quill pen in her hand has obviously been at work. There are visible lines written on the parchment that we see in the portrait. Perhaps the lines are the following ones:

1. For a discussion of the expressive cultural, or ritual, responses of Africans to the trade, see Sterling Stuckey, *Slave Culture* (New York: Oxford University Press, 1987). See also Lawrence W. Levine, *Black Culture and Black Consciousness* (New York: Oxford University Press, 1977).

2. For a discussion of Afro-American autobiography, see Houston A. Baker Jr., "Auto-biographical Acts and the Voice of the Southern Slave," in his *The Journey Back* (Chicago: University of Chicago Press, 1980). See also William Andrews, *To Tell a Free Story* (Urbana: University of Illinois Press, 1986).

3. *The Poems of Phillis Wheatley*, ed. Julian Mason (Chapel Hill: University of North Carolina Press, 1986). All citations refer to this edition.

The happier *Terence* all the choir inspir'd,
His soul replenish'd, and his bosom fir'd;
But say, ye *Muses,* why this partial grace,
To one alone of *Afric's* sable race:
From age to age transmitting thus his name
With the first glory in the rolls of fame?
(p. 4)

We do know that Phillis inscribed these lines in her poem "To Maecenas." In doing so, she wrote her male precursor's African name (Terence) and body into the discourse of eighteenth-century heroics. Further, she comes to us in these lines as African embodiment of Terence's precursorial spirit. She calls the question on the muses, as it were—with her pen. That question, finally, is one of metalevels and canonicity. What is it, Phillis queries, that privileges Terence's presence and why is there a situation of "partial grace" and perpetual exclusion?

The second image reads as follows:

The hearing of those wild notes always depressed my spirit, and filled me with ineffable sadness. I have frequently found myself in tears while hearing them. The mere recurrence to those songs, even now, afflicts me; and while I am writing these lines, an expression of feeling has already found its way down my cheek. To those songs I trace my first glimmering conception of the dehumanizing character of slavery. I can never get rid of that conception. Those songs still follow me, to deepen my hatred of slavery, and quicken my sympathies for my brethren in bonds.[4] (p. 58)

Here the precursors are legion, but it is their embodied *sound* that marks an expressive lineage. A self-conscious narrator of African ancestry can be envisioned staring straight ahead in the manner of Wheatley, hearing again from a position analytically outside the circle of song an informing sound. The tear on "these lines" is the unifying affective bonding between a spirited and singing text and the written autobiography of Frederick Douglass. Theory's intangible province is embodied in the image of the narrator writing black, lyrical, first principles that he has extrapolated from his meditations on song. "Slaves sing most when they are most unhappy." The tear, unhappiness, a soul-killing institutionalization of the African body, bring the narrator's present writing and the songs' past sounding together under the controlled pen of African autobiographical genius. We might say the spirit comes through;

---

4. *Narrative of the Life of Frederick Douglass,* ed. Houston A. Baker, Jr. (New York: Penguin, 1982), p. 58. All citations refer to this edition.

the vernacular resounds in brilliant coalescence with the formally literary. The metalevel prompting the African, slave impulse (an expressive impulse) to song is made readable.

The conflation of past and present, ineffable and readable, marked by Douglass's passage prepares the way for an entirely self-conscious translation of "unhappiness" in a soul-killing institution that brings the narrator into portrayed, pen-in-hand harmony with the Wheatley of *Poems on Various Subjects:*

I had no bed. I must have perished with cold, but that, the coldest nights, I used to steal a bag which was used for carrying corn to the mill. I would crawl into this bag, and there sleep on the cold, damp, clay floor, with my head in and feet out. My feet have been so cracked with the frost, that the pen with which I am writing might be laid in the gashes. (p. 72)

Deprivation, theft, commodification, the burlap (wool?) pulled over the slave's eyes, a sleep of reason that produces wounds ("cracked . . . gashes")—all of these merge in the meditation of a present narrator who has pen-in-hand. The spiritual bankruptcy of American slavery embodies itself as the wounded and commodified ("a bag which was used for carrying corn to the mill") body of the African. The spiritual significance of such a scene emerges only through the pen laid, as poultice and portrayal, on the wound. A single fissure gives rise to written signification of immense proportions as Douglass, like his precursor Wheatley, calls the question.

These images of Wheatley and Douglass are images of Afro-American theory in its self-embodying resonance. They could be multiplied tenfold through a survey of Afro-American literary critical history. One thinks of W. E. B. Du Bois's autobiographical situation at the close of his "Forethought" to *The Souls of Black Folk* as well as his lyrical autobiographical situation at the conclusion of that collection. One can summon to mind the autobiographical situation of the writer in Richard Wright's "The Literature of the Negro in the United States," or James Baldwin's narrator in the "Autobiographical Notes" that open his collection *Notes of a Native Son.* One thinks, as well, of Ralph Ellison's autobiographical introduction to *Shadow and Act* and of Amiri Baraka's opening autobiographical essay "Cuba Libre" in his collection entitled *Home.*

Such enumerations, however, are not theory. They are certainly metatheoretical, though, in a way that will helpfully clarify the project in Afro-American intellectual history that is at work here. For they serve to adumbrate the lineage of what I have designated as an "autobiographical negotiation of metalevels" that constitutes black discourse in its most cogent form.

II

At present in the United States there seems to have occurred a quite remarkable reversal of this form. Imagistically, this reversal displays itself in the person and voice of Afro-American critics, with pen in hand, suggesting that theory is *alien* to a founding Afro-American discourse. Such critics claim that black discourse is most aptly characterized as humanistic and unambiguously moral. Critics such as R. Baxter Miller and Joyce Joyce want, in fact, to suggest that Afro-American discourse *must* be taken as a palpable and simon-pure output of a loving, moral creature known as Man, or, more charitably and inclusively, Humankind.[5] Implicit in the claims of Miller and Joyce is the notion that Homo Africanus is somehow comprehensible by standards of scholarship and fields of rhetoric that are not implicated in the sphere of metalevels, or "theory."

That is, for Joyce, Miller, and their ilk, an adequate picture of Afro-American discourse can be achieved only via assumptions of a traditional humanism and methods of standard disciplines such as social history, philosophy, and group psychology. Claims of writers such as Miller and Joyce situate them with debunkers of a project in literary and expressive cultural theory that has been disruptively influential for, at least, the past two decades in American, French, and British universities. It also situates them, I believe, at some remove from discernible contours of Afro-American intellectual history as I have tentatively envisioned it in my foregoing remarks.

What I want to suggest is that the Afro-American's negotiation of metalevels, in combination with his or her propensity for autobiography as a form of African embodiment, enabled him or her to control a variety of levels of discourse in the United States. Such control has placed African Americans in a position that refutes, it seems to me, any claims for a simplistic humanity, humanism, or affective purity of black discourse.

The most forceful expressive cultural spokespersons of Afro-America have traditionally been those who have first mastered a master dis-

5. See *New Literary History* 18 (1986–87) for Joyce Joyce; see also R. Baxter Miller, ed., *Afro-American Literature and Humanism* (Lexington: University of Kentucky Press, 1978).

course—at its most rarefied metalevels as well as its quotidian performative levels—and then, autobiographically, written themselves and their *own* metalevels palimpsestically on the scroll of this mastery. The act of such mastery has sometimes moved hostilely *against* claims of a traditional humanism and has seldom been characterized by any sentiment that might unambiguously or simply be designated "love."

A case in point from black discourse is resonantly before us at this moment of celebration of the Constitution of the United States of America. When the black writer David Walker issued his *Appeal* in 1829, in the form of a revolutionarily African document containing a "preamble" and four "articles" and maintained throughout that document an autobiographical voice, he accomplished the type of founding, black, theoretical, discursive negotiation I have in mind.

As a document that, in a sense, writes itself on the enslaved body of the African, the Constitution of the United States contains both a foregrounded story of freedom and a variety of backgrounded narratives of suppression and enslavement. David Walker, like all theoretically adept Afro-American spokespeople, had absolute knowledge of one set of suppressions, and he took as his task an appealing writing (or re-righting) of the African body in the very foreground of the Constitution.

Walker, in Henry Louis Gates's sense of the word,[6] *signifies* with, on, and in the very face of the *meta* and performative levels of the founding discourse of Euroamerican culture. He knew, of course, that such discourse as the Constitution had to be survived and syncretically refigured if African freedom and community were to become American realities.

Now, whether Walker was more loving, humanistic, convivial, or inherently humane than, say, the average *white* Boston citizen of his day, is a stunningly irrelevant point where Afro-American expressive cultural theory is concerned. What is important is that he was both autobiographically astute and strikingly brilliant with respect to the foregrounded stories of such white citizenry. (His very title, in its long form, refers to colored *citizens*—a truly African, heretical invocation in 1829.) He was, in short, a successful Afro-American theorist who knew that simplistic assertions of a distinguishable African American cultural and discursive practice would yield nothing. He knew that he had to master the very forms of enslavement in order to write the African body in empowering terms. Walker's act, thus, constitutes an auto-

6. "The Blackness of Blackness: A Critique of the Sign and the Signifying Monkey," in *Black Literature and Literary Theory,* ed. Henry Louis Gates (New York: Methuen, 1984), pp. 285–321.

biographical revolution, an explosive superliteracy that writes the self not in terms of the other but in lines that adumbrate the suppressed story of *another*. The *Appeal* emerges as a new covenant, a new constitution embodied in the African. It repudiates a hypocritical constitutional humanism and urges a robust hatred of slavery. Theory understood in terms of David Walker's *Appeal* is, I believe, of the essence of Afro-American intellectual history.

What most discourages readers about "theory" in another form— specifically, as it has manifested itself in the academy in recent years—is its seeming self-absorption, its refusal to supply material examples and enumerations that make for general recognition and reading. Theory seems, perhaps to those like Miller and Joyce, merely self-indulgent, an endless spinning of personal webs, or the ceaseless construction of what Elizabeth Bruss calls "beautiful theories."[7] Not only do such efforts fail to yield material examples or general reading, they may seem, finally, to have no practical consequences whatsoever, refusing to translate complex expressive cultural texts into enumerative, catalogued, or syllabused forms.

There is much to be said in support of the suspicion and charges of theory's detractors. There exist, for example, forceful, comprehensive, and usable accounts of expressive texts that derive from such seemingly "theory-free" accountings as psychological and sociohistorical explanatory narratives. Still, the disparagement of theory by Afro-Americans who claim somehow to be nonobscurantist geniuses of racial love and/or knights of the order of humanism might be considered slightly bizarre. For it is, surely, theoretical discourse—conceived as autobiographical cultural commentary—that is the very foundation of Afro-American intellectual history. The incendiary deconstruction, defamiliarization, and signifying within the master discourse represented by Walker's *Appeal* or Du Bois's *Souls* or Baraka's *Home* (full as that text is of Wittgensteinian analytic philosophy) constitutes, indeed, the writing and informed ritualization of the African body in the New World.

Finally it is not theory, I think, that Afro-American detractors mean when they attack the Afro-American literary theoretical project, but rather *the politics of theory* as they have manifested themselves in recent years. Afro-Americans were the very first radically to call the question on the traditional exclusiveness of the American academy in recent years, and they called this question in traditionally Afro-American theoretical terms. At Yale, Cornell, and San Francisco State, for example, such

7. *Beautiful Theories* (Baltimore: Johns Hopkins University Press, 1979).

workers as Armstead Robinson, Roy Bryce Laporte, Michael Thelwell, James Turner, Sonia Sanchez, and Nathan Hare astutely, personally (writing, talking, and thinking out of their own lives) adduced a different idea of the *real* story of higher education in the United States. The embodiment—the very African embodiment—of their endeavors was *black* or *Afro-American* studies. We might say that where the founding of Afro-American studies was concerned, the personal was the theoretical. Such theoretically adduced studies have been for the past two decades the visible sign of African American spirit-work on university campuses. The results of black studies initiatives have included: revised and re-figured admissions policies, new courses, revised canons of study, and the creation of an atmosphere where myriad formerly suppressed or backgrounded discourses have taken to the open air in their unique significations.

From activist autobiography, or metalevel negotiation as it were, in the example of black studies, the academy has, on the one hand, moved to various other "studies," such as women's, Chicano, gay, Asian-American, etc. On the other hand, the actional character of theory that produced black studies has been recuperated by disciplines such as "English" as an occasion for sometimes esoteric and leisurely "readings" (for the eleven millionth time) of the same books by the same white, male authors who have marked syllabuses for decades. Theory, in this conservative manifestation, has been entirely adjectival—a project in which a mere *renaming* suffices for recuperation. Its work is held to be different or new because it is, say, "deconstructive." It goes by a different name, and a nominal modishness replaces metalevels' driving force. The traditionally privileged maintain their exclusive access to and control of scholarly rhetoric through perpetual renomination. And advancement is secured through rhetoric approved by these designers of the avant-garde. Today, a "new" generation in its forties and fifties looks just as white—if not as male—as its forefathers and foremothers. And the new generation remains just as uncommitted to actional theory as its forebears. Scarcely a socially active cohort, it represents itself as a coterie of white academicians traveling from place to place dropping deconstructive words.

Represented in the manner I have just described, theory does seem useless, and those Afro-American scholars and critics who are academicians must appear as traitors to fervid commentators such as Miller and Joyce. Further, Afro-American scholars who are adherents of an academic theoretical enterprise must seem resolutely to have turned away from some not-too-long-past clarity of purpose and prose. Who, after all, would deny that such a turning toward the adjectival groves of theory is a profitable—yes, even an entrepreneurially canny—gesture for an Afro-American intellectual?

Still, neither the remissness of white academicians—whether men or women—nor the entrepreneurial or careerist cunning of black academicians—whether men or women—should compel us to desert the most active traditions of theory in our own intellectual history in the name of a *return* to humanism or affectional moralism. Rather we should simply seek, in our own newly possible negotiation of metalevels to extrapolate what is actionally and autobiographically necessary and useful for us in order to move the founding and always resonantly in-action theoretical project of *our own* culture.

In short, the task seems to me one of negotiating the unseen and presuppositional domains of current popular white theorizing in much the same way that Walker, Douglass, Wheatley, Du Bois, or Baraka negotiated the heroics and analytics of their respective eras—pen in hand, listening to African sounds of precursors and mastering (both intellectually and rhetorically) the discursive forces and stories that suppress an African body. Like such spokespersons of our cultural past, we must be fully informed, indeed brilliant strategists of metalevels who trust our autobiographical impulses.

The most theoretically sophisticated act for the Afro-American scholar in our era is an autobiographical one—on the metalevels. For he or she is currently situated—by the very term "scholar" and the beneficence of Black Studies—within the very worlds of mastery. This *withinness* vis-à-vis the world of the masters is signified by Douglass and Wheatley with quill pens and by Walker's formal troping on the very Constitution of the United States. The autobiographical orientation of our past spokespersons is signified by their personal account of the *sound* of precursors, whether it is an African Terence or a plantation sorrow song. Douglass and Wheatley, like Walker and Baldwin, look toward the *unseen* and body it forth as rewriting, rereading, or, in some regard, the founding textuality of an African story in its syncretic primacy. Today, the Afro-American scholar's turn and eternal return is surely most usefully toward the type of founding theoretical project suggested by such traditional black, discursive efforts as those. The general goal is, finally, I believe, a family identity—a black, national script of empowerment.

There are several objections that can be envisioned to my proposal, with its great stress on an autobiographical prospect. First, there will arise the familiar and always paradoxical—considering its normal source—query about "exclusion." Does an autobiographical condition of existence and authenticity preclude non-Afro-American (say, "white") commentators from the domain of Afro-American expressive cultural theory: The answer is a painful No. Painful because the incumbency for the non-Afro-American critic is to finger the jagged grains of a brutal experience in which—if he or she is white—he or she is brutally implicated. (James Baldwin, in response to a white student's objection that his work was too full of "hatred," said: "Your objection shows exactly why we need a white history month. Only when there is such education will we achieve a new moral vocabulary.") "Autobiographical," in my proposal, means a personal negotiation of metalevels that foregrounds nuances and resonances of a different story. The white autobiographer who honestly engages his or her own autobiographical implication in a brutal past is as likely to provide such nuances as an Afro-American theorist. What has usually been meant, however, in raising the objection of "exclusion" is that a somewhat vaguely specified "we" should be concerned more with the universal (whatever that means) than with the autobiographical.

Which brings us to a second possible objection. The situation of theory in the domain of the autobiographical seems to privilege the merely personal, the delimited personal "experience" as a category of observation and analysis rather than the general, systematic, objective, empirical consideration of variables constituting an occurrence or an event. Usually objections against the "personal" are launched in the name of moral objectivism. Morality and objectivity demand transcendence of the merely personal, we are told. Here, we might enter a small meditation on the personal in criticism and theory as a way of addressing such objections and as a prelude to concluding considerations of a poetics of Afro-American women's writing.

III

There are few moralists who fail to discover in their own lives indisputable evidence of an unimpeachable morality. Similarly, there are few theorists who do not find in their own work evidence of a stunning fidelity to the "spirit" of their subject. Neither the moralist nor the theorist, however, is likely to see his or her evaluations as self-congratulatory. Both usually feel that they have proposed general or universal principles which, upon careful self-examination, they find reflected in the particulars of their own lives. Governed by standards of a general virtue or a universalist objectivity, neither the moralist nor the theorist wishes to acknowledge the determinacy of language, vested interests, privileged interpretive postures, or a will to power in the domains of value and evaluation.

At least since Samuel Taylor Coleridge's reservations in his *Biographia Literaria* about the merely idiosyncratic features of William Words-worth's verse—or, perhaps, it is at least since Socrates set the ideal vision of the state against the idiosyncratic and merely personal reveries of the poets—moralists, poets, and critics have been cautioned against the personal. We listen for a moment to T. S. Eliot: "One error, in fact, of eccentricity in poetry is to seek for new human emotions to express; and in this search for novelty in the wrong place it discovers the perverse. . . . Poetry is not a turning loose of emotion, but an escape from emotion; it is not the expression of personality, but an escape from personality."[8] Eliot not only brings the classical argument home with full force, but also states precisely the criteria by which any autobiographically situated theoretical project would be disqualified as standard or classical poetry and, perhaps, aptly characterized as "perverse." But before rushing to his judgment, let us pause for a moment, descending carefully from lofty heights of moralism and classical criticism to speak person-to-person— even off the record.

Theorists follow, always, a purely personal line. In their most self-aware moments they have no doubt whatsoever about the specifiable determinants of every one of their favorite essays, reviews, lectures, and pedagogical utterances.

Now if a theorist chooses never to be "personal," that simply means that he or she has made an entirely personal choice. Who, after all, in our most self-directing moments stands over us, saying "Now, Houston, you'll probably want to perform a search-and-replace operation when you're finished with the present essay, changing all of your 'I's to 'one's"? There are, to be sure, institutional conventions, career and market con-straints, that serve as implicit censors for us all. But, finally, we make our own choices and are seldom deceived, I think, about the "personal" determinacy of our work. The search-and-replace operation that fore-stalls recognition (sometimes even self-recognition) of the personal is the substitution of human or universal values for what actually operates any given theoretical enterprise—*my* values.

The substitution is always in the service of powerful interests (one's own included) that seek to maintain the status quo in the name of the

8. "Tradition and the Individual Talent." In *Selected Essays* (New York: Harcourt, 1950), p. 10.

general, the universal, or *la condition humaine*. But as a theorist normally works—even under such rigorously political circumstances as those of, say, Mikhail Bakhtin—the condition closest at hand is his or her very personal one.

For a theorist, then, to acknowledge autobiography as a driving genre of the theoretical enterprise is for him or her to do no more than tell the truth. When I "analyze," for you my reader, a poem or a novel, or set forth a large-scale trope for an entire Afro-American expressive domain, I am merely offering you a determinate recall of my experiences under the conventions of criticism or theory, a peculiar and covering style, as it were. This is not to plump down squarely for a return to journeys of sensitive souls among the masterpieces. Both "sensitive" and "master-pieces" were overdetermined in that form of impressionism. No, what "recall" implies here is a narrative, which begins, as Barbara Herrnstein Smith argues, with the founding condition "something happened."[9] My critical position or theoretical project is a personal posture marked by the narration of what happened, *to me*. The decisive emphasis (mine) on "to me" resurrects, of course, the British aestheticism of Walter Pater and others.

In his *The Renaissance*, Pater says that Matthew Arnold's injunction to see *the* object "as in itself it really is" demands qualified restatement. For Pater, the aim was to see *a* particular, unique object as it is, to him.

I am not, finally, advocating more in my own privileging of the autobiographical than an allowance which transforms the critic into a critic—a very particularly constructed and accounted-for expressive figure. Such an allowance opens, I feel, a space for what I call *personal poetry* in the critical field.[10]

Stated directly in terms of my own current theoretical and critical practice (a practice that I hope will be fully theorized and utilized in the nineties), an autobiographical allowance enables racial poetry to displace state philosophy. In a sense approved by Gaston Bachelard, *poetics*—a coding, as it were, of racial poetry—can be defined as the emergence of a poetic image (visual, tactile, or auditory) that displaces the causal explanations of investigative "sciences" such as psychology or psychoanalysis.[11] Poetics is a meditative enterprise that privileges the poetic image, or the unique expressive sound of a culture, as the founding or generative

9. Barbara Herrnstein Smith, *On the Margins of Discourse* (Chicago: University of Chicago Press, 1978).

10. See Houston A. Baker, Jr., *Racial Poetry and State Philosophy,* Occasional Paper 12 (Minneapolis: Center for Humanistic Studies, University of Minnesota, 1986).

11. Gaston Bachelard, *The Poetics of Space* (Boston: Beacon, 1969).

force of that culture. Such forces are held, in my reading of Bachelard, to be creatively spiritual and underdetermined.

For me, the very ability to move to an Afro-American poetics requires an autobiographical recall of the auditory. The image of Douglass and Wheatley *at writing tables* returns again. "Those songs still follow *me* . . . ," says Douglass. Only a *re-sounding* account of what happened "way down yonder by *myself*" delivered as an autobiographical, written negotiation of metalevels can yield a fully descriptive and predictively adequate theory of Afro-American discourse. Such a theory alone enables us to avoid Santayana's prophesied fate of reliving, rather than thoroughly revising, through our own person and practice, history. What I must do, in illustration of the autobiographical situationality that I have advocated, is to take a seat at the table of Douglass or Wheatley and listen. For Douglass not only speaks of songs that follow him but also maps a position for anyone who would like to verify his observations.

If any one wishes to be impressed with the soul-killing effects of slavery, let him go to Colonel Lloyd's plantation, and, on allowance-day, place himself in the deep pine woods, and there let him, in silence, analyze the sounds that shall pass through the chambers of his soul, —and if he is not thus impressed, it will only be because "there is no flesh in his obdurate heart." (p. 5B)

This *mapping of position* implies that the successful theorist not only understands the importance of his or her autobiographical situation but must also be able to direct attention to authentic sources of black expressive sound. That is, Douglass knows both how and where to listen.

Similarly, a theorist in our era would know that piney-woods observation and audition of male voices is far less effective for theory than a hearing of, say, women's supper-getting-ready songs, conjuring formulas, or communal storytelling. The metalevels of African embodiment today are most effectively discovered and negotiated in the sounds of Afro-American women's expressivity.

The master discourse that carries us most effectively toward such metalevels is poetics. Steering clear of causal accounts, enumerations, catalogues, and superimposed "deconstructionist" readings, an Afro-American theorist can turn his or her autobiographical attention today to sounds of mothers and sisters. Wheatley's calling the question on the Muses, which has already been mentioned ("Terence alone") thus can be read in gender terms. Poetics, drawn from a master discourse, become the inventive site of a hearing of Afro-American women's voices.

In many ways, to convert poetics to a feminist criticism is not only to

refigure the African body that emerges from a standard male theoretical
story, but also to revise all American stories in the person of the theorist—say, a teller of metalevels such as Janie Crawford Killicks Starks
Woods who poetically refigures everyday black woman's life in her own
autobiography.

So now, I will assume my own place at the writing table, listening,
pen in hand. My form is autobiographical. My task is to convert a master
discourse of poetics into a new story. I shall listen, autobiographically,
and then inscribe an emergent body, a new story, a black woman's text.
Poetics is the form and substance of my concluding section and my
projected theoretical forecast for work in the nineties.

IV

In the Introduction to his beautiful book *The Poetics of Space,* Gaston
Bachelard writes:

The image offered us by reading the poem now becomes really our own. It takes
root in us. It has been given us by another, but we begin to have the impression
that we could have created it, that we should have created it. It becomes a new
being in our language, expressing us by making us what it expresses; in other
words, it is at once a becoming of expression, and a becoming of our being. Here
expression creates being. (p. xix)

Conditioned by Bachelard's allegiance to a phenomenology of the imagination, this statement implies a virtually shimmering instant when
objective reality and all purely subjective experience are bracketed, compelling a reader to inhabit and to be inhabited by the being of the poetic
image. For Bachelard, poetic images are the origin of consciousness. As
reverberating products of poetic reverie, they enhance language and
renew both us and the world in which we live.

More importantly, poetic images such as *house* serve as analytical
tools. They allow us not only to map a topography of intimate human
space but also to follow moments of human consciousness to the very
functions (signaled by the verb "to inhabit") of intimacy and protection
that are coextensive and coterminous with an image such as *house*.
Similarly, the "objective" or "remembered" corner of a childhood home
is less important for an understanding of corners than felicitous images
of *corner* presented by poetic reverie.

Hence, when he uses the word "poetics," Bachelard does not intend a
peculiar set of conventions, rules, and procedures for the composition or
analysis of creative writing. "Poetics" signals images that comprise the
origin and foundation of a human world. "Space," for example, is con-

ceivable only in terms of poetic images (such as *house* and *corner*) that figure it forth from and intersubjectively to human consciousness.

Bachelard wages a polemic against psychology and psychoanalysis because those disciplines strive to explain the "cause" or the meaning of poetic images. For Bachelard, nothing prepares or "causes" a poetic image; its manifestation is something entirely new. Further, no psycho-biography of a poet can make more effective the shimmering import of even one of his or her felicitous images.

It is as though the felicitous poetic image is, for Bachelard, not an objective phenomenon but a reverberant event that one enters in the office of human renewal, comprehension, and liberation:

A great verse awakens images that had been effaced, at the same time that it confirms the unforeseeable nature of speech. And if we render speech unforeseeable, is that not an apprenticeship to freedom? What delight the poetic imagination takes in making game of censors! (p. xxiii)

Bachelard's poetics and an effective criticism of Afro-American women's writing converge at the site of the poetic image.

One of the most important essays on the efficacy of Afro-American women's expressivity in the United States is Alice Walker's "In Search of Our Mothers' Gardens"[12] in which the author recalls:

I notice that it is only when my mother is working in her flowers that she is radiant, almost to the point of being invisible—except as Creator: hand and eye. She is involved in work her soul must have. Ordering the universe in the image of her personal conception of Beauty. (p. 241)

This description—in its shimmering irradiance of subject and object—captures the kind of splendid intersubjectivity detailed by Bachelard. The word "invisible" suggests a pure sublimation or reverie in which the imaged *garden* is created as spiritual and eternal form.

Neither *flowers* nor *mother* is as important, finally, as the implied aboriginal creation in the *garden*. In a word, Walker as both reader and poet discovers through the image *garden* how the world is made anew.

By writing her mother's vernacular *garden* as literate poetic image, Walker opens the field of Afro-American women's consciousness in its founding radiance and claims for herself an enduring spiritual legacy. Beginning her essay with a discussion of Jean Toomer's *Cane,* a book in

12. Alice Walker, "In Search of Our Mothers' Gardens," in *Ms* (May 1974), and in *In Search of Our Mothers' Gardens: Womanist Prose* (San Diego: Harcourt Brace Jovanovitch, 1983).

which Afro-American women are beautifully and tragically mute in their
repressed spirituality, and Virginia Woolf's "A Room of One's Own,"
which discusses the traditional repression of women's creativity, Walker
discovers a cause for rejoicing, celebration, and hope in her mother's
imaged garden. If Bachelard's and Walker's formulations are combined,
the prospect emerges for a scholarly approach to Afro-American wom-
en's writing called a "poetics."

V

The "poetics of Afro-American women's writing" signals a theory that
seeks to arrive at the guiding spirit, or consciousness, of Afro-American
women's writing by examining selected *imagistic fields* that seem deter-
minative for selected texts. Space, as conceived by Bachelard, is an
imagistic field. It is a function of images (e.g., *house* or *corner*). We come
to know space through an examination of such images. Furthermore,
human space has attached to it both "protective value" and "imagined
values, which soon become dominant" (pp. xxxi–xxxii). By examining
imagistic fields that compose space, therefore, we also come to apprehend values and beliefs that govern our lives. Our cultural
geographies are, thus, comprehensible through images.

The word "cultural" must be taken as an independent variable. For
Bachelard's approach is only effective, I believe, when it is combined
with examinations of culturally specific creative or imaginative fields such
as Walker's "In Search of Our Mothers' Gardens." A general or universal
field such as space, is, finally, only a motivating area of examination—
one hypothesized as constitutive of all cultures.

We assume, for example, that space, place, and time as universal fields
are, indeed, rife with images that Afro-Americans have both inhabited
and been inhabited by. At the same time, we assume that there is a field of
"particular" or vernacular imagery unique to the Afro-American
imagination.

The task of a poetics, then, is to operate a universal category or
imagistic field through a culturally specific field in order to enhance both.
The project is, one might say, akin to the application of a course in
general linguistics to the specifics of, say, black English vernacular.
Again, it might be likened to the examination of Afro-American expressive culture under the prospect of general theories of textual
production and performance. The axiological results of such operations
include accessing the general, overarching, or framing images and values
of a culture as well as foregrounding the quite specific values or instances
that modify or expand a general field.

For example, one might attempt to show how a "poetics of Afro-American women's writing" applied to a text such as Toni Morrison's *Sula*[13]—a text determined by *place* from its opening phrase "In that place"—sharply modifies and expands the field of *place* and, at the same time, foregrounds distinctive values and aspects of an Afro-American expressive field. Place, in a poetics of *Sula*, differentiates into European and Afro-American. Within the Afro-American, it undergoes further gender discrimination into a "standard" male province and a woman's cosmetological territory.

Correlatively, "The Bottom," which serves as *Sula*'s vernacular setting, becomes a field where specifically Afro-American women's places— Eva Peace's and Helene Wright's houses, Edna Finch's Mellow House and Irene's Palace of Cosmetology—offer an energetic figuration of patterns of purity and danger, order and inversion in Afro-American life. The shack or place of Ajax's mother—where seven sons are taught respect, love, and admiration for women as well as the spiritedness of the art of conjure—becomes a generative image in the field of place and a foregrounded place of potential for rearrangements of Afro-American life.

VI

If one measure for determining the success of a poetics of Afro-American women's writing is the type of expansiveness and foregrounding just discussed, then surely another measure, indeed one implicit in any project conditioned by phenomenology, is a palpable or felt "shift" of critical horizons. A theorist may always feel that his or her work has been successful in producing such a shift, but the essentialness of the shift can only be confirmed by the response of another. An example of the type of intersubjectivity that I have in mind occurs at the conclusion of Zora Neale Hurston's *Their Eyes Were Watching God*,[14] when Pheoby, the friend to whom Hurston's protagonist, Janie, tells her autobiographical story of a black woman's life, responds:

"Lawd, . . . Ah done growed ten feet higher from just listenin' tuh you, Janie. Ah ain't satisfied wid mahself no mo'. Ah means tuh make Sam [my husband] take me fishin' wid him after this. Nobody better not criticize you in mah hearin." (p. 284)

13. Toni Morrison, *Sula* (New York: Knopf, 1974).
14. Zora Neale Hurston, *Their Eyes Were Watching God* (Urbana: University of Illinois Press, 1978).

A sense of growth and change, a sense of dissatisfaction with the given are combined in Pheoby's words with a resolution to pursue a different course of action. Here, it seems to me, is one clearly figured success of poetics.

For, in a sense, what Janie has done—in a fictive and precursorial foreshadowing of Walker—is transform the quotidian rites of a black woman's passage through the world into a series of figures or images that are so resonant that they catapult Pheoby into new consciousness. Janie's revealed images become occasions for Pheoby to both read and write the world in new and liberating ways.

The life of Hurston's protagonist has its origins in the derogation and sexual exploitation of her grandmother and mother. The life itself is essentially a meditative one. It is recuperated, however, by an imagistic, autobiographical telling that receives attentive response. From the utter mundanity of two marriages and a tragically brief and fleetingly happy third one, Hurston's protagonist creates a poetics of Afro-American woman's everyday life.

What might be called Janie's "poetics" are of inestimable transformative value. To make Sam take her fishing is for Pheoby to alter expected relationships, transforming the black woman from worker (mule) of the world to a participant in male, ludic rituals that provide leisure and a space for spiritual growth. (We have but to recall how powerfully instructive for culture the one-day fishing expedition is in Hurston's *Mules and Men*.) For Pheoby to forestall "criticism" of Janie is for her to exemplify a potential for the renewal of Afro-American tolerance and communality that is always immanent in black women's expressivity.

VII

The correlations between universal and particular, critic and audience that constitute measures of success for a poetics of Afro-American women's writing also suggest a third measure. Successful analyses, in their concentration on the essential spirit or imminent potential of Afro-American women's expressivity move the criticism and theory of black women's writing beyond merely interested readings. Heretofore, the potentially liberating effects of Afro-American women's creativity—like the poetic potential of Janie's autobiographical recall—have been hampered by the self-interested approaches of critical camps so busy, in Janie's phrase, "wid talk" that they have failed to provide the kind of comprehensive listening offered by Pheoby.

As early as the appearance in the 1970s of Gayl Jones's *Corregidora*[15] and Toni Morrison's *The Bluest Eye*,[16] some black male critics insisted that Afro-American women's writing was but an Amazonian show of divisiveness, despair, and violence.[17] Such critics were particularly distressed by what they considered the exuberant black-male-bashing of Afro-American women writers. This earlier critical impulse toward a self-interested concentration on aversive images in black women's writings persists in recent criticisms of Alice Walker's hugely successful *The Color Purple*.[18]

In response to such male criticism have come equally interested feminist responses suggesting that Afro-American women's writings are more amenable to feminist than to other kinds of critical readings.[19] The sound of this criticism is suggested by the guiding claim of some of its more notable essays: "Black women's existence, experience, and culture and the brutally complex systems of oppression which shape these are in the 'real world' of white and/or male consciousness beneath consideration, invisible, unknown" (Smith, p. 157). Here, a phenomenological "unintelligibility" or inaccessibility to other than committed feminist critics is assumed as a ground for privileging radical feminist readings of Afro-American women's writings.

Finally, there are interested readings by both theoreticians and ideologues who appropriate Afro-American women's writings as modish examples for abstract arguments. The interested reading here is, perhaps, the most colonizing form of all. It shows no allegiance or obligation to the field of Afro-American particulars. Practitioners are often critics who feel that it is unnecessary for them to read an entire text before delivering sweeping critical judgments. They also feel no obligation to inform themselves, through even minimal study of Afro-American cultural history or specific historical and cultural resonances of black women's existence, before holding forth on novels, poems, essays, and short stories that are, at least in part, functions of such history and culture.

15. Gayl Jones, *Corregidora*, (New York: Random House, 1975).

16. Toni Morrison, *The Bluest Eye* (New York: Washington Square Press, 1972).

17. The school of critics known as "The Black Aesthetic" was preeminent in such charges.

18. Alice Walker, *The Color Purple: A Novel* (New York: Harcourt Brace Jovanovitch, 1982).

19. See Barbara Smith "Toward a Black Feminist Criticism," in *All The Women Are White, All the Blacks Are Men, but Some of Us Are Brave: Black Women's Studies,* ed. Gloria T. Hull, Patricia Bell Scott, and Barbara Smith (Old Westbury, N.Y.: Feminist Press, 1982), pp. 157–75.

But surely nothing could be more intensely "interested" than pointing out the limitations or excesses of critical orientations different from my own. A poetics of Afro-American women's writing, as I advocate it, is indeed an interested enterprise. First, it proceeds from a theorist who began work under the aegis of the Black Aesthetic and whose nationalist orientation remains strong. Second, it derives from a male critic who has a decided interest in both expressive cultural theory and interdisciplinary approaches to cultural texts. These interests, obviously, condition my sense that there is a sui generis cultural spirit at work in quite specific womanist ways in Afro-American culture and that this spirit can be elucidated by theoretical analysis.

But having acknowledged the interestedness of my orientation, I want still to claim that the success of a poetics of Afro-American women's writing should be measured by the extent to which such an enterprise avoids limitations of a narrow self-interestedness and offers broadly comprehensive analyses of the guiding spirituality to be discovered in the imagistic fields of black women's writing. The spirit work that is imagistically projected by such writing is, I think, like what is called by the religion of voodoo—*The Work*.

In women's narratives such as Morrison's *Sula*, Zora Hurston's *Mules and Men*,[20] and Ntozake Shange's *Sassafras, Cypress, and Indigo*,[21] spirit work is frequently imaged by the space, place, and time of the conjure woman. One might say, in fact, that a poetics of Afro-American women's writing is, in many ways, a phenomenology of conjure. In any case, the field most decisively analyzed by such a poetics is decidedly not one where pathological or aversive images dominate. Rather, what are revealed are felicitous images of the workings of a spirit, as so wonderfully captured by "In Search of Our Mother's Gardens." Describing the task of her generation of Afro-American women writers, Walker asserts:

we must fearlessly pull out of ourselves and look at and identify with our lives the living creativity some of our great-grandmothers were not allowed to know. I stress some of them because it is well known that the majority of our great-grandmothers knew, even without "knowing" it, the reality of their spirituality, even if they didn't recognize it beyond what happened in the singing at church—and they never had any intention of giving it up. (pp. 237–38)

20. Zora Neale Hurston, *Mules and Men* (Bloomington: Indiana University Press, 1978).
21. Ntozake Shange, *Sassafras, Cypress, and Indigo* (New York: St. Martin's Press, 1982).

To discover the guiding spirit work of Afro-American women's expressivity through an examination of selected texts and culturally constitutive fields, is to transform a *garden* into an eternal and infinite image. Such a transformation tends dramatically, I believe, to refigure familiar and interested conceptions. It foregrounds a reverberant spirit work that offers both an example of and a hope for a perseverance and communality that have enabled a whole people to survive monstrously hard times in the past and to continue their forward movement in a weary land.

VIII

This is the sound and current sounding of Afro-American theory to which I listen and to which I subscribe. I think of alternatives such as a misty humanism or a water-clear appreciative mode and I know there is no escape from complexity. Our title as Afro-Americanist scholars, theorists, and critics makes us guardians of entitlements that require intelligence, trust in ourselves and one another, and bone-wearying (autobiographically astute) intellectual labor. We sustain our titles at a cost described by Amiri Baraka in "Titles":

> My head
> is a fine
> tangle. My soul, a
> quick note, settled
> in the flesh.
>   There are so many lyrics,
> so many
> others
> who will not understand
> I will say this to you tho,
> It is not as if
> there were
> any more beautiful
> way.[22]

Response: *Mae G. Henderson*

Entering from the garden, pen in hand, I assume a place at the writing table of Wheatley and Douglass to pen a response to Houston Baker's theoretic-discursive practice and call for imagistic fields. My form, too,

22. From *The Dead Lecturer* (New York: Grove, 1964), p. 34.

will privilege the autobiographical as I dialogically engage Baker's theory and poetics of Afro-American women's writing. Because my current theoretic and critical work privileges the personal voices and auto-biographical experiences of black women, I situate myself for this occasion in the space between discursive practices and imagistic fields.

Baker offers for our consideration the thesis that Afro-American dis-course, in its most eloquent and cogent manifestations, is constituted by what he calls an autobiographical "negotiation of metalevels." "The generative conditions of African life in the New World that privilege spiritual [or metalevel] negotiation," argues Baker, "also make auto-biography the premiere genre of Afro-American discourse." He concludes that "Afro-American intellectual history, therefore, is keenly theoretical because it pays a compulsory attention both to metalevels of cultural negotiation and to autobiographical inscription. . . . privileg-[ing] the unseen and the intangibly personal."

Afro-American intellectual history is characterized by engagement in the senses of being committed *and* interlocutory. Metalevel negotiation not only engages theory but praxis as well, culminating, Baker tells us, in actional theory. One of the strengths of such a thesis is that it expands the notion of syncretism—which has, in the past, embraced the domains of folk history and the oral tradition. Baker's thesis is successful in that it produces and privileges syncretism at the level of formal literature. In anthropological terms, his thesis implies a negotiation between two traditions—the hegemonic and nonhegemonic—that results in a change for both. Such an approach constitutes an emerging consensus in poststructuralist Afro-American criticism. We can no longer regard ei-ther Afro-American literature or criticism as separate and disengaged from other literary-critical discourses. Nor, I might add, can other liter-ary-critical discourses any longer be considered in isolation from Afro-American discourse. Finally, Baker's theoretic-discursive model builds on the tradition of studies of the slave community begun by such scholars as John Blassingame who, in effect, rereads slave religion as Afro-Chris-tianity and collective metalevel negotiation.

For the purposes of my response, I interpret Baker's autobiographical act, in its broadest sense, as a particular and personal discursive reading. In the spirit of this project, I would like to engage in an autobiographical negotiation not directly with a precursor but with Baker's reading of the brief excerpt from Phillis Wheatley's "To Maecenas":

> The happier *Terence* all the choir inspir'd,
> His soul replenish'd, and his bosom fir'd;
> But say, ye *Muses*, why this partial grace,

> To one alone of *Afric's* sable race:
> From age to age transmitting thus his name
> With the first glory in the rolls of fame?

Baker's interpretation suggests quite correctly that Wheatley conjures one whom the western muses do not typically invoke, the African slave-poet Terence. In doing so, Baker tells us that Wheatley writes "her male precursor's African name . . . and body into the discourse of eighteenth-century heroics"—that she becomes, in effect, "an African embodiment of Terence's precursorial spirit." I would submit, however, that Wheatley accomplishes something over and above a negotiation with the master discourse of western heroics; she not only writes Terence into literary history, but (like her successor Douglass) performs the equally important task of writing *herself* and *her story* into *history*. This act of self-inscription is achieved through what I have elsewhere described as a dialogic engagement with both the dominant or hegemonic discursive tradition as well as the subdominant or (to use Rachel DuPlesses' admirable term) "ambiguously (non)hegemonic" discourse. What I am proposing is that Wheatley, in the subsequent tradition of black women writers, engages in *multi*-metalevel negotiations with a tradition that privileges not only white but male discourse. Thus, the "partial grace/To one alone of *Afric's* sable race" calls into question not only the exclusion of other African voices, but the privileging as well of "the happier Terence" (the expression begs a comparison with the author herself).

It is, after all, *his* name transmitted "from age to age . . . With the first glory in the rolls of fame." My point here is that Wheatley's complex autobiographical negotiations are not only racially but sexually strategic. Her situation positions her in a doubly marginalized relation to traditions from which she is excluded by race as a black and by gender as a woman. It is on the basis of this multi-metalevel negotiation—or what I describe as dialogic engagement with the various and multiple discourses of the other(s)—that I affirm Baker's racial reading of Wheatley's discursive dilemma but propose a simultaneous gendered rereading of the same text.

Baker's poetics of Afro-American women's writings is based on the notion of "imagistic fields," generated by Walker's metaphor for the roots of black women's creativity—"our mothers' gardens." Baker argues that the critic's autobiographical negotiation in relation to the imagistic fields inscribed in Afro-American women's writings yields "a unique inscription of the Afro-American self as woman" and "a refiguration of the African body that emerges from a standard male theoretical story." It is noteworthy that the image of woman and the female principle have long been associated in western thought with "the dark continent." From Freud to Suleiman to Cixous, scholars and critics have conflated the image of Africa with that of the female body, images suggesting the mysteriously unknown: the erotic and the exotic, the natural and the spiritual, the primitive and the pristine. Baker, it would seem, reverses the conventional western metaphorical construction of the female body in terms of the African (continental) body by suggesting that the works of contemporary Afro-American women writers inscribe the African body in terms associated with the female—spirituality, nurturance, and fertility.

Gaston Bachelard's "felicitous poetic image" becomes, for Baker, a generative metaphor for an Afro-American women's poetics. Alice Walker's image of the garden, in her essay "In Search of Our Mothers' Gardens," is a prototype of the "felicitous image" which Baker employs to formulate a poetics of black women's writing. The project is an elegant one which assumes that universal fields or categories such as space and time can only be meaningfully experienced through a culturally specific field of "particular" or vernacular imagery unique to the Afro-American imagination—and, implicitly, the Afro-American woman's imagination.

The significance of this field in the Afro-American woman's imagination is clearly suggested in Robert Stepto's interview with Toni Morrison, "Intimate Things in Place." The interview not only hints at the meaning of place—i.e., "geographical landscapes"—but more precisely, the importance of "places . . . set in time"—that is, the specificity of place read through time read through the Afro-American woman's novelistic imagination. In what we might call an autobiographical negotiation of spatiality, Morrison explains to the interviewer what it is like to create a racially defined space ("the community"), and further, what it is like to create a woman's place within that community:

I felt a very strong sense of place, not in terms of the country or the state, but in terms of the details, the feeling, the mood of the community, of the town. In [my] book, I was clearly pulling straight out of what autobiographical information I had. I didn't create that town. It's clearer in my memory than when I lived there. . . . Also, I think some of it is just a woman's strong sense of being in a room, a place, or in a house. Sometimes my relationship to things in a house would be a little different from, say, my brother's or my father's or my sons'. I clean them and I move them and I do very intimate things "in place": I am sort of rooted in it, so that writing about being in a room looking out, or being in a world looking out, or living in a small definite place, is probably very common among most women anyway.[1]

1. Michael S. Harper and Robert B. Stepto, eds., *Chant of Saints* (Urbana: University of Illinois Press, 1978), p. 213.

From a somewhat different perspective, Julia Kristeva, in her essay on "Women's Time," takes the position that "when evoking the name and destiny of women, one thinks . . . of the *space* generating and forming the human species. . . ." The very notion of space, maternal space, in the examples Kristeva cites, is elaborated not only by writers and theorists such as Joyce and Freud, but by western thinkers extending back to Plato, whose *chora,* or "matrix space," "provides a ground for all that can come into being." Moreover, as a spatial trope for a ground of being, a source of nourishment and fecundity, Walker's garden is associated with Bachelard's birth and renewal imagery in *The Poetics of Space.*

Indeed, so compelling is this connection between women's subjectivity and space for Kristeva that it modifies her conception of the fundamental categories of time and space as they are filtered through women's perceptions and experiences. Time, for Kristeva, can only be understood within the dimensions of spatiality. She formulates a kind of space-time ratio, "monumental temporality," that conceptualizes "the problematic of a time indissociable from space"—a notion of time that, as she puts it, "has little to do with linear time" and more with an "all-encompassing and infinite like [sic] imaginary space."[2]

I confess to a certain seduction by Baker's theory for all the above reasons. Yet, while Baker is, in some respects, very much in accord with Morrison and Kristeva, the danger is not only that of essentializing but of reinforcing the most conventional constructs of (black) femininity. An equally interesting strategy would be to read these notions of female space and female body in a way that destabilizes the idealization of women.

I have a second confession—and that is to a certain sense of dis-ease with the *specularity* of this rather spectacular theory. Both the Arnoldian injunction ("to see 'the' object as it is"), Pater's revision ("to see 'a' particular, unique object as it is to me"), and Mary Russo's more specific view of woman as spectacle, are problematized for the black woman as a privileged object of discussion in the formulation of a poetics of Afro-American women's writing. The privileging of the visual image, in particular, from the "autobiographical situationality" of the male poses certain conceptual and theoretic problems.

My concerns are twofold and interrelated, and involve both the adjectival and the nominal referents in "felicitous image." Baker defines his task as "comprehensive analyses of the guiding spirituality to be discovered in the imagistic fields of black women's writing." In a further

2. Julia Kristeva, "Women's Time," *Signs: Journal of Women in Culture and Society* 7, no. 1 (1981), pp. 15, 16, 16n, 17.

delimitation, however, he explains that "the field is decidedly not one where pathological or aversive images dominate." Continuing, he observes that "what are revealed are felicitous images of the workings of a spirit, as so wonderfully captured" by Walker's garden imagery.

It is this meditation on the image (as opposed to negotiation of metalevels of discourse) that raises the problematic of the gaze. The privileging of the image—that which we can see—resides uncomfortably in Luce Irigaray's "dominant scopic economy." "In this logic, the prevalence of the gaze," writes Irigaray, woman is once again "[relegated] to passivity: she will be the beautiful object."[3] In other words, if theoretical activity connotes discursive engagement, performance, and praxis, then "imagistic fields" connotes woman as spectacle—objectified and inscribed by the male activity of scopophilia. Moreover, if black/female subjectivity is constituted by the gaze by the other(s) (just as, I would suggest, the subjectivity of the (black/male) other(s) is constituted by the (black/female gaze), what happens to those aspects of (black/female) self from which the gaze is averted? If, as Lacan suggests, "the gaze is the instrument through which light is embodied and through which . . . I am *photo-graphed*," if what "determines me, at the most profound level, in the visible, is the gaze that is outside," then I am at the mercy of what the other(s) determine is the appropriate "scopic field."[4] It is the appropriate scopic field, the grid which separates the "pathological or aversive" from the "felicitous," that constitutes the most disturbing aspect of Baker's approach. What happens, one might query, when the eye is averted from the "nonfelicitous" image?

Parenthetically, and by way of a transition from the noun *images* to the adjective *felicitous,* I would like to rephrase Baker's own question to non-Afro-American commentators on Afro-American expressive cultural theory. My question is addressed to those excluded by gender and/or race from the autobiographical experiences of black women: "Does an autobiographical condition of existence and authenticity preclude non-Afro-American women commentators from the domain of Afro-American women's poetics?" Rephrasing Baker's own response, "I must answer a painful No." Painful because the incumbency for the non-Afro-American-woman critic is to finger the jagged grain of a brutal experience in which—if he or she is white and/or male—he or she is

3. Luce Irigaray, "This Sex Which Is Not One," in *New French Feminisms,* ed. Elaine Marks and Isabelle de Courtivron (New York: Schocken, 1981) p. 101.
4. Jacques Lacan, *The Four Fundamental Concepts of Psycho-Analysis* (New York: W. W. Norton, 1981) p. 106.

implicated. The nonblack feminist critic/theorist who honestly engages his or her own autobiographical implication in a brutal past is likely to provide nuances such as that of the black feminist scholar. What, however, are the preconditions or precautions for the nonblack feminist critic/theorist who dares to undertake such a project?

The critical act, for Baker, is "the mapping of position" or the "autobiographical situationality" which allows the "successful theorist" to know "where and how to listen," or in terms of "the poetics of space," "where and how to see." Thus, the first requirement for the critic or theorist of black women's writing must be the deconstitution of the gaze of the other(s)—i.e., an alteration of perception, or revision, in the sense of approaching the discursive subject or object from a new perspective or angle of vision. By confronting not only the felicitous in the imagistic fields of women's literature, but the nonfelicitous as well, one is able, as Laura Mulvey proposes, to "disrupt the male gaze by interrupting the pleasure of the visual. . . ."[5]

The real status of black women and their relationship to the rest of society, I would argue, cannot be captured in "felicitous images." Such a representation would suggest that black women inscribe themselves in nonadversarial relationships with both the community and the society at large. Such images have the potential to reinforce and maintain the status of currently marginalized and subdominant groups. The power of black women's writing is precisely its ability to disrupt and break with conventional imagery. If, for example, Walker's mother in the garden symbolizes birth and renewal, then Morrison's mother who burns her son to keep him from reentering the womb evokes death and destruction. If Hurston's Tea Cake can be, for her protagonist Janie, "a bee for a blossom," he is subsequently transformed into a rabid creature whom she must kill in self-defense. If Jessie Fauset's "Old Philadelphians" represent the achievements of the (black/female) middle-class, the secular rewards of race uplift, and the values of material redemption, then Gloria Naylor's *Linden Hills* explores at what spiritual and emotional cost their objectives are attained. If Maya Angelou triumphs over rape and near-incest, then Morrison's Pecola succumbs to the madness resulting from the incestuous rape of a young black girl.

What do we readers learn from these *non*felicitous images—positive images that elide into their opposites? What is the danger of a poetics that locates black women within a prelapsarian Edenic garden, a poetics

---

5. Laura Mulvey, cited by Juliet F. MacCannell in *Figuring Lacan: Criticism and the Cultural Unconscious* (Lincoln: University of Nebraska Press, 1986), p. 135.

that does not take account of the negative or aversive images? Do we run
the risk of concealing from ourselves very real problems resulting from
generational, class, gender, color, or racial difference and disharmony by
limiting our focus to felicitous images? Dare we risk reducing the complexity and misconstructing (or misconstruing) the totality of our
experiences? Although the reading suggested by the felicitous-images
approach is critical and descriptive, in some respects, it seems a more
sophisticated and refined reformulation of the more prescriptive
positive-images approach. Black women's lives and literature are much
too complex to be limited to the duality of positive and negative images.

These eliding and ambivalent images have the effect of defamiliarizing
images of quotidian experience and producing what Fredric Jameson
calls a sense of "dialectical shock," the transitional moment in which,
according to William Dowling, the reader is forced "out of customary
and comfortable positions and into painful confrontations with un-
suspected truths."[6]

In conclusion, I would like to address the issue of difference—"critical
difference." The black literary-critical tradition, as Baker has demonstrated elsewhere, has been subject to periodic shifts as we discover new
critical paradigms to organize and structure our readings. As a result of
these sometimes seismic shifts, earlier paradigms lose their immediacy—
I do not say value, but immediacy. Older critical and theoretic approaches become wrapped into tradition, as we privilege that which
Roland Barthes, in "What Is Criticism," describes as "a construction of
the intelligibility of our own time."

Part of the commitment of the black feminist project, however, is the
privileging of difference. It is, after all, the rhetoric of universality that
has excluded gender, race, and class perspectives from the dominant
literary-critical discourse as well as the socio-political centers of power. It
is the reduction of multiplicity to undifferentiated sameness that has
empowered white feminists to speak for all women, black men to speak
for all blacks, and white males to speak for everyone. What I propose is a
multiplicity of "interested readings" which resists the totalizing character of much theory and criticism—readings that can enter into dialogic
relationship with other "interested readings"—past and present.

We must deconstitute the notion of *the* black tradition. Our literary
history speaks to dialogue and debate among various and competing

6. Fredric Jameson, cited in William C. Dowling, *Jameson, Althusser, Marx: An Introduction to "The Political Unconscious"* (Ithaca: Cornell University Press, 1984), p. 11.

critical camps from at least the Harlem Renaissance to the present. We engage not only in intercultural metalevel negotiations, but intracultural metalevel negotiations as well. Just as we must move away from the hegemony of the dominant discourse, we must move away from the hegemony of the dominant mode(s) of literary criticism within our own tradition. To suggest a pluralist resolution is perhaps too simple; we must, however, promote rival critical paradigms which critique each other's theories and readings, for despite pretensions to wholeness, there will always and forever be inadequacy in models and paradigms. They are, after all, explanations and constructions of reality based on "strategies of containment" and "boundaries of exclusion."

What has sustained us in the past in our attempts to construct a whole tradition has been dialogue among rival and, at times, antagonistic models. It is the differences among these contestorial and critical models—as they speak to and critique each other—that enable us to return again and again to the notion of a black critical tradition. We must continue to recognize and respect that dialogue is necessary to fill in the lacks or deficiencies within and among different and competitive paradigms. In pursuing this critical dialogue, we engage not only our peers but also our predecessors. This critical connection with both past and present is in the spirit of the Afro-American community. We are a people who have survived through recognizing and respecting each other and the ancestors.

6

Performing Blackness:
Re/Placing Afro-American Poetry

Kimberly W. Benston

The Postal Official was taken aback: he was on a routine inspection of a
sorting office on Chicago's Southside, but what he saw was definitely *not*
routine. Off to one side, without ostentation or fanfare, a young worker was
sorting his pieces as if he were Dr. J. giving a clinic: around the back—
shump!, into the box; through the legs—*swish!,* into the bag; and so on. The
Official couldn't forbear: "Young man," he intoned, "that's truly amazing!"
"Aw, man," the worker shot back, flipping another piece over his head neatly
into a slot, "This ain't nuthin . . . you just wait 'til I can *read* this jive!"

I first heard this Dick Gregory tale when growing up in Chicago in the
1960s. Now Gregory told the story to our predominantly black high-
school audience with an undertone of sardonic bitterness at its implicit
dichotomy of blackness and literacy. At the same time—and no doubt
Gregory had this too in mind—we in the audience recognized humor in
the delicious irony of style's triumph over the alienating technology of
officialdom: the trickster over the chump, the gouster over the Man.
With perhaps too little appreciation of Gregory's cautionary tone (or of
his appended maxim: "Get from the playground to the proving-
ground") the tale made the school-yard rounds for many months, and
even if we used to speak of Earl-the-Pearl and Chet Walker instead of the
Doctor, it answered exultantly to some rebellious need we all felt as we
crawled our way through the labyrinthine nightmare of urban educational decay. Little did I suspect that the story could be redeemed twenty
years later as an allegory of my professional life—not in the niches of the
post office, but among the more differentiated spaces of Afro-American
literature. For at the time I was first encountering Gregory's little fable as
a schoolboy in Chicago the state of Afro-American literary interpretation
was well reflected by the tale: obscured by the shadow of a hermeneutical
technology produced as much to confine as to illuminate black ex-

164

pression, pieces of Afro-American literature were casually, if elegantly, sorted into categories (of period, genre, and "sensibility")—but few were actually being *read*. Since then, a veritable explosion in interpretive activity and acumen has taken place, so that we find ourselves on the threshold of an entire reevaluation of the very image of Afro-American literary tradition.

Now, when we seek a revised account of Afro-American tradition, and we turn to the area of criticism specifically devoted to the poetry of that tradition, what we find is perhaps somewhat less satisfactory, less theoretically compelling and practically instructive than the critiques offered in the realm of narrative and dramatic studies. There are, of course, many excellent studies of specific works and authors (among them Vera Kutzinski on Jay Wright, Peter Erickson on June Jordan, Melvin Dixon on Robert Hayden, Betty Parker-Smith on Carolyn Rodgers, Billy Joe Harris on Amiri Baraka), but those efforts I know of which attempt to provide a comprehensive scheme or explanation of the poetry lack the depth, variety, and sophistication we have generally come to expect of the criticism. Most strikingly, to take the cue again from Gregory's anecdote, a division persists between our knowledge of the poetry as text and our awareness of it as performance—a gap which I think our criticism must address with utmost rigor if we are to begin an enlarged account of the poetry's ever-widening activity and ever-deepening complexity.

It may be, in fact, that the poetry's relative susceptibility to discrete analyses resists theoretical efforts that move toward totalization, toward recuperation and ideological closure. I hope to speculate a little about this toward the end of my essay, but in order to arrive at a reasonable position from which to do so I would like to begin by suggesting that a polar opposition is at work in those critical narratives that do aspire to a synoptic sweep: on the one hand, the Afro-American poem is measured against a privileged notion of "blackness" which is posited as external to both the Euro-American "mainstream" and, in a political sense, to the poem itself; on the other hand, the poem is tested for conformity to a universally applicable norm of "the poetic" which is supposed to exist both in and outside any notion of "blackness." I would argue that these views share a basic philosophic supposition—that the poem's meaning may be located in some standard both prior and external to the poetic act itself, a supposition rooted in a common political implication—that the critic's role is to discriminate the "proper" from the "failed" or foolish, the correct from the deviant.

Let me quickly illustrate by contrasting two justly well-known appraisals of Afro-American poetry. Haki Madhubuti's (Don L. Lee's) *Dynamite Voices* may be taken as a representative of what I will term the "hermeneutics of blackness": for him, black poetry ranges on either side of the great divide of the Black Arts movement, which created, in his view, the first thoroughly "Black" Afro-American poetry. While acknowledging the influence of earlier periods, especially of the Harlem Renaissance, upon the new black poet's sense of purpose and seriousness, Madhubuti measures the "unique" status of the contemporary, originary black poem by a standard of didactic commitment, "concrete" subject matter, and orality, a standard that no earlier poetry had fully realized. Against Madhubuti, we may place a representative of what I would call the "hermeneutics of recuperation"—Blyden Jackson, who, in his contribution to *Black Poetry in America* (cowritten with Louis D. Rubin), sees likewise in the modern black poem a "world of blackness" where every utterance "sounds alike," a plainness which Jackson sees threatening the reduction of the poetic to "a cartoon quality." However, where Madhubuti sees in the modern discourse of blackness a salutary disjunction, Jackson offers to reassimilate the era's disharmonious outcries to the presumed continuity of a "synthetically American" tradition, allowing us to "think of recent black poetry at least as much in the context of poetry as of propaganda."

In a sense, Madhubuti and Jackson share a crucial presupposition for the interpretation of Afro-American poetry: that the critic's role was radically reshaped or threatened by the emerging poetic of contemporary practitioners, a poetic which asserted that the peculiar power of black verse was its refusal of difficulty and the accompanying need for professional exegesis or "translation," and, concomitantly, that the poet, in questioning the authority of tradition, conceived his or her work as not merely experimental but as an exploration of radically alternative cultural constructs.

Curiously, both critical camps I have been outlining respond to this potential subversion of the uses and reception—indeed, of the very category—of poetry by reaffirming the rather traditional assumption that literature is an inevitable consequence of being, and that its "natural" role is to mime an experience whose authenticity is guaranteed by being enacted independently of any reflection upon it. Both Madhubuti and Jackson thus accept the opposition of the poem-as-structure and the poem-as-event, and each undertakes the task of maintaining the purity of one notion against the iniquity of the other. Behind this opposition stand a host of other, rather familiar, dualities which permeate both interpretive fields: oral vs. written, craft vs. politics (as in Jackson's dichotomy of "poetry" and "propaganda"), and so on. It is the burden of my argument that unless we shift the ground from underneath a criticism erected on such contraries, locating our discussions at some *juncture* of ideological and aesthetic concerns, we will be doomed to retrace the conceptual do-si-do marked out by the secret partners of recent years, the schools of blackness and universality; further, we will fail to perceive the poetry's own dynamic lesson of its upheaval, that it is not an inevitable object but rather a motivated, constructed, corrosive, and productive process.

Having said this much, I feel myself to be at a crucial methodological crossroads; for many of us, the next move has inevitably been either to take up one side or the other in revisionist fashion or, in cursing both houses, to adopt some version of the (post)-structuralist/New Critical bromide about meanings, whether rhetorical or discursive, being "in the poems themselves." Given the choice, I would (as I have just hinted) choose the course of rhetorical least resistance and argue for such withinness, but I will be suggesting that the choice so constructed has been misconceived. In any case, I would like to defer that gesture (in a manner, I hope, that also makes the gesture *different* once performed) by proposing two other ways to look at critical polarization in studies of Afro-American poetry.

First, I would observe that the argument between Madhubuti and Jackson concerns a very real historical and ideological issue, one in which, I believe, we are as critics as much enmeshed today as are the artists of whom we dare to speak: that is, what is the continuing meaning of the Black Arts movement of the 1960s and 1970s; on what terms shall we calculate its aims, achievements, and legacy? For our current disputes in the late 1980s over, on the one hand, the propriety of extratextual criteria, and, on the other hand, the political motivations of various neoformalisms, should be seen as displacements or extensions of an earlier inquisition of the "poetic" as a valid category of value, a questioning to which writers such as Madhubuti and Jackson were responding. The positions represented by Madhubuti and Jackson can be read as variant responses to the claims of rupture and resistance that were at the core of the "black aesthetic," claims which, whatever their absolute philosophic and material validity, fundamentally altered the framework (conceptual and institutional) in which we operate today. Thus, one lesson of the fracturing of commentary into the poles I have been describing is that the tactics we employ in decoding and recoding black poetry still turn in some measure on our interpretation of the ferment which stands now at a generation's remove, on our attitude toward the

programmatic declarations and practical performances which carry the
Black Arts movement's freight of aesthetic, ontological, and political
visions.

Second, I think it would be helpful to understand the polarized
arguments I have outlined as a derivative of the literature's own contemporary struggle for self-definition. Indeed, I would suggest that the two
critical positions outlined above—one embracing the Black Arts' ideological claim for an autonomous black poetics, the other seeking to
situate black poetics within a larger and more continuous framework of
American/Western/Human creativity—are in some sense parodic reflections of an argument taking place in the literature itself, an argument
about the nature of blackness, performance, and the modern Afro-American self.

To establish a paradigm for this discourse, I shall briefly contrast two
passages which offer brilliantly compressed reflections of the key issues
involved: the sermon on the "blackness of blackness" in Ralph Ellison's
Invisible Man and Clay's famous concluding monologue in Amiri Baraka's *Dutchman*. Each text privileges the relation of blackness to
performance as a vision of Afro-American identity, grouping around
that topos a complex of problems integral to any discussion of Afro-
American poetry (problems concerning the relations of history to tradition, modernism to elegy, textuality to orality). Both texts do so, I will
argue, in order to figure quite distinct theories of black selfhood and that
selfhood's formation by and in the "play" of language. Let us begin with
Ellison's passage:

I not only entered the music but descended, like Dante, into its depths. And
*beneath the swiftness of the hot tempo there was a slower tempo and a cave and I entered
it and looked around and heard an old woman singing a spiritual as full of
Weltschmerz as flamenco, and beneath that lay a still lower level on which I saw a
beautiful girl the color of ivory pleading in a voice like my mother's as she stood before a
group of slaveowners who bid for her naked body, and below that I found a lower level
and a more rapid tempo and I heard someone shout:*
"Brothers and sisters, my text this morning is the 'Blackness of Blackness.'"
*And a congregation of voices answered: "That blackness is most black brother, most
black . . ."*
"In the beginning . . ."
"At the very start," they cried.
" . . . there was blackness . . ."
"Preach it . . ."
" . . . and the sun . . ."
"The sun, Lawd . . ."

" . . . was bloody red . . ."

"Red . . ."

"Now black is . . ." the preacher shouted.

"Bloody . . ."

"I said black is . . ."

"Preach it, brother . . ."

" . . . an' black ain't . . ."

"Red, Lawd, red: He said it's red!"

"Amen, brother . . ."

"Black will git you . . ."

"Yes, it will . . ."

"Yes, it will . . ."

" . . . an' black won't . . . "

"Naw, it won't!"

"It do . . ."

"It do, Lawd . . ."

" . . . an' it don't."

"Halleluiah . . ."

" . . . It'll put you, glory, glory, Oh my Lawd, in the WHALE'S BELLY." . . .

"Black will make you . . ."

"Black . . ."

" . . . or black will un-make you."

As if deliberately reversing the illusionary, dematerializing movement of humanist metaphysics, Ellison ironically displaces "white my-thology's" myth of origin with a story of *the beginning-as-blackness*. At such a black beginning, the passage suggests, we find enacted a series of complex differences and dislocations, first imaged here as a "descending" through cultural realms (hence Dante, flamenco, and yiddishkeit are invoked even as the "spiritual" world of Afro-American descent is evoked). In what the novel will later teach us to call a Rinehartean questioning of the fluid world beneath any textual field, Ellison's hero plunges toward a site where language, in the crucible of national and family romance, has both the impulse to summon a presence and the power to declare its own absence, to proffer a story of the past while thematizing the performative or fictional character of all such telling.

In the performance of his preacher, Ellison thus stages the strategy of the topos of beginning as an interrogation of received cultural abstrac-tions, assertions like those mythic ones that declare an absolute place of origination, those privileged allegories of foundation by which histor-icism (à la Brother Jack) and mythography (à la Homer A. Barbee) alike declare their mastery. And by denaturalizing "history" as an essential, teleological display, the passage forces us to consider even blackness as a mediated, socially constructed *practice,* a process in and not a product of discursive conditions of struggle.

The generative energy of the passage thus emanates from a dialogic site-ing (in the root sense of *sermo*), the preacher's public speech on blackness. But in noting Ellison's demystification of a beginning which would stand beyond any revisionary performance, we might well note that the passage is itself a critical repetition, a slyly belated quotation, of another "primordial" sermonic beginning in American literature: the "blackness of darkness" briefly heard and quickly shunned by Melville's Ishmael at what "seemed the great Black Parliament sitting in Tophet" (vide "The Carpet-Bag" chapter of *Moby Dick*).

The blackness of Melville's preacher is an outcry of utter negation, a cacophony of "weeping and wailing and teethgnashing" which must be at once glimpsed and then escaped as the enabling, "stumbling" prelude to the more thunderous preachments of authorized whalers. For Melville's privileged figures, be they questers or questioners of the Primal Name, "blackness" remains "profound" and "awful" but always chthonian, while the more resonant ambiguities of "fluid identity" are ascribed to the "grand hooded phantom" of a "whiteness-of-whiteness."

Accepting the ambiguity of his own beginning, Ellison at once cites Melville's text as an inescapable element of the American scene and appropriates its authority over that scene by reshaping it toward a new "end." Ellison, in effect, forces Ishmael (and, with him, the quintessential American reader Ishmael implicitly mirrors from the moment of *his* inaugural "calling") to re-enter the arena of the preacher's dark pronouncement, and then suggests that the text of blackness is precisely about the internal contradictions, necessary repetitions, and transgressive revisions of any beginning per se. But, further, Ellison's text thematizes the problematic of beginning as performed repetition by declaring its own divided status as expression.

"Black will make you . . . or unmake you":

understanding its existence as irreducibly heterogeneous, *blackness* establishes and yet also destabilizes relations, dislocating its own privileged status as arch-signifier of Afro-American expression. Embracing the "is" and "ain't" of the being-of-blackness, announcing a kind of dark Law of Contradiction *in place of* the dominant representations of black discourse, this topos presents the possibility of a differential principle of identity which refuses any effacement of the dissimilar by a totalizing theory of Afro-American existence (as in Ishmael's hurried critique of the "negro preacher's" sermon as "Wretched entertainment").

Thus Ellison's sermon works by differential tensions, defining the ever-shifting "scene" of Afro-American language as dialectical: "In the beginning" was the sign of the End, the bloody sun of *Revelations* (cf. Rev. 6:12); black will and it won't; love enfolds hate; laughter echoes moan—a doubleness experienced both rhetorically (won't/don't) and dramatically (the "ivory" whiteness-of-whiteness calls for the preacher's "black" response). Primordial blackness, then, is not a node of absolute essence but, rather, the (re)discovery of the subversive ambiguity of any expressive act. "Blackness" is the endlessly enigmatic name for a ceaselessly elusive agency; it is that which "puts" a reluctant prophet into the dark cave of the WHALE'S BELLY as a precondition for his deliverance through (and for) testifying.

This theory of blackness clearly has profound implications for poetic and interpretive practices alike. But let us explore such possibilities in concert with a Barakan vision of blackness. Here is an excerpt from Clay's angry, and ultimately fatal, disputation with his "ivory" antagonist, Lula:

Just shut up. You don't know what you're talking about. You don't know anything. So just keep your stupid mouth closed and let me talk. . . . you wanted to do the belly rub? Shit you don't even know how. You don't know how. . . . Belly rub is not Queens. Belly rub is dark places, with big hats and overcoats held up with one arm. Belly rub hates you. . . . They [whites] say, "I love Bessie Smith." And don't even understand that Bessie Smith is saying "Kiss my ass, kiss my black unruly ass." Before love, suffering, desire, anything you can explain, she's saying, and very plainly, "Kiss my black ass." . . . Charlie Parker? Bird . . . would've played not a note of music if he just walked up East Sixty-seventh Street and killed the first ten white people he saw. Not a note! . . . You don't know anything except what's there for you to see. An act. Lies. Device. Not the pure heart, the pure pumping black heart. . . . You understand? No. I guess not. If Bessie Smith had killed some white people she wouldn't have needed that music. She would have talked very straight and plain about the world. No metaphors. No grunts. No wiggles in the dark of her soul. . . . all it needs is that simple act. . . . Ahh Shit. But who needs it? I'd rather be a fool. Insane. Safe with my words, and no deaths, and clean, hard thoughts, urging me to new conquests.

Clay's speech is a vision of blackness in relation to being and performance; it is like the preacher's sermon in constituting an ideological and epistemological theory of signification. But if in Ellison we see the un-

masking of myths of idealized presence and the disclosure of the
diacritical dispersal of linguistic force, in Baraka we feel a countermove-
ment from the impure to the essential, a deliberate and violent reversal of
Ellison's descent that points beyond the realm of figure to its corrected
meaning in a "proper" form.

For Baraka, the expressions of language and the body of blackness are
diametrically opposed; discourse and being are not, as for Ellison, inextricable, and the possibility of "knowing" begins with an emphatic
refusal of eloquence's prestige. Blackness, far from being inextricable
from the paradoxes of its articulation, finally transcends representation.
Afro-American cultural *expression* is not, in fact, the *Ding-an-sich* of the
blackness which its pronouncements would invoke.

Clay's blackness "hates" the representational realm of *as if* in which he,
as a mere preacher of the Word, remains enclosed in spurious "safety."
His blackness longs for incarnation as literal presence, for the singular
revolutionary act that would "murder" self-difference and heal the
breach between black identity and discourse that the original violence of
whiteness opened. The essential effusions of a "pumping" blackness
replace Ellison's projection of an endlessly mediated black performance.
They suggest a "pure" center around which the empowered meanings of
Afro-American being coalesce. This center becomes the authentic
"heart" of performance, redeeming black expression from its condition
as diasporic, even burdensome "device."

Clay's polemic against the "lie" of "metaphor" would shatter the
Ellisonian scene of textual construction. This scene Clay sees as *itself* (and
not simply the hidden white master) weaving the "mask" of blackness-as-
being. Ellisonian discourse, Clay seems to propose, points to the self-
repeating act of signifying (cf. the play's subway in its mock-heroic
quests of endless return) rather than to the longed-for signified. Thus the
image of destruction, of smashing the idols of the tribe, yields not silence
but "plain talk." Speech is deployed as a present act that cancels the
emptiness of performances that are sometimes heard merely as ends in
themselves; and the sacramental violence of desire is at last fulfilled.

We may, in fact, note that where Ellison is concerned with the twist-
ing of ends into their "possibilities" as beginnings, Baraka is
revolutionarily more apocalyptic. Where Ellison's questioning of origins
gives to language a productive capacity realized only in its performance,
Baraka's invocation of a longed-for end envisions play as either a pre-
revolutionary diversion or, more radically, a postemancipatory
sacrament in which the coded meaning of historical black expression
would become "very straight and plain." Poetic activity, in *this* world in

which we perforce have our beginning, is at best only an approximation of the continuous ideal of lived experience. In the vision of a "simple act" of liberating violence, Baraka's hero in fact assigns a signal role to the pure gestures of performance. But the authenticity of such gestures is realized only through a termination of the self-questioning (or, to fully accept Baraka's polemic against Ellison in this drama, self-falsifying) theatricality of Ellison's subterranean preacher.

Performance is not, then, inescapably dissonant and aporetic. But until it is directed to invocation of a primal name of blackness, becoming both the site and mechanism of a revolutionary transubstantiation, performance can only be a mockingly faint shadow of a more "real" expression. (Clay's speech, after all, understands itself to be yet another "text" of Afro-American literary tradition, and its citation of Ellison's preacher, unlike the preacher's revision of Melville's Ishmael, reinscribes a sign of self-enslavement, not self-enablement.) Thus the prophecy of revolutionary blackness must supersede the Ellisonian story of performed blackness as necessary fiction.

The Ellison/Baraka argument over the nature and telos of performed blackness brings us back to the question of interpretive strategies with which I began. Ellison's view of blackness as perpetual beginning suggests that the meaning of blackness does not inhere in any ultimate referent but is renewed in the rhythmic process of multiplication and substitution generated from performance to performance. This is not in the least to say that, for Ellison, performance is arbitrary or empty, just as it is not abstracted or objectified. It is, rather, a construct of desire, mobilized at a site of struggle against various forms of closure. As interpretive respondents to its performative call, we are asked to accept the continuously unsatisfying and contradictory character of its enunciations. As compensation, we are offered a notion of the black text as a dynamic producer of richly differing signifying perspectives—a fashioner, in fact, of a world (as the hero puts it near the end of *Invisible Man*) "seething with possibilities."

Baraka's vision, by contrast, asks us to negate the effects of such temporizing textual displacements. It urges us to materialize a presence that is dissimulated in performance. It pushes us to move *through* the text to the truth of blackness beyond (one might say, to *literally* per-form!). Baraka's dance of blackness here (his essentializing belly rub of signifying) is, to those who embody it, spectacularly unconcealed. It possesses sense and sensuality that precede "anything you can explain." In a sense, the Black Arts poet's blackness stands beyond a need for exegesis as such; Clay's sermon is ironically directed to an auditor (i.e., Lula) who, ipso facto, can't "understand" it. Indeed, until the "simple act" of revolution provides a palpably comprehensible epistemology of black presence displacing partial performances that inadequately prefigure it, we may surmise that it is the *audience* (here imagined to be more like Clay than Lula) rather than the performance that requires scrutiny. We also assume that the preacher's task is visionary annunciation of the *is,* not dialectical engagement of the *is and ain't,* of blackness.

For Baraka, the Ellisonian play of language's doubleness is a duplicitous discord that screams the burden of black modernism. And in a curious sense, representation is finally not problematic for Baraka as it is irresolvably for Ellison, because representation can never quite erase blackness in order to mark (in repetition) its absence. Instead, representation temporarily, if hurtfully, hides or encodes blackness, allowing for the possibility of its becoming present as a history—a history that would not be a fiction.

We are finally in a position to return to the contrast of interpretive modes exemplified by Haki Madhubuti and Blyden Jackson. Madhubuti, like Baraka, invokes the extralinguistic standard of "correct" blackness in erecting a vision of the poetic canon, while Jackson, like Ellison, refocuses attention on the verbal medium in which a rather more eclectic or "synthetic" vision of blackness evolves from generation to generation. But Ellison and Baraka are *alike* in a crucial respect that sets them apart from Madhubuti and Jackson. For the creative writers' accounts of the topos of performed rupture, loss, and the consequent desire for restored plentitude—even if they disagree about the destination of desire's projects—differ significantly from Madhubuti and Jackson's in that they see no immediately available cultural authority that could *stabilize* blackness's performances. In this sense, the Ellison-Baraka contrast offers us a mechanism—an enabling allegory, if you will—for resituating the critical opposition of "blackness" and "universality" on a ground internal to Afro-American discourse itself. Ellison and Baraka offer models of the black text which imply that such an opposition is, indeed, constituent of Afro-American poetics. If this is so, then criticism might make the opposition its own subject. What might such a critical project look like in practice?

At this point I would like to turn back to the contemporary criticism of black poetry and admit that I have neglected one global analysis which offers insight into this critical dilemma/opportunity—that is, Stephen Henderson's Introduction to *Understanding the New Black Poetry,* a work whose foundational value for cultural criticism has been richly explored by Houston Baker in *Blues, Ideology, and Afro-American Literature,* and which I now take up as a complex and rare instance of theoretical praxis. In its amalgam of conceptual and practical reflection, this work generates a series of tensions and juxtapositions which are at once fruitful and, I think, in need of further deliberation. I am particularly interested in the apposition of Henderson's strategy for decoding the poem's performative enunciations (the structural investigation of music as "poetic reference")—a strategy that opens up the poem as a potentially infinite realm of play—with his concept of "saturation," which seems to operate simultaneously as a goal and limit of the critic's own performance.

Henderson's observations on the uses of music as poetic device collectively suggest that poetic form, through the topos of performance, has become an arena of possibilities rather than a fixed datum. The language of blackness thus becomes a practice of open-ended signifying, so that the category of "structure" yields a more complex idea of structuration—i.e., a power to continuously rethink and revoice centers of poetic vision celebrated by Ellison's preacher.

At the same time, however, Henderson's own, rich tabulation of tactics and devices begins to formulate a mechanical or instrumental mode of reading, hinting at a desire to reify intention and agency through a critical codification of written forms and oral formulas. As if answering this objection that poetic performance cannot be reduced to a category of precise structural explanation, Henderson proceeds to his theory of "saturation," that arena of a blackness which texts somehow "manifest" and proper readers somehow "simply know." It seems to me that a potentially self-disabling theory is at work here. The black poet is "saturated" by that which he demonstrates, asking his audience to identify with what they already are. The poet becomes thereby a curiously reactionary figure, for the poem's performative activity is denied any transformative force, whether didactic or subversive. The energies unleashed by performance are finally neutralized or contained by the privilege of a mutually "saturated" subject. The poet/audience merges into the stabilizing order of a priori, external, reified "blackness."

What are we to make of this apparent division in Henderson's critical project, this double perspective on performed blackness as both energized by its processual nature and confined by an extrinsic, if impressionistic, touchstone?

In fact, there are other issues at work in Henderson's critique which might illuminate this tension. Throughout his essay, Henderson takes pains to orient analysis of the poetry's logical structure in ideological terms, continually observing that interpretive acts are never merely aesthetic, never free from the desire for power and cultural authority. Most important, he notes that this authority is not given but constructed and contested, although it secures its prestige precisely by presenting itself as inevitable. In some sense, it seems to me, the tension between structuration and saturation is a product of this ideological critique, expressing as it does a bifurcated evasion or subversion of "Western" critical authority. We are given a guide to a *science* of interpretation as well as a mode of *engaged* interpretation which authenticates the black critic's very cultural being as the enabling condition of his activity. Henderson simultaneously delivers a canon for "understanding" the textual practices of black poetry and re-idealizes these forms as residing among "things unknown."

Henderson's balance of objectives is, I believe, unsettled, but it is also unsettling in a very useful manner. The danger it courts is that of dismantling one metaphysical/ideological system by erecting another, thus recapitulating the political structure underlying textualist-idealist aesthetics. At this point we might have recourse to historical explanation, noting that the uncertainty of Henderson's double proposition arose in part from the circumstances of an institutional critical voice seeking to negotiate a register somewhere between the ignorant hostility of mainstream standards and the sometimes equally hostile anti-academicism of the poets themselves. It is undeniably, however, only Henderson who brings us back to the poetic itself as a realm of *theoretical* as well as aesthetic/political activity. And in order to move my discussion toward a tentative proposal for a qualified "agenda" for interpretation of Afro-American poetry, I shall now offer a particularized deployment/displacement of Henderson's commentary, an interrogative response, as it were, to his sermonic call.

My subject will be A. B. Spellman's "Did John's Music Kill Him?" an example of what we may call the Coltrane poem, that genre of modern black poetry in which the topos of performed blackness is felt most resonantly. I begin, however, with a passage from another instance of the genre, Jane Cortez's "How Long Has Trane Been Gone":

> John Coltrane's dead & some
> of you
> have yet to hear him play
> How long how long has that Trane been gone.

To the Afro-American elegist, the death of Coltrane is not experienced as an event; it is a recession of Coltrane from the minds of the living. It is an enforced deprivation, a radical discontinuity, the chill

of absence—and, hence, it is both an instigator of Afro-American alienation and a provoker of the black poet's crisis of expression.

The mourner's questioning of vacancy and death, becomes, inevitably, the poet's meditation on chaos and silence, the antitheses of
language. How, each asks, can the paralyzing pain of loss be transformed
into collective progress and productive speech? For the mourner the task
is to find celebratory praise where only lamentation seems possible; for
the poet, the quest is for expression that dispels the silence, for a re-
storative *poiesis* that reestablishes culture as possibility.

Re-membering becomes re-collection: the recovery of a lost being
depends upon a figural resanctification of history and, finally, of the
being himself. What we witness is the metamorphosis of Coltrane into
"Trane," of man into archetype. The death of Coltrane becomes, in
modern black poetry, a central topos of renewal and is accepted ultimately as beginning—as a question: How long how long has that Trane been
gone?

The Coltrane poem traverses the path of loss, outrage, and restitution
through a series of beginnings and prevented closures. It attempts to
reorder a world from which Coltrane's spirit is suddenly withdrawn. Yet,
it also undertakes this task as a struggle in and with received poetic form,
specifically, the classical mode of pastoral elegy.

Let us turn now to Spellman's "Did John's Music Kill Him?" which I
quote in full:

> in the morning part
> of evening he would stand
> before his crowd. the voice
> would call his name &
> redlight fell around him.
> jimmy'd bow a quarter hour
> till McCoy fed block chords
> to his stroke. elvin's thunder
> roll & eric's scream. then john.
>
> then john. *little old lady*
> had a nasty mouth. *summertime*
> when the war is. *africa* ululating
> a line bunched up like itself
> into knots paints beauty black.
>
> trane's horn had words in it
> i know when i sleep sober & dream

> those dreams i duck in the world
> of sun & shadow. yet even in the day john
> & a little grass put them on me clear
> as tomorrow in a glass enclosure.
>
> kill me john my life eats
> life. the thing that beats out of
> me happens in a vat enclosed
> & fermenting & wanting to explode
> like your song.

>> so beat john's death words down
>> on me in the darker part
>> of evening. the black light issued
>> from him in the pit he made
>> around us. worms came clear
>> to me where i thought i had been
>> brilliant. o john death will
>> not contain you death
>> will not contain you

From the title's opening question to the poem's concluding prophecy of transcendence, "Did John's Music Kill Him?" displaces loss by a dialectic of death, a dialectic that transmutes the apparent finality of extinction into the creative deliverance of a perpetual dying. As in pastoral elegy, the lamenting poet so closely identifies with the dead musician that he becomes a reflection or "shadow" of the departed: "kill me john. . . . "

The poet and Coltrane are alike restricted; the musician's strife-tormented "ululation" is an image of the poet's own constrained expression, i.e., the poem itself. This complex identification with the dead, a fixation which becomes as problematic as it seems beneficial, will lead to the poet's own nocturnal meditations. Before the consequences of such doubling and division are apparent, the opening of the poem attempts to envision a shared moment of fullness and presence, imagining musician, ensemble, and community convened by the promise of Coltrane's "song," a ceremony of invocation now rendered uncertain and conditional by the hero's imminent vanishing:

> in the morning part
> of evening he would stand
> before his crowd. . . .
> jimmy'd bow a quarter hour
> till McCoy fed block chords
> to his stroke. elvin's thunder

roll & eric's scream. then john.

then john. . . .

The poem begins by returning to a time before Coltrane's disappearance; and yet, as the many caesuras suggest, it anticipates the hero's entrance with as much apprehension (perhaps, indeed, half-acknowledged foreknowledge) as attentive expectation. The off-stage figure becomes more distant, it seems, as the déja vu of the setting becomes more populous, resonant, and precise. Within this scene-painting, the "calling" forth of Coltrane initiates the poem's pattern of beginning *again,* evoking as it does a kind of supplicatory recuperation or restitution of the figure without whom performance is all mere prelude. But, despite these hesitations and a curious uncertainty of tense, the nourishment of the collective's call does at last appear to bring forth the longed-for being: "then john."

The repetition of the phrase "then john" is the first, and indeed the signal crisis of "Did John's Music Kill Him?" What value might we assign it? On the one hand, it may be a kind of stammer, a disembodiment of voice for both poet and musician expressing not merely the latter's extinction but the former's paralysis or ambivalence in the face of bereavement. On the other hand, it might indicate the poet's capacity to begin once more despite the sudden shock of dislocation. The poet cauterizes the wound of John's denial by resituating the opening scene, moving it forward to the playing of familiarly funky sound. The stutter of repetition becomes the sly triumph of poetic grace.

Such a positive reading of the repetition is encouraged by the music's own evolution, from the jocular and sassy *little old lady* through the revisionary appropriations of *summertime* to the massive profundity of *africa* which, in its self-interpreting essence, gathers around the reimaged performance a fully saturated blackness ("bunched up *like itself*. . . paints beauty black").

The second stanza thus asserts that what might have been a terminal rupture is but a stage of development, wresting through the acoustic power of echo the possibility that seeming loss can be transformed to unenvisioned gain. The shift in emphasis from visual to aural traces of the scene of performance is one dimension of this pursuit of a more authentic manifestation of Coltrane's essence. Another is the poet's acknowledged implication in the dynamics of immanence, a descent which, prefigured in the gap between the first two stanzas, is accomplished through recognition of the hero's actual past-ness: "trane's horn had words in it / i know. . . . "

With this attachment to the fate and force of the hero's expression, the poem begins yet again, while the substitution of "trane's horn" for "john" begins the process of renewal by redefinition. Such displacement is only literally reductive, for the articulate horn is revealed as a kind of synecdoche of the musician's capacity of self-realization. Through its mechanism, the poet attains a freedom from the constraints of time and space which so bedeviled existence in the opening stanzas. The resultant dream-vision, reversing classical elegy's priority of illumination to darkness (with a witty troping of nostalgic pastoralism by nocturnal reefer), answers the prior stanza's howl of discovered blackness with an easeful prospect of repose.

At this point, the poem achieves stillness and composure. It seems itself to have become a crystalline sepulcher, a final form which formulates and sequesters an elusive, almost expended identity.

But simile betrays the element of hypothesis ("*as* tomorrow . . ."). The dialectic of loss and recovery has been frozen by a gesture of self-consolation, and the poem's arrival at the period closure is like a deadening monumentalizing of Coltrane which the poem's own attainment of "clear" structural containment presages.

The poet and his subject are equally constricted by the "knots" of completed identity. Physical demise has been redressed only by the tyranny of delimitation. The poet tears himself free, this time not merely miming but actually invoking the ruptures of discontinuity in the service of a paradoxically lethal continuity.

> kill me john my life eats
> life. the thing that beats out
> of me happens in a vat enclosed
> & fermenting & wanting to explode
> like your song. . . .

The complacent assurances of delimited vision give way to a harsher "clarity" of self-effacement.

Baraka has written of Coltrane's music that its underlying thrust was simply, "Find the Self, then Kill it." Freeing himself from the impossible, if "beautiful," need to "paint" the hero's absent form, to reincarnate the literal body of his performance, the poet finds self-negation becomes a self-abnegation. He is violent and fertile, self-consuming and self-emerging. The identification with Trane is transformed into a liberating, self-dispersing participation in music, just as the poem itself is about to dissolve structure into a futile death-wish for identity. Hence, poet and Trane emerge as dark voyagers (more wailers that whalers, undertaking re-quests for meaningful presence), and the "self" remains occluded and unspirited as they plunge into an ambiguously Ellisonian-Barakan underbelly of being.

The poet, then, descends with Coltrane to the "pit" of deathly negation, seeking to deliver the classically oxymoronic "issue" of dark-light for both self and community:

> . . . black light issued
> from him in the pit he made
> around us. worms came clear
> to me where i thought i had been
> brilliant. . . .

The poet journeys through the underworld, submitting his own "brilliance" to the corrosive challenge of the worms, seeking to restore the brilliant image of john, to envision him no longer enclosed either by death or poetic artifice. Such speculative adventure leads toward a furious act of emancipation, but it is one held in suspension by the ambiguous syntax of constrained desire and the submerged transumption of words by worms:

> o john death will
> not contain you

Thus the poem at once acknowledges the threat to sacramental liberation and attempts to marshall its energies to renew the opening stanza's image of resourceful, improvisational vitality.

The poem, in one clear sense, can be read as reestablishing *life,* life as a vigorous engagement and elimination of death (note the insistent enjambment and lack of closure in the last lines.) *Life is the defiant, effervescent gesture of death dying.* Song—musical *or* poetic—must be both discharge and product of this confining process; and the resumption of song in the repetitive conclusion is both formal and performative evidence of catharsis. This song creates in ceremonial form an ending and a beginning and is effective as an enriched *repetition* of the earlier truncated performance: the "crowd" is reassembled with the "named" hero; a given order of words, expressions, and values is affirmed once again.

Far from being either an unimpeded narrative or a static lament, then, Spellman's Coltrane poem must be read as a series of provisional or transitional hypotheses linking an actual to a virtual being. In some sense each verse paragraph arises as response to premature closure which the poet either fears (as in the "then/then" episode) or miscasts (as in the projected plentitude of stanza 2). Coltrane's absence, Spellman's poem tells us, is an integral element of his presence. The poet's quest is thus a movement to catch a vanishing "Trane," an effort to (re)construct what was originally heard and felt by treating the scene of performance as a kind of communal palimpsest.

The uneasy progress from stanza to stanza in "Did John's Music Kill Him?" represents just this pursuit of linguistic continuity in the face of experiential rupture; and the salient unifying element throughout the poem is nothing other than "john," the invocation of the hero's elusive essence. It is an absent *name*. Or alternatively—it is the disclosure of a *process* of naming which never finds absolute embodiment in a determinate shape. In one reading, "john" becomes the Proper Name which, while authorizing the act of poetic recovery, stands beyond the strictly poetic domain; it is the singular and un-"contained" word assuring the musician (and the poet who mirrors him) a possible reappropriation of refined or refocused being. (Here we infer Clay's vision.) Coltrane becomes a longed-for absent center, the recovered ground to collective history and revolutionary progress behind the bounds of transactions and inscriptions. His death is seen as a kind of primordial violence, a splitting from original wholeness which the opening stanza images in its unfragmented state. The poem's task is therefore to be seen as a working through and against its own materiality in order to re-embody the salvific spiritual totality which obtained prior to the hero's particular performances and "words."

An alternative reading would remind us that the desire for the unifying effect of a logos beyond temporal discourse is truly a *sign* of the will-to-expression. It is a necessary fiction. The opening scene is the first in a series of reconstructions of Coltrane-as-performance; his being is seen from the beginning as nothing more or less than the possibility of performance itself, always inscribed into the cultural space which it itself also creates by playing "then," as "called" upon.

Spellman's poem *performs* the tension, or, better, the dialogue of these two notions of expressive practice. But my main point is that an engagement with both views at once will involve us in the critical choices staged by our earlier juxtaposition of Ellison and Baraka, the ideological stakes of which are discernible in Stephen Henderson's writing.

Following what is implicit in Henderson and central in the Coltrane poem, I think we need to see Afro-American poetry not as a static alignment of proclamations (reflecting either some preconstituted "reality" *or* its own stagnant pool of tropes) but rather as a performative activity that sees itself in struggle with other practices. A corollary point: we must recognize our own relation to this process, understanding interpretation as an inescapably mediatory act that will itself be a transformative process. Thus, as we contemplate our movement past the juncture of Black Arts and formalist impulses that situates much of our work today, we must be careful not to retreat into a nostalgic humanism which ignores the differences *within* black discourse(s) as well as their conflicts with other discourses. Conventional oppositions of praxis/theory and history/discourse which occupy so much of our internecine exchanges will no longer serve. Our readings *are* performances which theorize their relations to other readings. They, too, continuously (re)construct their "subjects."

More specifically, we need to investigate further the nature of "textuality" in black poetry, a problem initiated by such Black Arts speculators as Larry Neal but not adequately pursued until quite recently. I think it particularly important that we reexamine the dichotomy of "oral" and "written" from conceptual and political perspectives, shifting attention from a literalist charting of vocal versus written techniques to an understanding of the values black authors ascribe to each. Thus, for example, Ishmael Reed's notion of "writing," with its emphasis on the mobility and openness of expression, has more in common with Neal's "orality" than does, say, Haki Madhubuti's evocation of an ideal, even numinous "musicality." By extension, we need to pursue discussions of the *body* in poetic discourse, that third term between textual and metaphysical "figurations" which, as a locus, might resist the division of the mute and the known, the quotidian and the meta.

A revaluation of textuality, and the accompanying terms of "oral" creativity, should lead us also to further explorations of the vernacular as part of the terrain of Afro-American poetry. Indeed, the evocation of the vernacular as a criterion of Afro-American theoretical discourse has become almost de rigueur (I have obviously succumbed myself!). Perhaps it is time to *discriminate* among these touchstones which, as the contrast of Ellison and Baraka is meant to show, do not necessarily call into being a common set of assumptions and desires.

We need, moreover, to begin to treat vernacular material as more than just an enabling agent of other critical or aesthetic practices. The vernacular itself constitutes an important element of the poetic, and our relative silence about it suggests a covert motive for constructing a particular form of the Afro-American literary "canon."

We might, for example, begin to speak at one and the same time of Ishmael Reed and Ramm-El-Zee, of Carolyn Rodgers and Run-D.M.C. Indeed, we might begin to ask whether the very category of Afro-American "poetry" is especially enlightening or whether it has become a barrier to more fruitful juxtapositions of expressive material. Much of the force of black poetry derives either from its resistance to the rules of genre or from its absorption of seemingly discontinuous idioms (from classical elegy to collective improvisation). Thus, as I noted earlier, any general theory of Afro-American poetics must be willing to see itself continuously disrupted and revised.

A final point is, at least partially, a point of self-criticism. If the category of black poetry is in some sense a specious (certainly, at best, a heuristic) instrument, then I think it follows that we must attempt in the future to situate black poetical works in a *variety* of contexts, generating thereby new critical topoi for our study. Afro-American "poetry" can, in the nineties, be conceived as a continuously destabilizing and unsettled *set of relations* rather than as a determined "order" of statements and positions. I have offered in my essay *a* reading of *a* problem in Afro-American poetics, primarily through the topos of performed blackness. This has led to a particular narrative construction of an Afro-American poetic "tradition," one emphasizing the elegiac modernism underlying a group of specific performances. But other narratives are possible: a feminist construction, for example, might focus on the obsession with proper *naming* as a concealed discourse of the father, and the contestation of the scene of performance figured by Ellison and Baraka as an agon of patriarchal succession. (Or it might not—it might rather seek, à la Shange's *For Colored Girls*, to intervene in this performative scene in order to appropriate, not simply dispel, its authority and power: to assert the performative presence of *ntozake*, the woman voicing her *own* "stuff.")

In any case, I will leave my readers to imagine other narratives—but be they psychoanalytical or Marxist, New World (e.g., Afro-Cuban), or Pan-African, I hope that in the mutual dance of difference performed by such narratives we may find the means to resist any closure of the "tradition" conceived as struggle and renewal.

Works Cited

Baker, Houston A., Jr. *Blues, Ideology, and Afro-American Literature*. Chicago: University of Chicago Press, 1984.

Baraka, Amiri [LeRoi Jones]. *Dutchman*. New York: Grove, 1964.

Brisman, Leslie. *Milton's Poetry of Choice and Its Romantic Heirs*. Ithaca: Cornell University Press, 1973.

Ellison, Ralph. *Invisible Man*. New York. Random House, 1952.

Henderson, Stephen. *Understanding the New Black Poetry*. New York: William Morrow, 1973.

Jackson, Blyden, and Louis D. Rubin, Jr. *Black Poetry in America*. Baton Rouge: Louisiana State University Press, 1974.

Madhubuti, Haki [Don L. Lee]. *Dynamite Voices*. Detroit: Broadside, 1971.

Spellman, A. B. "Did John's Music Kill Him?" In Henderson, *Black Poetry*, pp. 261–62.

I would like to acknowledge the kindness of C. Stephen Finley and Robert G. O'Meally, who offered me spirited and insightful critiques of earlier drafts of this essay. Should they fail to see the effects of their analyses in the present version, I trust they will take this as a sign of dimness, not recalcitrance, on my part.

Response: *Cheryl A. Wall*

If Kimberly Benston's perception is accurate that the criticism of Afro-American poetry has been less theoretically compelling than the critiques offered in the realms of narrative and dramatic studies—and I believe it is—then his essay takes several giant steps toward redressing the balance. What Benston argues for is a new reading of the critical debates that blazed forth when the Black Aesthetic was proclaimed almost two decades ago and that continue to delimit our poetic analyses today. That the effects would manifest themselves most strongly in the poetic sphere is perhaps to be expected, since poetry along with drama was the touchstone for the Black Arts movement. Benston's rereading locates these debates firmly in the province of literature, not politics, while at the same time it recognizes the complex interactions between art and ideology. The anticipated result is the clearing of a site from which we can apprehend and define a new and truer poetics, one that recognizes Afro-American poetry for the "motivated, constructed, corrosive, and productive process" it is.

The clarifying insight which takes the discussion of the "hermeneutics of blackness" and the "hermeneutics of recuperation" to a new level is Benston's perception that the critical debate reflected and reflects an argument taking place *in* the literature itself. Much is gained from seeing the critical debate as one which grows out of the literature rather than one imposed on the literature by sociopolitical concerns. Benston's critical vocabulary prompts a less happy personal observation. Repeating the references to "hermeneutics," "texts," and "canons" makes me, the daughter of a Baptist minister, think I'm too much about my father's business.

As Benston sees it, one major argument that goes on within the literature concerns the nature of blackness, performance, and the Afro-

American self. In a brilliant critical maneuver, Benston invents an enabling allegory to resituate the critical opposition of "universality" and
"blackness." The aptly chosen protagonists, Ralph Ellison and Amiri
Baraka, are often appropriated as standard-bearers for the critical schools
Benston evokes; but as he demonstrates, the ideas for which they battle
are not synonymous with those their putative disciples champion.

Ellison's preacher may nevertheless get an "amen" (as we were taught
to say), and perhaps an especially heartfelt one from a poststructuralist
new critic, for defining the "ever-shifting scene of Afro-American language as dialectical." The conception of "blackness as a mediated,
socially constructed *practice,* a process and not a product of discursive
conditions of struggle" would seem to free us from clearly essentialist
and perhaps inherently racist definitions of "blackness." Equally compelling is Ellison's view of blackness as "endless beginning," whose meaning
"does not inhere in any referent but is renewed in the rhythmic process . . . generated from performance to performance." Moreover, for
critics of whatever school, the Ellisonian view of the black text as "a
dynamic producer of richly differing signifying perspectives" is a wel-
come one. And yet, just as Ellison's preacher seems ready to make
converts of us all, Benston introduces Baraka's countervision of
blackness.

Baraka's protagonist cuts Afro-American expressions off from the
endless play envisioned by Ellison's preacher. Clay's blackness "longs for
incarnation as literal presence, for the singular revolutionary act that
would 'murder' self-difference and heal the breach between black identity and discourse that the original violence of whiteness opened." Clay's
pained awareness that words are no substitutes for deeds and his consequent longing for the singular revolutionary act prefigure his creator's
later call for " . . . 'poems that kill.'/Assassin poems, Poems that
shoot/guns. . . " Perhaps we might reread "Black Art," the poem quoted
here, both as a manifesto and a meditation (like Clay's speech) on the
(im)possibilities of a truly black poem in a world unchanged by black
revolution.

Ultimately, Benston locates a crucial commonality in the Ellisonian
and Barakan views. If Baraka's speaker proclaims the need for black
people to liberate themselves, a liberation that would in turn give rise to
an art, a poetry that would speak in terms "very straight and plain," the
text he creates, no less than that of Ellison's preacher, is shaped by the
paradoxes and ambiguities of Afro-American life. Early in the essay,
Benston refers to the disjunction between our knowledge of poetry as
text and our awareness of it as performance, but he does not fully pursue

the implications here. Certainly, Baraka's plays and his performances of his poems, no less than the sacred and secular sermons of *Invisible Man,* act out and through the meanings of blackness, "renewed in the rhythmic process."

To some degree, I suspect, the critical debate to which Benston responds and which he seeks to defer is less the universality/blackness agon of the 1960s than the ongoing debate about the place of "theory" in Afro-American literary criticism. The work of Amiri Baraka is central to the essay's strategy, because Baraka's vision is a powerful reminder that Afro-American literature remains an engaged literature. Part of our duty and challenge as critics is, I believe, to honor that engaged spirit, regardless of the mode of criticism we individually adopt. From its introductory anecdote onward, Benston's essay demonstrates an acute awareness of this obligation. He recognizes no conflict between it and the abstractly theoretical method he employs; indeed, he finds corroboration for his method in the texts themselves. The debates that take place in the literature are richer and more complex, Benston convinces, than those which critics have staged.

To return to that enabling allegory, I would argue that suggestive and useful as it is, it is nevertheless more applicable to the literature of the period it invokes—and I say literature since the examples themselves suggest how Benston is "re/placing" poetry as a genre—than to more recent writing. Several of the arguments within the literature have changed. To some extent, blackness is, as Baraka asserts, "the always present, yet always coded subject of Afro-American cultural expression." But, to take just one example, verbal gestures by certain Afro-American women poets over the past two decades suggest various ways in which they attempt to move beyond the "blackness is and blackness ain't" debate Benston so adroitly configures.

Perhaps the most striking pronouncement of this endeavor comes in Ntozake Shange's titular statement, "For *Colored* Girls Who Have Considered Suicide When the Rainbow Is Enuf." Reflecting on Shange and on what Hortense Spillers has named "the community of black women writing," a community that has achieved visibility since the 1960s, I hear Ellison's preacher in a new way. In his explication of the beginning-as-blackness, he does in fact image difference and violence. But the initial difference which he and Benston both subsequently elide is gender—the old *woman* singing a spiritual, a beautiful *girl* the color of ivory, pleading in a voice like my *mother's*. It is, of course, this unwritten space that Shange and her sister poets have been filling in.

Like their better-known counterparts in fiction, black women poets have been insistent in their attempt to inscribe an Afro-American female self into literary discourse. In so doing, they have complicated the terms of the debate. Blackness must now be defined as a mediated, socially constructed, and gendered practice. The definition is, needless to say, applicable to male and female writers, past and present. If we were to compose an allegory, for example, that dramatized the relation between Ralph Ellison and Gwendolyn Brooks, we would inevitably apprehend the dynamics of gendered blackness in the 1950s.

Beyond changing the (male) subject, those female poets who also want to explore the traditions of performed blackness that Benston identifies confront an intriguing formal challenge. Women were, of course, historically denied participation in many of these traditions; for instance, speechifying, whether in the pulpit or on the block, has been a mainly male prerogative. The necessity of recovering and inventing female traditions of performed blackness has led, I think, to some of the more striking formal innovations in this poetry. Among the examples that *For Colored Girls* brings to mind are the children's rhymes that end the prologue, the representation throughout of those discursive strategies for negotiating respect that folklorist Roger Abrahams has termed "talking smart" and "talking sweet," and the improvisation of new rituals such as the "laying on of hands" with which Shange concludes her choreopoem.

The blues is one celebrated tradition of performed blackness, crucial to Afro-American poetics, in which women and men have participated equally. It is important to note, too, that the blues provide another means of backgrounding the nature of blackness argument. In the blues blackness is not debated, is is assumed. While only a few women poets incorporate the formal structures of the blues in their work, many transform those structures, and most treat blues allusively. Critics should begin to analyze the various reclamations of this tradition in more detail. Clay's response to Bessie Smith is shared by a black woman poet like Sonia Sanchez, particularly in her early poems. But for Sherley Anne Williams, the proposition that had Bessie killed some white people she would not have needed that music is irrelevant, if not plain wrong. At the least, Williams's speaker would need the music Bessie makes, no matter what.

> 39. Bessie on my wall: the thick triangular
>   nose wedged
>   in the deep brown
>   face nostrils
>   flared on a last
>   long hummmmmmmmmm.

> Bessie singing
> just behind the beat
> that sweet sweet
> voice throwing
> its light on me.

This is the first in a cycle of poems, "Regular Reefer," written in tribute to the great blues singer; indeed, Smith's presence is felt throughout the volume, entitled *Some One Sweet Angel Chile*. Here, the photograph denotes the iconic importance that the singer has for the speaker, but the relationship between priestess and devotee is far more intimate than ceremonial. It is not, after all, the Empress of the Blues whose photograph we see; it is simply "Bessie" on the wall. Readers have no more need of a last name or title than the speaker does. The face, unadorned and unashamedly Negroid, the inimitable voice that we hear "just behind the beat," the warmth and enlightenment it bathes us in are all immediately recognizable. The "hummmmmmmmmm," the poem's verbal sign for Smith's vocal gesture, can be heard in any register the memory supplies. One reader might hear it as the cathartic moan in "Young Woman's Blues," while another replays the ecstatic cry in "New Orleans Hop Scop Blues." The structural device which Stephen Henderson identifies as an appeal to "tonal memory" enables readers to complete their own versions of the text. Talking straight and plain, or rather, as in Baraka's poem, seeming to do so, the speaker expresses our collective gratitude for the light and life-giving art of Bessie Smith.

Speaker and subject in Williams's poem stand in similar relation to speaker and subject in "Did John's Music Kill Him?" (Let me say parenthetically that my own reservations with respect to Benston's critical method were finally allayed by his reading of Spellman's poem. For me, an interpretation that rich and supple validates the method that produced it.) The difference is that "Bessie" is a far more approachable, less exalted figure than "John." Several factors may account for this, but the most pertinent one is that in addition to embodying the traditions of and possibilities for female creativity and autonomy, the blueswoman for many black women writers is the foremother who must be embraced.

Finally, I have some thoughts on the concerns with which Benston began his meditation on Afro-American poetics. It seems to me that the studies of individual poets such as those of Baraka, Rodgers, Hayden, Jordan, and Wright necessarily precede the design of broader paradigms. In addition, we have seen considerable refinement of Henderson's groundbreaking theories by, among others, Houston Baker, Sherley Anne Williams, and Henderson himself. The field is far from fallow.

Rather more urgent than the need to invent new paradigms is the need to identify a canon. What constitutes Afro-American poetry today? While, on the one hand, we have reclaimed Phillis Wheatley, we have not done a good enough job in bringing together the poetry of the last twenty years. Issuing from small and university presses, in regional and local journals, published under the auspices of Afro-Americanists, feminists, post-modernists, et al., the work is widely dispersed. How the multitude of voices speak to each other is, at present, impossible to say. As Henry Louis Gates's essay in this collection makes clear, scholars make canons, and the textbook/anthology is the instrument of their formation. In 1973 Stephen Henderson, perhaps signifying on Brooks and Warren's *Understanding Poetry,* gave us *Understanding the New Black Poetry;* he offered one configuration of the canon as it then rested. We need re-visions for the nineties.

Works Cited

Abrahams, Roger. "Negotiating Respect: Patterns of Presentation Among Black Women." *Journal of American Folklore* 88 (January–March 1975): 58.
Baraka, Amiri [LeRoi Jones]. *Black Magic Poetry.* New York: Bobbs-Merrill, 1969.
Henderson, Stephen. *Understanding the New Black Poetry.* New York: William Morrow, 1972.
Williams, Sherley Anne. *Some One Sweet Angel Chile.* New York: William Morrow, 1982.

Response: *Stephen E. Henderson*

In the 1960s everyone, it seems, was a poet. Poetry and drama, for a while, were the two dominant literary genres for black writers. The audiences were enthusiastic and the poets were prolific. Today, many of those poets are either silent or have turned their attention and their loyalties to other concerns. Today, tastes and standards have changed. A new generation of poets has quietly emerged, and, despite the prodigious activity of critics of Afro-American literature, relatively little attention is being paid to the poets or the poetry of the 1960s.

Kimberly Benston observes these facts and further notes that, as a rule, the criticism of Afro-American poetry is "less satisfactory, less theoretically compelling and practically instructive than the critiques offered in the realm of narrative and dramatic studies." Despite the presence of "many excellent studies of specific works and authors," most of the efforts that he knows of "which attempt to provide a comprehensive scheme or explanation of the poetry lack the depth, variety, and sophistication we have generally come to expect of the criticism." Benston speculates that this may be due to "the poetry's relative susceptibility to discrete analyses" and may tell us something about its resistance to "theoretical efforts that move toward totalization, toward critical recuperation and ideological closure." He suggests that "a polar opposition is at work in those critical narratives that do aspire to a synoptic sweep: on the one hand, the Afro-American poem is measured against a privileged notion of 'blackness' which is posited as external to both the Euro-American 'main-stream' and, in a political sense, to the poem itself; on the other hand, the poem is tested for conformity to a universally applicable norm of 'the poetic' which is supposed to exist both in and outside any notion of 'blackness'. " He argues that both views "share a basic philosophical supposition—that the poem's meaning may be located in some standard both prior and external to the poetic act itself" and that "the critic's role is to discriminate the 'proper' from the 'failed' or foolish, the correct from the deviant."

He analyzes two appraisals of Afro-American poetry, one which views the poetry as a new historical phenomenon with its own distinct characteristics; the other as having some of the same features but capable of reintegration into the American tradition. Benston argues that criticism should be shifted from contraries such as form vs. content, "craft vs. politics," to be relocated at "some *juncture* of ideological and aesthetic concerns." The two positions are a legacy of the Black Arts movement and "the tactics we employ in decoding and recoding black poetry still turn in some measure . . . on our attitude toward the programmatic declarations and practical performances which carry the Black Arts movement's freight of aesthetic, ontological, and political visions."

Benston further argues that these two positions above are "in some sense parodic reflections of an argument taking place in the literature itself, an argument about the nature of blackness, performance, and the modern Afro-American self." As a paradigm for his discourse, Benston contrasts and analyzes the "blackness of blackness" sermon in the prologue of *Invisible Man* and Clay's climactic speech in Baraka's *Dutchman*. His analysis and contrast of Baraka and Ellison offers an "enabling allegory," "for resituating the critical opposition of 'blackness' and 'universality' on a ground internal to Afro-American discourse itself." They—Ellison and Baraka—"offer models of the black text which imply that such an opposition is indeed constituent of Afro-American poetics. If this is so, then criticism might make the opposition its own subject."

Benston next considers my own *Understanding the New Black Poetry* and singles out the juxtaposition of my notion of "saturation" and the listing of formal elements in the poetry.

He finds this "unstable" synthesis useful because it "brings us back to the poetic itself as a realm of *theoretical* as well as aesthetic/political activity," while reminding us that determinations of power and authority have a methodological priority over discriminations of taste or truth.

In his dialogic response to Stephen E. Henderson's "call," Kimberly Benston analyzes A. B. Spellman's "Did John's Music Kill Him?" and this imaginative and altogether admirable reading discovers in the dynamics of the "Coltrane poem" a black variant of the pastoral elegy. I think that Spellman would be highly pleased with Benston's reading of his poem; however, I would caution against universalizing or particularizing the "Coltrane poem" as a type, not only because it does not encompass the range of such poems, but also because it shares features with many poems on the death of such musicians as Eric Dolphy and Charlie Parker. In addition, the pastoral includes specific features such as the procession of the mourners, which this poem omits. I am struck by Benston's reaction to the "state" of criticism of black poetry because some eight years ago I addressed similar issues in "Black Poetry: The Continuing Challenge" at the Melvin Butler Poetry Festival (April 30, 1979) at Southern University, Baton Rouge, Louisiana.

Briefly, in "Black Poetry: The Continuing Challenge," I saw the challenge as having three parts: (1) the cultural base, or the folk and popular roots of the poetry, (2) the challenge of the tradition, i.e., of Afro-American poetry and other traditions which may have influenced it, and (3) the challenge of the modern world, which requires the kind of sophisticated criticism that Benston calls for today. In addition, the challenge summons readers and poets alike to study the moral and political issues with which the poetry is engaged. They certainly are found in Ellison's prologue and Baraka's play, and they have not been intellectually metabolized, as Benston suggests.

As a step in the direction of exploring the conflicting dimensions of blackness to which Benston alludes, I cite two specific examples of textual challenge: (1) Skip James, the blues man, sings: "I lay down last night trying to take my rest. And my mind got to ramblin' like a wild geese from the West." Notice that he said "a wild geese," not a wild goose. And it was singular, not plural. If we are properly tuned in, we don't "correct" his grammar, for if we do, we miss the poetry of a "geese" existing in its self-generated and directed ambience. There are many such examples in the oral tradition, which elude self-righteous analysis.

Another example comes from Carolyn Rodgers' "Poems for Some

Black Women." The poem is about sophisticated, successful, beautiful women, who still feel a void in their lives, which, paradoxically, may derive from their success. They "Know too much," they are too understanding. They buy too many things. And the poem continues:

> we need ourselves sick, we need, we need
> we lonely we grow tired of tears we grow tired of fear

What is important here is the grammar. We recall that the women are educated, sophisticated, complex, and modern. Yet here in the last despairing stanza the poet elicits a note of pathos that reveals worlds about the condition not only of black women but of millions of people, male and female, in the modern world. These two lines consists of six simple clauses which on first glance appear to be parallel. Examination, however, shows that the pattern is broken up at the beginning of the second line, where the speaker shifts to a black vernacular construction, "we lonely," with the so-called zero copula retained from West African language patterns. The effect of this grammatical "lapse" (which is really an orchestration of the lines) is to add poignancy to the situation by stripping away all vestiges of masquerade, even those of standard English. The realization is intensified by black in-house references to "bitchy" and "Sapphire," negative extensions into the vernacular, and the stammering repetition of "not too dumb not too not too not too." And finally, as Dance observes, the poet reinforces the thematic intensity "by setting that last word *lonely* on a single line by itself and placing a period before and after it."

> we need ourselves sick, we need, we need
> we lonely we grow tired of tears we grow tired of fear
> we grow tired but must al-ways be soft and not too serious . . .
>   not too smart not too bitchy not too sapphire
>   not too dumb not too not too not too
> a little less a little more
>   add here detract there
>   .lonely.

What black poetry needs today and in the nineties is our close and sophisticated critical performances of a blackness that is always elusive . . . but always, as well, "on time."

7

Biography and Afro-American Culture

Arnold Rampersad

I want to discuss the place of biography in Afro-American culture, but to do so from a particular and I hope crucial perspective—that of the role of psychology in the structure of Afro-American biographical writing. I do not propose here to investigate the field of black biography in a thorough or systematic way, or even to cover all the important biographies, except perhaps obliquely, in the course of speculation about the place of psychology in the form. On the other hand, it would be useful to bear in mind a short list of what we may take to be some of the more important biographies and near-biographies produced so far, with the emphasis on writers: Robert Hemenway's portrait of Zora Neale Hurston; the biographies of Richard Wright by Constance Webb, Michel Fabre, and Addison Gayle; Wayne Cooper's Claude McKay; Faith Berry's Langston Hughes and my own two volumes on the same figure; Nellie McKay's Jean Toomer, which has been followed by Cynthia Earl Kerman and Richard Eldridge's more detailed account of the same life; L. K. Wiggins's study of Paul Laurence Dunbar; Nathan I. Huggins's brief work on Frederick Douglass; Louis Harlan's prize-winning two-volume Booker T. Washington; and the various portraits of W. E. B. Du Bois by Elliott Rudwick, Francis Broderick, and myself. Other books may come to mind.

Before turning to the question of psychology, however, I would like to make a few observations about biography and Afro-American biography as subjects in general. Remarks about biography should be made only with caution. Scholarship in biography is a neglected and perhaps intrinsically narrow business, and contrasts sharply with the fertility of related fields. Scholarship in autobiography, in contrast, is large, contains multitudes—although that field is not nearly as grand or multitudinous as the general field of literary theory. Certain aspects of biography make it a difficult area about which to theorize. For instance, an actual autobiographer is not likely to be a scholar of autobiography, and a scholar of autobiography is almost never asked to offer evidence that he or she has written or, indeed, can write an autobiography. A theorist about biography, on the other hand, is almost inevitably someone who has written a biography and then feels a need, or sees an opportunity, to reflect on the genre. Perhaps as a result, biography has generated comparatively little important scholarship concerning itself. The would-be biographer sits down to the task with little formal or informal instruction in the field, and less that is likely to be useful. Such a person also can learn little from his or her mistakes, since one may write—at most—two or three biographies in a lifetime, and most biographers write only one such book.

The entire field, it seems to me, is surrounded by an aura not of mystery but of uncertainty. The standards are unclear, the provenance uncertain. A basic question arises: Is biography valuable to the study of literature, in particular, Afro-American literature? This is a pressing matter, since much of the most exciting discourse generated in recent years in literary theory (both within and outside Afro-American literature) seems to me not only of conspicuously little application to biography but in some ways in direct opposition to its vagueness of standards, values, and techniques. For the moment, and perhaps for the foreseeable future, biography is and will remain the poorest relation in the family of Afro-American literary enterprises—being neither the fundamental fish that is art nor the (winged) fowl of theory and criticism. In fact, as more and more of our younger scholars are drawn to literary theory, which is in great vogue as a field of study, biography may be increasingly slighted. Theory is almost always compulsively elitist, and sometimes never more so than when it attempts to press the claims of democracy. Biography may affect elitist manners, but its business is essentially democratic; it is a leveler, it introduces the great to people who are little (the little people) by comparison, and who are curious not so much about other people's art as about other people's business. (To put it another way, while a typical scholarly journal for theoreticians may be *Critical Inquiry,* the natural organ for biography sometimes seems to be the *National Inquirer.*)

If we assume, however, that biography is an important aspect of our literary enterprise, then I would like to advance certain notions concerning our approach to it.

First, there is no real substitute for the full-scale portrait. Terms such as "literary biography" and "intellectual biography" are probably, in most cases, confessions of partial portraiture, and partial failure. (This is not true of all cases; Hemenway's *Zora Neale Hurston* calls itself a "literary biography," but it virtually revolutionized the field of biography in Afro-American literature.) To borrow from what Henry James said about the distinction between novels and romances, there are probably only good biographies and bad biographies. "Literary" and "intellectual" biographies should be attempted before full-scale biographies only when there is an acute and most likely permanent shortage of data. After a full-scale biography, of course, anything is possible. Above all, the terms "literary" and "intellectual" should not be taken as signs of a greater depth or seriousness on the part of the biographer. A biography is not the place for elaborate discussions of artistic texts, especially artistic texts the reader probably has not read. Such an approach is an abuse of the form—unless the unavailability of evidence makes these discussions necessary.

Secondly, the biographer working in Afro-American culture must not curtail his or her work out of a sense of protectiveness either toward the subject or toward the race—a natural sense, given our history, but one that should be overcome in this instance. The example of Alain Locke (the influential Howard University professor and one of the major presiding figures of the Harlem Renaissance as a mentor of younger artists and as editor of *The New Negro*) is helpful here. Often peevish and even vindictive, Locke nevertheless carefully preserved for posterity even those documents that appear to show him in a poor light. Similarly, the black biographer can hardly allow himself or herself to imagine that the reputation of the race can be affected by what he or she writes about a particular subject. In time, everything will out, and the concealing biographer merely postpones the inevitable. No topic is too intimate for treatment by the biographer—whether that topic is sexuality or politics or racial apostasy. A free and frank investigation, within the bounds of reason and the basic rules of evidence, is needed.

The biographer working in as controversial an area as the Afro-American literary tradition, or in any area, should set the highest standards of evidence. In one aspect in particular, the oral tradition, this may be a truly significant point. Much has been made, and deservedly so, about the value of the oral tradition to black culture. It needs to be remembered that a biographer must deal in specifics—and that the strong suit of the oral tradition, whatever it may be, is not the specific but the gloriously general. Gossip passed down through the generations is not superior to gossip passed over a telephone line, and is hardly the same as the oral tradition. The biographer must be on guard to distinguish one from the other, and on guard to save the reader from that most dangerous of interviewees—the person who knows little or nothing but is eager to help.

As for the basic question of overall form, I believe that there is certainly no one design that would accommodate the lives of black writers, who cover the entire spectrum of human personality, politics, sexuality, and artistic sensibility. By "form" here I mean, for example, the epic, in which the subject is a hero; or the approach of scientific, Zola-like detachment; or the novelistic; or even the approach taken in certain commercially successful biographies—though not of blacks—in which excerpts from interviews form the entire biography, without a narrative of any kind. (No doubt, one could write a biography in blank verse, or even *terza rima*.) The most tempting form in the context of black or minority culture in general is that of the epic, in which the hero or heroine advances his or her fortunes simultaneously with those of the race against almost insuperable odds that are usually identified with racism. There is indeed a deadly undertow that pulls many biographers of black subjects (or of subjects belonging to other politically and culturally aggrieved groups) towards propaganda and hagiography. But the most casual acquaintance with the lives of black writers should tell us that few of them—certainly few of the major writers—have been centrally impelled in their careers by a desire to champion the race. Many, indeed, have worked against the racial grain, and attempted to prove in their art the unimportance of race by showing their art to be somehow "above" race. A few have even detested the race, even as their careers have been taken, ironically, as triumphs of the race.

The black biographer, like any other biographer, must gather as much evidence as possible, and remain as open and pliable as possible, while thinking vigorously and independently all the while. Only then is he or she likely to be rewarded with the emergence of the form that is inevitable to the particular biographical situation. In this respect, biography is a passive exercise; in other respects, it is anything but passive. The biographer has a smaller range of choices than one perhaps imagines; the material, I think, chooses the form—when the form is well chosen. The suggestion by a friendly critic to me that there may be a form akin and attuned to the rhythms of jazz and the blues and other predominantly black artistic achievements, and that the black biographer should seek it out, is charming, but not likely to be very useful. In fact, it is likely to be useless unless one is approaching biography as if it were an art itself. But biography, even the biography of an artist, is definitely not an art, it is only in part an art. Nor is it a science, it is only partly a science. There should be no doubt, however, that the biographer must face his or her subject more like a scientist than an artist. Without an attempt to pursue the elusive and unattainable truth within recognizable rules of evi-

dence—the heart of the scientific method—the biographer is a menace
to literate society.

Hence my particular interest in the subject of the role of psychology in
Afro-American biography. To many people, psychology still raises the
specter of a flagrant violation of the intimate. In one of the finer novels
written by an Afro-American, John A. Williams's *Sissie,* the attitude of a
black man to a certain doctor might be instructive as we look at this
subject. The man, Ralph, is meeting for the first time Dr. Bluman, a
white psychiatrist. After some verbal fencing the doctor asks:

> "Can we get started now?"
> "I feel a little awkward about this," Ralph said.
> "Ummm, yes?" Bluman gave Ralph an interested, open look.
> "I feel a little defeated too"—Ralph turned his eyes quickly toward the doc-
> tor.—"I mean, finding it necessary to come here."
> "Why did you find it necessary?" . . . Bluman's eyes twinkled. He waited this
> time.
> "I'm out of dreams . . . . I'm at a dead end—" He broke off, thinking with a
> sudden suspicion that even his speech patterns would be under analysis here.

Many of us, faced with a psychoanalytic or a psychotherapeutic initiative—not to mention a psychiatrist—respond as Ralph does: We "feel
a little defeated . . . finding it necessary to come here." The same quality
of reticence is noticeable when we look at the field of black biography—
by which I mean the biographies of black Americans by anyone—and try
to determine the extent to which books in the field have been influenced
by, or have taken into account, the insights, discoveries, and methods of
psychologists. If biographies of blacks have not been so influenced to a
marked degree, should they be? And what are the major problems and
difficulties involved in the incorporation of psychological approaches in
the field in general? Is there an alternative to Freud and his opponents
within the field of psychology?

I believe it is fair to say that, far from being influenced by psychology,
black biography has kept a vast distance between itself and that discipline. If one looks at even the most acclaimed books in the field, one sees
hardly any attempt to link the art of biography to what I call—if only in
provocation—the science of psychoanalysis. Methodologically, insofar
as black biography is concerned, we have really not advanced beyond W.
E. B. Du Bois's historic description of the black American mind in the
The Souls of Black Folk—the oft-invoked description of Afro-American
"double-consciousness, this sense of always looking at one's self through
the eyes of others, of measuring one's soul by the tape of a world that
looks on in amused contempt and pity. One ever feels his twoness,—an

American, a Negro; two souls, two thoughts, two unreconciled strivings, two warring ideals in one dark body, whose dogged strength alone
keeps it from being torn asunder." As biographers, we have hardly
reached Du Bois's second significant formulation or description of the
black mind, or of a mind like his own, which came in his autobiography,
Dusk of Dawn (1940). The passage begins:

It is difficult to let others see the full psychological meaning of caste segregation.
It is as though one, looking out from a dark cave in a side of an impending
mountain, sees the world passing and speaks to it; speaks courteously and persuasively. . . . One talks on evenly and logically in this way, but notices that the
passing throng does not even turn its head, or if it does, glances curiously and
walks on. It gradually penetrates the minds of the prisoners that the people
passing do not hear, that some thick sheet of invisible but horribly tangible plate
glass is between them and the world. They get excited, they talk louder, they
gesticulate.

Then some persons, Du Bois goes on, may become "hysterical. They
may scream and hurl themselves against the barriers. . . They may even,
here and there, break through in blood and disfigurement, and find
themselves faced by a horrified, implacable, and quite overwhelming
mob of people frightened for their own very existence."

To repeat: I do not believe that biographers of Afro-Americans have
moved in psychological terms past Du Bois's image of the two souls to
his image of the plate glass between the races. And it goes without saying
that the latter image, published in 1940, has been itself superseded by
other images from the arts. Our biographers have thus lagged far behind
our artists—a fact that should not be a revelation to anyone. Some years
ago, I suggested that all of Afro-American literature has, in a sense, come
out of *The Souls of Black Folk*—and most precisely from Du Bois's image
of the divided souls. I would add that the greatest of postwar black
fiction, notably that of Richard Wright and Ralph Ellison (Wright of
"The Man Who Lived Underground" and Ellison's *Invisible Man*), had
as their symbolic antecedent Du Bois's image of the plate glass and the
invisible, increasingly enraged black who smashes his way out. Richard
Wright, unlike our biographers—indeed, unlike even some of his biographers—had a deep interest in psychiatry, which sprang from his own
relationship with Dr. Frederic Wertham (author of "An Unconscious
Determinant in *Native Son*," first published in the *Journal of Clinical and
Experimental Psychology* in July 1944). This relationship led Wright to
help set up the first psychiatric clinic in Harlem, and to write his novel
Savage Holiday, which is explicitly psychiatric in its approach.

If one goes beyond postwar fiction, one sees in at least one place—

John A. Williams's *Sissie,* which I cited earlier—the black novelist un-
afraid to take psychiatry seriously and in its most proper, clinical form.
The truth is that some of our best artists have forged ahead in their
interest in psychology—while their biographers have lagged behind.
Clearly there have been difficulties in the way of a working link between
psychology and black biography. Take Du Bois, for example. In *The
Souls of Black Folk,* which is about a people, he borrowed the concept of
"double consciousness" from academic psychology, or what passed for it
in its dawn. Nevertheless, this concept was not twenty years old—a short
time, in academic and intellectual terms—when Du Bois adapted it from
the scientific currency of William James and his colleagues in the field.
But Du Bois did not see fit to make a similar appeal to psychology when
he himself became a biographer in his *John Brown,* published six years
later. There he fell black on hoary methodology—the historian Hippo-
lyte Taine's pseudo-scientific notion that the great determinant factor in
the emergence of a leader is the trio of *race, milieu,* and *moment.* Du Bois
used this approach to explain the mind of man who, clearly, according to
even his own brother, was crazy at least part of the time. Du Bois's
disloyalty to psychology was unfortunate. Double-consciousness, as a
term, facilitates entry into the human mind. *Race, milieu,* and *moment,*
however, are as external as dialectical materialism, for example, in ex-
plaining it—not completely invalid, not impossible of insight, but
nevertheless almost inherently external, one might say, to the working of
the mind.

One recent book by a black litterateur turned veteran social scientist
has addressed this problem directly (in fact, apart from the black histo-
rian Earl Thorpe's efforts in psychohistory, I do not know of anyone else
who has come close to the subject). That book is by the late Allison
Davis: *Leadership, Love, and Aggression,* published by Harcourt Brace
Jovanovich in 1983. In attempting four distinct psychological studies, of
Frederick Douglass, Du Bois, Richard Wright, and Martin Luther King,
Jr., Davis does not conceal his hostility to most of their biographers. On
Douglass: "None of his biographers has studied the central paradox in
Douglass's personality—the conflicting hatred and love for a powerful
father who treated him as a son at times, but never emancipated or
publicly acknowledged him. Only Dr. Stephen Weissman, in a short
article, has explored this early, ambivalent bond." And later: "From the
ages of seven to fifteen he had been reared by Sophia Auld and loved by
her as her own son. It seems extraordinary that his biographers have
ignored so central a fact in his emotional life and identity development".
On Du Bois: "He was an enigma to friends as well as to enemies. Faced

with his inscrutability, his biographers have dealt only with symptoms."
On Wright ("the angriest, and yet the most influential of all black writers"): Michel Fabre, the leading Wright scholar, and author of the
biography *The Unfinished Quest of Richard Wright* (1973), is "a man of
good intentions but of incredible naiveté both about black life in Mississippi and about the psychology of personality. [Fabre] is not equipped
to deal with Wright's emotional development. He has no knowledge
whatever of Wright's basic emotional conflicts, and apparently no interest in learning their continual working in his behavior, his fantasies,
and his writing." For King, no such direct attack is mounted against a
biographer, but we may infer Davis's sense of the inadequacy of King's
biographers by noting that the books he praises most for an understanding of King were written by King's widow and by a man who lived with
the family for many years: Coretta Scott King's *My Life with Martin
Luther King, Jr.* (1969) and L. D. Reddick's 1959 study, *Crusader without Violence: A Biography of Martin Luther King, Jr.* ("All other
biographers have depended upon Reddick's book for a knowledge of
King's first thirty years.")

As far as I can tell, Davis's book is the first to attempt a psychoanalytical reading of black leaders. If it is not required reading for any
other reason, it should be for *that* reason. A published psychological
study of a black leader is an act of courage in itself, so entrenched is the
opposition to such work. (The fear of theory runs deep, as I found out
some years ago when, after a mildly Freudian analysis of an aspect of
Langston Hughes, I was publicly rebuked by two senior black scholars—
one who asserted that his only interest was in the work, not the life, and
another who urged me to leave Freud alone and instead consult the
African gods for my insights. To the former, I protested that biography
is about the life first and foremost; to the latter I should have said that,
among other things, his statement was Olympian.)

Davis's model in *Leadership, Love, and Aggression* is more than mildly
Freudian; it is strongly so. Originating in a paper first delivered before a
meeting of the American Psychiatric Association, it depends heavily on
Freud's discussion of aggression—which takes many forms, of which
anger is "the simplest, most normal." Davis distinguishes between "realistic anger" and the nourishment of resentment, most often by the
conflict between "the wish to be loved and an angry desire to avenge a
lack of love." The manner of handling aggression falls into three basic
types: sadistic, masochistic, and affiliative, or *"reality-oriented."* Davis
cites Freud's "War and Death" on the closeness between the human
desire to kill and the drive to love; anger must be vented or it will destroy.

He also cites Freud's "On Narcissism": "In the last resort we must begin to love in order that we may not fall ill, and must fall ill if, in consequence of frustration, we cannot love."

Davis's book received scant attention. As far as I can tell, it went unnoticed by the *New York Times;* no academic literary journal reviewed it. To some extent, this treatment was deserved. For example, Davis undertook to discuss Martin Luther King, Jr.'s, toilet training without, to say the least, sufficient evidence. And in treating Richard Wright, he defied the many indications that the autobiography *Black Boy* was in many ways an unusually wide manipulation of the facts of Wright's life— as Michel Fabre showed conclusively—and quotes Wright's words there as evidence of the truth. Thus he takes it as a fact that Wright was reared in "a clan of obsessively religious and sadistic women," in "a family of infinite sadistic inventiveness." "I have never read," Davis writes, without irony, "of so violent a clan of women." On the other hand, it was on something akin to firsthand experience (they had known each other in Chicago) that Davis declares of Wright that "he never enjoyed life among Negroes"; and on grounds justifiable by an intelligent reading of Wright's work—although asserted by none of his biographers—Davis asserts that "Wright hated blacks as deeply as whites did."

At least two of the few reviews of *Leadership, Love, and Aggression* were wildly contradictory. One, in the *Library Journal,* thought the book "not likely to change history's view of these men." On the other hand, the *School Library Journal* believed that it filled "a giant gap in the knowledge and understanding of these men." The latter may be overstated, but I think it errs, if it errs, in the right direction. To those who say that to impose Freud on the black mind is to extend European hegemony over blacks I would answer, first, that any analysis is better than none, and anti-Freudian blacks have offered no countersystem or antisystem worthy of the name; second, that the Freud–Erik Erikson model does not so much declare itself as final truth as it raises questions of enormous value to ourselves. We need to remember, in examining our reservations about psychiatry and psychobiography, that as scholars we have no real hope of reconstituting the past, and therefore should have no immobilizing fear of misrepresenting it. We investigate and recreate the past, ultimately, in order to understand better our own lives and society. For that reason alone, we should proceed with less caution.

In his essay on King, for example, Davis's burden is to uncover how King was able to turn hate into affiliative love. If one does not make this psychiatrically inspired attempt, fraught with danger as it is, the consequences can range from simple dullness as a biographer to a range of errors—the greatest of which would be to support the idea that such a turning of hate into love is really impossible, and that the love-gestures of King were superficial and strategic, like the advertising campaigns of our ambitious, image-building politicians. We need to approach our leaders not with reverence for them but with a degree of reverence for complex methodology, or at the very least without the primitive fear of complex methodology that assails many of us. (One of the great ironies here is that, as Davis points out, the most anti-intellectual black position, that of the cultural nationalists, was most effectively fueled in the 1960s by a psychiatrist, Frantz Fanon, notably in his *Wretched of the Earth*.)

In King's case, as seen by Davis, psychology reinforces our sense of his goodness by demonstrating that that which made him good to the point of greatness was also psychologically possible. In the case of Du Bois, the observation is different. Du Bois is seen as the grand crusader that he was, but the will to crusade is linked to the force of aggression within him, and to his almost impenetrable loneliness, his fear of women, and his early fear of illegitimacy. According to Davis, Du Bois hated his mother because, among other reasons, he so feared the stigma of illegitimacy, and then was guilt-ridden over his hatred. I mention Davis's treatment of Du Bois and King to underscore a point—that politics are involved, or a basic position concerning power and people. If Freudian psychology is conciliatory and integrationist, I hasten to add that I do not think it, for that reason, sinister. Neither does Davis. And it is not necessarily authoritarian as a methodology. Davis prizes King's reconciling quality of forgiveness and love over Du Bois's scourging hatred, but he is never so haughty or so foolish as to ignore the fact that Du Bois was an extraordinary force for good in the history of black America.

One recent book on black American literature, it seems to me, draws creatively on a psychological approach for its insights into the literature: Michael Cooke's *Afro-American Literature in the Twentieth Century: The Achievement of Intimacy* (1985). In it, Professor Cooke sees four steps in the unfolding of black literature. First is "self-veiling," marked by an "unasserted, undemanding adaptation to the environment. . . . Its motive—to survive—is positive, but its vision limited." Second is "solitude," "in which the black character stands out from the veil [separating the races] and survives, but survives without sustaining or amplifying connections." The third is "kinship," when "relationships come into play, as the conditions of life become ampler and more varied"; but the enrichment comes "without relief" and the literature that results cannot escape a sense of "something deliberate, rather than fluent, and defensive, rather than spontaneous." Last of all is "intimacy," marked by "an openness towards the turns of inner life as well as the force of things without, and by a conviction of being at home in any dimension of the human experience." Robert Hayden's poetry and Alice Walker's *Meridian* exemplify the last category. James Baldwin and Ishmael Reed, on the other hand, stand for "tragic and ironic denials of intimacy." Another evolving stage is "beyond intimacy," marked by a kind of full-scale plunging into black experience, "axiomatic and comprehensive," as opposed to plunging into *the* black experience, which is called "dogmatic and political."

What we have here, I think, is a loose but intelligent adaptation or recasting of Erik Erikson, surely the most influential and effective of the Freud-based biographer-psychologists, and his eight stages of human development: trust (learned at the breast); autonomy (toilet-training, control of the anus); initiative; industry; identity (the sum of all previous identities); intimacy (the ability to love and surrender in love); gener-ativity; and integrity. (Erikson's essay is now at least twenty years old, I should mention here for those scholars who like their theory hot.) This adaptation or recasting on Professor Cooke's part is quite sweeping, but I do not think that anyone familiar with Afro-American literature and culture, and Afro-American life, can deny that his stages parallel certain prominent features of the evolution of the literature and culture over the past century. Indeed, I would go so far as to say that his book offers one of the more provocative and engaging statements on the psychology of black expression since Du Bois's *Souls of Black Folk* in 1903.

However, one question raised by Professor Cooke's work seems to me particularly challenging. Does literature "improve" to the extent that the text proposes what we the readers consider to be more advanced human development, greater psychological maturity? Or is such a consideration, in the final analysis, virtually extraliterary? From a literary or artistic point of view, something is obviously questionable, I think, about any scheme that proposes Robert Hayden's poetry, fine as it is, at the summit of black literature, even if we are tempted to see Hayden, with his gentle, inclusive Bahai philosophy and his patient, literate craftsmanship as pos-sibly the wisest and most admirable of our writers. I am not certain that we can reliably evaluate the work of writers according to our sense of the state of mental health of the major narrative voice or narrative presence in the writing. Our typical psychological tools are not politically or racially neutral, it seems to me, and we should be wary of being swayed in artistic judgments by writers whose works suggest temperamental and intellec-tual calm and pliability, together with integrationist politics—even if we admire such calm and pliability, and practice such politics.

In other words, if there is a questionable element in Professor Cooke's argument, it lies in the apparently linear and progressive nature of his scheme. I suspect that each of his four areas will continue to generate literature to the end of time, and that no one area is by definition more likely than the others to produce what objectively can be called good literature. Allison Davis ends by praising each of his four leaders for what they achieved; he had tried to explain the contours of their behavior, its origin and development, and not to see them in some scale of evolution. No doubt he clearly admires most of all the apostle of love, Martin Luther King, Jr., who reflects Cooke's and Erikson's common stage of intimacy and Erikson's generativity and integrity. King was also by far the most influential and successful of the four men (Douglass, Du Bois, Wright, and King) as a leader. But Davis never argues that King's speeches or writings were superior to those of the others because of his greater psychological maturity. They were not. As an artist in words, and although he wrote several books and was renowned as a public speaker, King is decidedly inferior to Douglass, Du Bois, and Wright.

In my zeal to insist that we need to take psychology more into account, I do not want to cover up the limitations of the field, or even to underestimate them, or to avoid acknowledging that possibly, just possibly, the man who was pushing the African gods might be on to something, in the sense that Freud and Erikson, say, might be all wrong for blacks. Of enormous help here, though not definitive help, is the thinking of certain feminists on the question of autobiography and the related and greater matter of identity. In her essay "On Female Identity," published in Winter 1981 in *Critical Inquiry,* Judith Kegan Gardiner quotes Carolyn Heilbrun, Sandra Gilbert, Susan Gubar, Elaine Showalter, and other critics on female identity and suggests that "the quest for female identity seems to be a soap opera, endless and never advancing, that plays the matinees of women's souls." I would say that the stabs by black cultural nationalists of a generation ago at defining black identity was often another version of the soap opera, or should I say another feature at the matinee—not so much *As the World Turns* but *Apocalypse Now.* But in the notes that Professor Gardiner offers toward defining the answer to the question, "Who is there when a woman says, 'I am,'?" we should find something useful for our own question today.

Using the psychological insights of Nancy Chodorow (*The Reproduction of Mothering,* Berkeley 1978), Gardiner concludes that "for every aspect of identity as men define it, female experience varies from the male model." The cornerstone of male definitions of identity is, of course, Eriksonian, and Gardiner makes much of the fact that, for him, "the paradigmatic individual achieving a mature identity is male, whereas the female has a specialized role as childbearer." A rival theory of identity—the main rival, and of great appeal to litterateurs, as Gardiner points out—is Heinz Lichtenstein's theory of "primary identity," on which Norman Holland, for one, has drawn for his strongly psychoanalytical criticism involving, of course, reader-response. Gardiner links the three men for the purposes of indictment. "Neither Holland, Lichtenstein, nor Erikson," she writes, "uses gender as a significant variable in his basic theory; none offers a theory of female identity as distinct from male identity." The thrust of the rest of her essay is an attempt to repair this inadequacy. I would argue that it is pretty clear that she repairs very little—her ideas are generally vague and tentative, but perhaps necessarily so, as mine certainly would be if I tried to talk about black identity. However, it also doesn't take much to see that the damage she inflicts as she tries to do her repairs is valuable in itself, for the damage is done mainly to male-dominated theory of allegedly human, allegedly gender-free identity that manages at the same time to slight women.

I applaud, finally, not her conclusions but her process. (Ironically, she summarizes that "female identity is a process, and primary identity for women is more flexible and relational than for men.") Explorations of this sort are badly needed in black biography. Of course, such explorations, in connection with black culture, should be in the hands of black American psychologists above all, but litterateurs apparently can expect very little help from that quiet quarter. Incidentally, I have shifted from Judith Gardiner's theorizing about women to theorizing about blacks, and I know that this sleight of hand slights the topic of black women. I slight the question of black women here only because you can observe me doing so, and can venture to repair that damage yourself. My point is that if we can separate men from women, we should be able, at least in theory, to separate blacks from whites. But we will do nothing at all on these scores if we do not accept the investigation of the mind as a proper province for the intellectual.

Why has black biography been so wary of psychology? The answers are many. A prejudice exists against psychoanalysis—ironically not unlike the prejudice against biography itself. But are there reasons peculiar to black culture? One reason could be that most of the leading biographers of blacks are white, and write under diplomatic constraints in the more intimate areas of their subjects' lives—and diplomacy is often the art of deceiving. But black scholars are really no more blunt or brave than their white counterparts. They are, indeed, at least as timid in the face of the potential black readership. Additionally, many undoubtedly feel the overriding need, in a racist national culture, to keep black heroes scrubbed and shining and heroic, and to conceal any evidence that may "tarnish" their reputations.

For myself, I find that I share the general suspicion of psychology in biography that I write myself. Some time ago, a friend who had read a large part of my biography of Hughes in manuscript form, and also had read an essay of mine called "The Origins of Poetry in Langston Hughes," published in the *Southern Review,* expressed some bewilderment at the difference of approach between the two. Not only was the latter—the essay—written at a more intense pitch than was the biography itself, but it seemed to be more "intellectual." In the essay, I wrote of a contest between will and passivity in Hughes, springing out of anger and a sense of isolation on the one hand, and a desire for a stasis like death on the other; I tried to argue that Hughes's poetry often showed the flaring of one or the other of these polar oppositions, but that his best work marked a compromise between the two because of the annealing context of the black race, which had entered into the boy's consciousness in lieu of his parents.

I do not believe that in my biographical work I ever write boldly about such factors as will and passivity. I would hesitate to write about neurosis and aggression, although I may betray a literary weakness for identifying guilt and shame. Why am I so reticent as a biographer? Biography, it seems to me, is an art insofar as it encourages genuine storytelling, and not many tales would survive the introduction of terminology borrowed from the sciences. Those tales that survive easiest are science-fiction, which depends on scientific terminology. Which is perhaps why so many explicitly psychoanalytical biographies read like—science-fiction.

Where does this leave us? I do not think it leaves us ignoring psychology. Rather, we have the burden of recognizing the validity of psychology and of using its methods to understand our subject. Then we have to translate those insights into a language appropriate to our discipline. In the process, something will be lost, and the room for error is potentially great. But we really have no choice in the matter. Let me end with a suggestion and then two observations.

Just as a psychiatrist must go through analysis in order to be certified, perhaps it should be the case that no one should attempt the biography of an artist, and perhaps the biography of anyone, if the aim is serious biography, without having become acquainted, in some form, with the basic psychoanalytical approaches. If this means entering a course of therapy, or the more expensive and time-consuming analysis, so be it. Surely we all can use a little psychotherapy.

Also, the fear of the political consequences of psychiatry and psycho-analysis needs to be reexamined. What we may fear, from a political point of view, is only the American version of Freud. As Sherry Turkel has pointed out in *Psychoanalytic Politics: Freud's French Revolution* (1978), while American psychiatry has maintained itself historically as the an-tithesis of progressive politics, or of politics at all, in recent years the French overcame their historic hostility to Freud and underwent a kind of conversion experience and a reinterpretation of Freud that have made his teachings, especially as interpreted and challenged by Lacan, not only compatible with socialism and feminism, for example, but a prime source of inspiration to both movements. One may see Fanon's work as part of this process.

And lastly, as biographers of blacks we should not forget the simple truth that being a Negro or colored or even a black in America is above all a psychological state. I believe that the effects of *direct* racism on the personality are trivial and relatively powerless compared to racism's *indirect* effects, which can be crippling. The damage of racism is often done long before someone is finally called a "nigger"—and many of us now go through life without a personal experience of that thrilling moment. Thus one explains very little as a biographer if one does not attempt to explain the mind, and to do so—in the absence of a rival model—according to some model derived, as Erik Erikson's and Allison Davis's are, from the works of Freud, or from some articulate opposition to Freud.

Response: *Michel Fabre*

I wish to start by saying that I have no essential disagreement with Arnold Rampersad's carefully worded and stimulating call for a more consistent use of psychology in Afro-American biography. I have never investigated that field in a systematic fashion, but his remarks are accu-rate: most biographers of black leaders and writers—myself included—have concentrated more upon the unfolding of public careers or on the development of literary works than upon providing a structured, co-herent psychological pattern of explanation for them; they have seldom gone beyond suggesting possible psychoanalytic keys.

Concerning Allison Davis's book, *Leadership, Love, and Aggression,* I am ashamed to confess that I never read it to the end. At the first Richard Wright Conference, organized at the University of Iowa in July 1971, Professor Davis gave a paper on Wright's relationship to black people which, I believe, served as a basis for his chapter on Wright in the book. I arrived one day too late at the conference to hear the paper, but I distinctly recall the dissatisfaction it evoked among participants, a reflection of one reason for the resistance to psychoanalysis which Arnold Rampersad hinted at: that Richard Wright, according to Davis, could have indeed hated black people and himself, was perceived as somewhat preposterous, even sacrilegious at the first major academic celebration of his work. I only leafed through the book in 1986 when Mercer Cook, whom I was then visiting in Washington, called my attention to Davis's allusion to my work. I told Mercer: "You know, I was really naive about race relations in the U.S. when I first did research in Jackson, Mississippi, in 1961." I may be less naive today and slightly better equipped to deal with Wright's emotional development. But I'm afraid my interest in learning about the repetitive working of the basic conflicts in his behavior has hardly increased.

For a while, I was attracted, however, by French critic Charles Mauron's theories of "psychocriticism." If it seemed preposterous to endeavor to psychoanalyze a dead writer, he claimed, one still could attempt to make some sense out of the reiterated, sometimes obsessive, patterning of certain words, phrases, or scenes recurring in the different texts the writer had produced. The writer's idiosyncratic use of these words and scenes harked back to his deep-lying or half-conscious obsessions. They helped provide a meaning, according to Mauron, insofar as "writing is the projection of phantasms on a page," as Alain Robbe-Grillet likes to put it.

I was so genuinely interested in recurrent patterns or obsessive images in Wright's prose that I wrote a psychocritical essay, published in 1980 under the title "Fantasies and Style in Richard Wright's Fiction." In an otherwise flattering review of my book, *The World of Richard Wright,* in a recent issue of *Callaloo,* Rudolph Byrd finds the piece "pedantic and tedious." It only "proves that if one knows well the features of a particular literary landscape, the connections one can make are almost infinite and that a symbol or object may contain a multitude of meanings, some fanciful and others that deepen a text's power and ambiguity." It appears that my attempt was inadequate; or, maybe, the whole psychocritical approach was wrong.

Arnold Rampersad's questions about the prevailing reluctance to use psychology and psychoanalysis in black biography are far-reaching indeed, and one might best respond to them in a roundabout way.

A biographer, especially a literary biographer, is generally caught between many dilemmas. One of them has to do with the balance between fact and art, or what Virginia Woolf liked to call "granite and rainbow." Whereas the writer is the only authority concerning the so-called "facts" of fiction, biographical facts can be verified by other people. However, since the biography develops through the mustering of such facts, it is not the writer's actual life, Woolf seems to imply, which becomes increasingly real to us, but his fictitious life "which dwells in the personality rather than the act." ("The New Biography," in *Collected Essays,* London, 1967, p. 234.)

In other words, factual data are the necessary basis of biography, but a chronological reporting of actions fails as biography if it lacks the necessary insight into the subject's mind, and fails to render the outlook, or zest for life, of the creative person. In order that the light of the personality may shine through, certain facts must be foregrounded, others must be merely mentioned or shaded. The ideal biographer is a creative shaper or interpreter of carefully researched and mustered facts. (In this respect, Arnold Rampersad's own biography of Langston Hughes could easily be cited as a model; it is indeed a splendid achievement in deft and balanced interpretation.)

A crucial point in writing biography is the relationship between the biographer and his subject, not to speak of the biographer's deliberate development of a thesis. How can the biographer know the subject's "interior" in order to sort out the conflicting evidence collected? The accurate fact-finder must also, to a degree, identify with his subject. He looks at him but he also attempts to look out from him in order to view the world as he viewed it. Avoiding excessive factual objectivity and being caught up in his subject to the extent of being unable to stand aside, the biographer must find a particular point for himself in the portrait between foreground and background. A good biography, as a consequence, should manifest implicitly the biographer's particular vision of the writer, a vision growing out of the research material and being gradually defined by it; it must also, unavoidably, reveal the biographer's worldview with its built-in ideological and hermeneutic choices and limitations.

A century ago, biographers often started from the romantic notion of inexplicable artistic genius; then they resorted to Taine's assumption that the artist was the product of a race (meaning "nation"), a period, and a place. More recently, Marxism and Freudianism have more or less taken over, overturning the assumption of genius unrooted in specific historical conditions. Yet both the Marxist view of history and Freudian psychology have tended to imprison the artist in deterministic ideologies. Both are dedicated to the unmasking of "latent" and thus supposedly more "real" determinants of a life, whether they lie in the repressed sexual conflicts of early experience and/or in the socioeconomic components of a historical period.

It is only too easy to point out how, among the kinds of creative interpretation which claim to get at the "inner mystery" of the subject of a biography, the psychoanalytical approach can lead to a caricatural reductionism. As I was recently reviewing a collection of essays gathered by Doireann McDermott on *Autobiographical and Biographical Writing in the Commonwealth* (Sitges, 1984), I came across a fascinating instance of interpretive approaches concerning Olive Schreiner, the white South African author of *The Story of an African Farm*, which can serve as an illustration. In her essay "Olive Schreiner: Approaches to Her Writing Through Biography and Autobiography," Cherry Clayton of Randse Afrikaanse University tries to determine whether Schreiner was above all "a colonial woman" or a Victorian neurotic. She notes that the crux of the disagreement among the biographers of Schreiner is the way in which they handle the asthma she suffered from. Vera Buchanan-Gould, in 1948, and D. L. Hobman, in 1958, simply accepted Schreiner's recurrent story that she "got wet" while traveling. In 1924, S. C. Crownright-Schreiner was characteristically concerned to impeach Olive Schreiner's accuracy as to the date of the coach trip, her traveling companions, and their destination. In 1980, First and Scott used a Freudian model of repressed sexual conflict: "was this because Schreiner's awareness of her sexuality and its passion appalled her?" they asked. Cherry Clayton wonders, "Who knows?" and she adds in a footnote: "Perhaps Havelock Ellis knew. At any rate, his case-history of Schreiner's sexual development, in *Studies in the Psychology of Sex* (1928) does not indicate that she was any more appalled by her own sexuality than the woman in the street" (in McDermott, ed., Sitges, 1984, p. 54).

The real question may lie there. What was it that made Schreiner, or Richard Wright, or any black writer different from the man or woman in the street? Indeed one could easily have used Dr. Frederic Wertham's analysis of "An Unconscious Determinant in *Native Son*" (1944). Wright himself believed for years that he could use the key of psychoanalysis not only to know his own creative process better but to explain historical events (like colonization) or to structure his fiction, like *Savage Holiday*. It would be embarrassing to list all the critics of *Pagan Spain* who took him to task for discovering phallic symbols in the dripping candles during the Holy Week procession in Seville or in the natural stone erections on which Montserrat Monastery was built.

Maybe the basic question is not "why" he became Richard Wright, but "how." By this I mean that the "self" of the *writer* should not be explained away by infantile fixations. Not that they are unimportant, but does the exploitation of the process, which can be applied to any individual, illuminate what makes the specificity of the artist? Another reason, to recall Jung's argument against Freud, is that all psychic processes constitute a teleological chain as well as a causal one. Psychic conditions should not be reduced to causes in the individual's past. In simpler terms: we all go somewhere and come from somewhere. From this angle, I think that James Olney's *Metaphors of Self: The Meaning of Autobiography* (Princeton University Press, 1972) and the collection of essays he edited under the title *Autobiography* in 1980 are of great interest for the biographer as well as the critic. In the latter volume, George Gusdorf's essay on the conditions and limits of autobiography is illuminating. When he claims that "there is a never-ending dialogue of life with itself in search of its own absolute" (p. 85), I readily share this existentialist viewpoint. Indeed, this process is everywhere evident in Wright's writings, especially in his early interviews, in his journals of the late 1940s, in the different drafts of *Black Boy,* in the correspondence with Margrit de Sabloniere. One could even interpret his contradictory impressions about the black situation in the U.S. or about his discovery of France as an oscillation between a stronger (progressive) and a weaker (regressive) self. Of course I believe that psychoanalytical perspectives carry valuable hints for literary critics as well as literary biographers. Wright's fiction can be read as a symbolic conflict between opposing selves; his life is thus transformed into a narrative both in his openly autobiographical writing and in his fiction. V. S. Naipaul states that novels are more revealing of a writer's inner truth than autobiographies. This would tally with George Gusdorf's statement that "every novel is an autobiography by intermediary."

But, I repeat, what makes a biography worthwhile to me is the discovery of a life that develops, opens up to new horizons, unfolds its potentialities. Growth, achievement, the restless quest that drove Wright to his own degree of greatness were elements which appealed to me. I feel that, by reducing a lifetime's evolution to a repetitive pattern of basic emotional conflicts, whether enacted in behavior or in writing, one would offer at best one case study among others, at worst an extended psychiatric diagnosis.

Such questions as which school of psychoanalysis is more fecund than the others, or whether Lacan is a disciple of Freud or his antagonist, are important. But they may be secondary to their ideological implications. There is a serious reason to be wary of psychoanalysis in the case of black biography, and it is certainly ideological in nature.

Psychoanalysis is supposed to help the individual know and accept himself; it tends to reconcile him with his environment. As it is generally practiced, it stresses social adjustment. It helps explain and excuse "delinquent" behavior. But it tends to project the maverick, the outstanding individual, as marginal and deviant. And here one can guess why black biographers have not been inclined to use a consistently psychoanalytical approach. Insofar as it purports to be a science, psychoanalysis has a totalitarian discourse. It excludes other explanations.

I suspect that Allison Davis himself shared the assumptions of his generation, those of American sociologists like E. Franklin Frazier, who functioned along the lines of integrationist thinking. (I mean "socially" as well as "racially" integrationist.) Such a view invites the biographer to interpret the subject's life in deterministic, even pathological terms. In psychology, this approach corresponds to the sociological approach which explained black American culture as a failure to reproduce white culture instead of seeing it as a counterculture or a culture of resistance.

I am surprised that Arnold Rampersad did not mention one "biography" of a black leader written with great literary skill from a psychoanalytical perspective: *The Confessions of Nat Turner* by William Styron. Whether Styron's historical data were accurate or not, starting from the premises he had chosen he could explain Nat Turner's rebellion only as a personal revolt and find its roots in infantile fixations and sexual desires. *A contrario,* this may explain why W. E. B. Du Bois chose *not* to write on John Brown from such a perspective; he could only have added grist to the mill of those who claimed that Brown was a madman. The choice of methodology is ideological.

If we bear this in mind, it does indeed greatly matter whether psychoanalytical theory is used as "the antithesis of progressive politics" embodied in American psychiatry or as a source of inspiration for feminism or socialism, as evidenced in Jacques Lacan's or Frantz Fanon's writings. Rejecting psychoanalysis as a whole certainly deprives the biographer of valuable instruments. But is it possible to borrow concepts and instruments piecemeal without implicitly subscribing to the claim of global explanation made by any potential science?

Admittedly, valuable models can be derived from Erik Erikson, innovative intuitions can be generated by the reading of Michel Foucault, and so on. However, in the last analysis, it appears that the best literary biographies have not been written by social scientists or psychologists but by literary critics-cum-historians. As Arnold Rampersad himself beautifully manages to do in *The Life of Langston Hughes,* the biographer should avoid reductive "keys" and try to present the changing outlines of the writer's career, provoking the reader to speculation as well as providing conclusions. The risk may consist in bringing out a riot of confusion instead of a richer unity. But is it not better to run that risk than to preclude from the start the possibility of multiple interpretations? Call this an eclectic approach, if you like. I would be prepared to defend it against the too frequently totalitarian assumptions of a narrowly "scientific" exploration of a writer's life and works.

Response: *Nellie Y. McKay*

In "Biography and Autobiography, and Afro-American Culture," an essay published in the *Yale Review* in 1983, Arnold Rampersad summed up the current state of the art and speculated aloud on future directions for the field.[1] Among other things he called attention to differences in black and white cultural perceptions of biography and autobiography, to the previous dearth and recent increase in the scholarly production of biographies of black people, including those of writers; and he reflected on the cultural implications of this development within the Afro-American community. A central question raised concerned reader responses to new trends which might develop in respect to the terms on which black biography might be produced in the future. Rampersad called for acknowledgment, on the part of those involved in this production, of the force of "modern" biography in the larger world and its application to black American biography. He strongly encouraged an investigation of these issues as a prelude to new approaches to contemporary work in black biography.

The essay was timely. For several years, scholars in the field have noted and pondered various reasons for the significantly small number of biographies that have been written on black subjects. Some blame for this paucity has fallen on the academy, which, through its system of rewards (tenure, promotion, salary increases, and research awards for work completed, as well as implicit devaluation of the lives of certain groups of people), discourages young scholars, particularly those from among people of color, from embarking on biographical studies. On the other hand, as Rampersad pointed out, and as new studies confirm, Afro-American autobiography has been the privileged choice of expression in black culture throughout American history, while biography has been a sort of country cousin. The "I" of the one receives considerably more cultural

1. Arnold Rampersad, "Biography and Autobiography, and Afro-American Culture," *Yale Review* 73, no. 1 (October 1983):1–16.

respect and admiration than the "she" or "he" of the other. The reasons for this, as others have indicated and William Andrews's recent book on Afro-American autobiography brilliantly demonstrates, are complicated, but turn largely on the axis of reclaiming personal identity.[2] Given the cultural bias toward autobiography, on the one hand, and the intellectual needs for the knowledge that biography inscribes, on the other, the central question that Rampersad raised in that essay was: to what extent are scholars of black biography prepared to embrace scientific theories of "modern" biography for their work, recognizing that such a step would make significant differences, not only in the kinds of books they write, but in their relationship to Afro-American culture through the responses of their readers?

As I see it, that 1983 essay represented the sound of one falling shoe. Diplomatically, it mounted a challenge to at least one group of scholars in Afro-American literature, urging them to move in a direction they had not previously taken. As the only literary biographer of W. E. B. Du Bois, and then in the process of writing the life of Langston Hughes, Rampersad was in an excellent position to evaluate the nature of the new work in the field. Within Afro-American literature, biography was a strategic front on which to issue this challenge, since the perimeters of the field offered containment against any threat of large-scale unwanted changes in the profession. Nonetheless, it presented a call for a bold examination of the place and role of biography in the Afro-American literary canon and, to a certain extent, for the first time brought the "idea" of biography into the limelight of our general concerns for the future of this literature.

Given the large number of available subjects, writing black biography might well be the new frontier in Afro-American literature in the twenty-first century. There is a great deal to be done in this area. For instance, no published biography of a black woman has yet been authored by a black woman, although Thadious Davis's on Nella Larsen and Margaret Wilkerson's on Lorraine Hansberry have been in preparation for some time. If as Robert Hemenway observed in his superb biography of Zora Neale Hurston, and as feminists would agree, gender is an important aspect of literary/historical representation, then scholars of both sexes and races bring different and valuable perspectives to the lives they

2. William Andrews, *To Tell a Free Story, The First One Hundred Years of Afro-American Autobiography* (Carbondale: University of Illinois Press, 1985). This is the most recent and most detailed of a number of studies, including those of Houston Baker and Robert Stepto, to show that slave narratives were rhetorical devices through which black slaves articulated their humanity in the search for freedom from the physical and psychological bondage of white oppression.

attempt to elucidate through biography. Thus it is important that black women, as well as others, examine the lives of women of their race in this area of research and writing.[3]

Rampersad's essay in this volume represents the sound of the second falling shoe. Here, potential biographers of black subjects are asked, even more directly, to reevaluate their conceptions of Afro-American biography on all of its fronts and to look toward the feasibility of particular approaches to the field. Rampersad points out that, even today, Afro-American biography essentially remains a form that has not taken advantage of theoretical methods of analysis for its production. What he calls for is the serious contemplation of psychological approaches in scrutinizing the black life. How do we answer that challenge?

As he suggests, this is no doubt a very good time, historically, to take a bold new step into the future. Several new biographies have been published in the interim between his *Yale Review* essay and our present conference, including Rampersad's own brilliant volume on Langston Hughes, with a second to follow soon. There are also works on Melvin Tolson, Claude McKay, and Jean Toomer, to name three of the most well-known literary figures. Rampersad is modest about his own work, but of the new biographies only his on Hughes attempts to apply psychological theories to interpret the life of a gifted writer. This text qualifies for his definition of "modern" biography. It is an example that others should well follow.

While many biographies of black subjects are still being written by white scholars (a commendable situation), many more black scholars are now engaged in the venture as well. This is a good time for the integration of new perspectives into the discourse. On another level, Afro-American Studies (literature, for our purposes), introduced into most northern white colleges and universities in the mid to late 1960s, has now come of age, and at this point we have an unprecedented opportunity to strike out in new directions and define new agendas.

Indeed, theoretical approaches are not new in Afro-American literary criticism, although there has been resistance to their adoption from some critics. And psychology and psychoanalysis are reasonable tools to employ for understanding some of the workings of the black mind and as

3. Ann Petry's biographies of Harriet Tubman and Tituba of Salem are juvenile books, and do not qualify for inclusion in this discussion. However, aside from Davis and Wilkerson, whose books are anticipated shortly, other biographies of black women by black female scholars are in various stages of planning. These include Nell Painter's study of Sojourner Truth, and Nellie McKay's study of Ann Petry.

ways of interpreting the black life. I suspect other critics have thought of additional new and interesting ways of examining a life, and it might be well to explore these. Still, the issue here is that theoretical approaches have been slower to make inroads in black biography than in other areas of Afro-American critical thought. Rampersad suggests a number of reasons for this, among them:

1. the biographer's fear of accusations of European hegemony over black consciousness;

2. the biographer's fear of misreading the materials, and thus misreading the life;

3. the biographer's timidity, in the face of a black readership with prejudices against both psychoanalysis and biography, in writing about the intimate areas of the lives of black subjects in other than certain ways. (After all, even Du Bois admitted that it is difficult to let others see the full psychological meaning of caste segregation.) Yet Rampersad asks that biographers become bolder than they have been, that they take risks in the face of reader accusation and rejection, and that they use these new tools to bring Afro-American biography into the modern age.

Reasons such as the above for "holding back," give us, as biographers and literary scholars, an opportunity to ask ourselves questions about the limits of Afro-American biography. What do we want it to be? What do we want of and from it? From my perspective, biography is about the life of its subject (albeit from one individual's point of view), and an understanding of the subject's work is only one way to get at a part of that life. Consequently, I am interested in promoting whatever resources are available to a biographer that will illuminate the mind of the subject. In dealing with black subjects, one is always aware that race, and as Rampersad also suggests, the psychological aspects of race much more than its physical manifestations, must be taken into consideration. In dealing with a black female subject, both race and gender are variables in the application of approaches that do not naturally include them as factors.

However, it is also important to give careful consideration to the implications of moving into psychological biography—to be wary of concealed pitfalls. There is more to the Afro-American position on biography and psychology than the accusation that the field has simply lagged behind more progressive areas of Euro-American biography. For one thing, as other critics have noted, there has been a long and uneasy history between other kinds of biography and psychology in general, although the literary past is littered with significant writers like Coleridge, Dickens, Dostoevsky, and others who recognized the importance of dreams long before Freud formulated his now commonly known theories. Part of the uneasiness between biography and psychology comes from the wide differences separating the two areas.

Psychology is the study of the entire field of human behavior, and psychoanalysis is a technique used to explore the unconscious in therapy. As critic Leon Edel, who uses psychoanalytic theory in his work, points out, the "biographer cannot psychoanalyze [the] documents" of the life she or he is exploring, and the work of the psychoanalyst and the biographer are to different ends.[4] What literary critics, including biographers, do with the knowledge that comes from these fields is very different from what the scientific practitioners in their areas do. Edel calls what we can do "literary psychology."[5] At the same time, he feels that the biographer learns almost nothing about the proper use of psychology from the study of theory, and that the most successful biographies using these tools are those whose authors have been exposed to psychotherapy. Even then, he sees a danger for many writers in the confusion between conscious, rationalized motivations and the promptings of the unconscious. Another area in which he advises thought and work concerns the use of language. The biographer who uses literary psychology must learn to translate the scientific terminology into literary language. Biographers who expect to use this approach need to learn the basic Freudian knowledge on ways of "thinking, dreaming, and having fantasies."[6] As Rampersad also points out, feminist critics have been busy separating out the ways in which women do these things differently from men and setting up their own framework for using psychoanalytic theory. This makes it incumbent upon Afro-American biographers or others doing Afro-American biography to work through the processes as well, setting up their own framework for use of psychological theories in their books. But this can only be done in the wake of a good deal of preparation and serious thought.

Having also read Allison Davis's *Leadership, Love, and Aggression,* I have my doubts that black literary critics/biographers will come to the kinds of conclusions that Davis does regarding the men in his book anytime soon. Of course, Davis was protected by the fact that he was a psychologist. And I must also add, that without the protection of that profession, but having read a good deal of Du Bois's writings, I disagree

4. Leon Edel, *Writing Lives, Principia Biographica* (New York: W. W. Norton, 1984), p. 46.
   5. Ibid., p. 148.
   6. Ibid.

with Davis on the issue of Du Bois's hate for his mother. Still, I understand and applaud the impulse in Rampersad's paper to encourage biographers to attempt to probe beneath the surface of behavior and search out conscious and unconscious motivations for action. There is a very good attempt to do this in the Hughes biography. As its author tells us, we cannot possibly reconstruct the past, so we ought not to feel paralyzed in misrepresenting it, if what we are doing is recreating it as a means of trying to further understand our own lives and society. The idea is bold and daring.

And finally, I think that biographers of black subjects cannot simply ignore or reject, out of hand, the apparatus of psychology in the writing of future black biography. I think it would be unfortunate for writers to turn their texts into case studies, since that is not the point of the challenge. But I suspect that more and more we will find biographers insinuating psychological theory into literary criticism. To leave it out completely is to leave the work undone, for this is modern knowledge which is now available to all of us. No one believes that human beings live only an exterior life. The internal life is hidden, and we can never capture it fully, but we now have the tools to discover some of what takes place in the reflective inner self. As Leon Edel says, we can get glimpses of it.

Response: *Robert G. O'Meally*

Arnold Rampersad's essay raises the classic contrast of "science" versus an uncertain art; or, as he would say, specifically, the method of Freudian psychology (as well as of Erikson's and others') as against what Michael Harper has called the "Explain School of Criticism," the lazy lack of systematic method, the deathwalk of "nostalgic humanism." Rampersad turns up traces of "cultural lag" among our literary biographers. Here it is as if the biographer reacts and overreacts to doubting white John of Chesnutt's *The Conjure Woman* tales:[1] the dully mechanical and hence comic rationalist, the boring white man of science whose frosty thoughts—and whose refusal to yield to the near-perfect truth in Uncle Julius's lies—connects him with the mad calculus that was the slave trade itself.[2]

---

1. See, in particular, Charles Chesnutt's "Sis Becky's Picaninny" and "The Gray Wolf's Ha'nt," in *The Conjure Woman* (Ann Arbor: University of Michigan Press, 1972; first published, 1899).

2. See Robert Hemenway, "The Functions of Folklore in Chesnutt's *The Conjure Woman*," *Journal of the Folklore Institute*, 13 (1976):283–309.

If we have been what Brer Rabbit calls "suscautious" of too much science (and here of course I mean critical science too), then our doubts go at least double for social science and social-science-oriented criticism where racial reductionism has so violently shrunken and misshapen the black image. Let's not forget Albert Murray's signifying, tables-turned name for social science's version of truth: social-science *fiction*.[3]

Let me vote yes with Rampersad and "science." First, though, a few "suscautious" observations.

1. I am one who always believes it to be a mistake to underestimate the effects of racism. Rampersad is just, in my view, in differentiating between what the Harvard psychiatrist Chester Pierce terms racism's micro-aggressions as against its macro-aggressions.[4] The cross-burning or the lynching is one thing; and the change flung on the counter or the delayed promotion is another. In one paper, Pierce has shown that referees in football games almost invariably look to the white team captains to call the tosses of the coins that start games. Such micro-aggressions (some are intensely private, individual attacks, unwitnessed by the unwitting perpetrator; others, like the albeit "unintentional" and largely "unseen" football ritual, of extraordinarily wide effect) are, Pierce points out, immensely damaging in their insidious, half-visible way. In this context I recall what Sterling Brown told a white student at Yale who said he thought the black poet sounded somewhat paranoid. "In America," Brown quickly rejoined, "any Negro who is not paranoid is *crazy*."

Not just Freud but the often beleaguered students of black psychology have offered telling formulas for looking at black life in white America. Pierce, among others, has considered stress and techniques of managing stress among his black patients: herein lie keys and secrets for the biographer of the black writer.

2. On the specific question of Freudian models, many and fast have been the warnings against Freud's biases and adhesions. (Feminist critics have been very helpful in setting Freud in perspective as a *male* psychiatrist.) For the biographer, I would suggest that Wordsworth's child-is-father-to-the-man sense of life—reinforced by Freud and then slavishly followed by generations of biographers—betrays a weakness not often considered. As Phyllis Rose reminds us, contrary to what most biographers seem to think, people are not potted plants—cast into fertile

---

3. Albert Murray, *The Omni-Americans* (New York: Outerbridge, 1970).
4. See Pierce's "Offensive Mechanisms," in Floyd Barbour's *The Black Seventies* (Boston: Porter Sargent), pp. 265–82.

soil, showing the inevitable early promise, budding shyly, breaking into blooms and fruits, fading at the last.[5] Here the dangerous temptation, aside from the aesthetic problem of the horrid march through shop-dulled steps and stages, is that the critic will lay waste his or her powers sifting through the subject's shadowy first days, poking at his or her parent's bed and around the first training toilet, and then leaving out the artist's more significant years of mature artistic production. Billie Holi-day, according to a worst scenario in these terms, may appear as a gone-wrong Catholic girl or just a crazy dopester, not as what she was: an artist of towering stature.

Having struck this jazz note, I should say that I would recommend *Good Morning Blues*, Count Basie's autobiography as told to Albert Mur-ray. Murray knows Freud's strategies and counterstates them or overlays them with strategies and questions of his own: How did young Basie develop his understated sense of style? How did his band act as a com-posing vehicle? How did he learn to play the band as his "instrument"? The great saxophonist Lester Young has said that every good jazz soloist must tell a story; that indeed an instrumentalist who would play a ballad with feeling must know its lyrics. "You're technically hip," Young was famous for telling fast young players. *"But what is your story?"* What, in this peculiarly jazz-oriented sense, was Basie's story? How did he develop his artistic voice with which to tell it?

3. My fear is that too rigid a Freudian treatment can trivialize or ignore an artist's truly great years; it can have no sense of the discon-tinuities of personal development, the uncharted reverses, the seeming miracles, the weird breaks in the pattern that seem truer to life's own criss-crossed way. (Novelists, to be sure, have been mindful of the jagged changes and surprises that shape human fate.)

Erikson's model of personality, with its markings of the stages of adult development, is in my view much more suggestive, more dynamic than Freud's for the 1990s literary biographer. Erickson sees adult life as a series of crucial adjustments and self-definitions.[6]

4. Following Kenneth Burke's lead, Ralph Ellison gives us still an-other dynamic model of constructing the self. Ellison routinely speaks of his own life (as well as the lives of his characters) in dramatic—Burke

---

5. For the general view of biography expressed in this paper, I am greatly indebted to my colleague and friend Phyllis Rose. Note especially her fine collection of essays, *Writing of Women: Essays in a Renaissance* (Middletown, Conn.: Wesleyan University Press, 1985).

6. See in particular Erik H. Erikson's *Childhood and Society* (1950), *Young Man Luther* (1958), and *Identity and the Life Cycle* (1959).

would say "dramatistic"—terms. One lives out a layered drama involving the Burkean touchstones of act, scene, agent, agency, and purpose. In an autobiographical essay, Ellison gives us his portrait of himself as a youngster who, along with adventurous co-conspirators, chose heroes that certainly were not chosen for them: "And our imaginations processed reality and dream, natural man and traditional hero, literature and folklore, like maniacal editors turned loose in some frantic film-cutting room."[7] He and the others were piecing together strips of images to suit their unfolding needs and motives: splicing, editing in, editing out. Here again it is the discontinuities, changes, and switches of all sorts ("crabways and crossways and around in a circle")[8] that challenge the personality-as-plant model. As jazz players tell us in their autobiographies (and here it is crucial to recall that young Ellison saw himself as a musician who wanted to master not just the classics nor just jazz; typically, he wanted it all), you emulate, you exceed, you steal from unlikely sources, you seek your own way, you go—as they say in the vernacular—for what you know. Ellison confesses that he acquired his bouncy way of walking from Milton Lewinsohn, a Jewish businessman in Oklahoma City, a man whose values—and whose bouncy walk!—Ellison admired.[9] Here Ellison takes aim at social science formulas which consider blackness as a mark of being forever locked out and inevitably victimized. And of course he also calls out those who see the black or the white American as all, or only, black or white.

5. But whatever scheme we apply to the lives of the black poets, I would suggest that we resist being too like Chesnutt's John in our science. Our novelists and poets do not learn their craft from psychologists and sociologists but from other novelists, and our biographers need to take heed of this. Read Freud, Erikson, and their critics. Then read Johnson, Strachey, Bate, Wilson, and Justin Kaplan. Read the great biographers. Recall Freud's remark that it was not he that discovered the unconscious but poets and philosophers. I would add that since biographers are not so much theorists as storytellers, radical at their best, they would do well to study James, Murray, Ellison, and other radical taletellers, too. We need more stories of our writers that do much more than compile facts; that have more and more of the fire of art in them.

6. Which brings me to the question: Why has biography, "white" and

7. Introduction, *Shadow and Act* (New York: Random House, 1964), p. xvi.

8. This phrase comes from Ellison's *Invisible Man* (New York: Random House, 1952).

9. See "Notes from the Academy," *Daedalus* 95, 1 (Winter 1966):435.

"black," so often lagged behind fiction and film in experimental storytelling? Why has there been so little play with time, in light of the examples of Faulkner and Toni Morrison? Why so little play with narrative structure? One thinks here of the examples of Gaines, Ishmael Reed, and Alice Walker. Why, in light of work by these same writers, has there been so little play with point of view? As Phyllis Rose has observed, if a filmmaker told a life history waltzing a-b-c-d-e from birth to maturity to death it would be so startling as to seem an innovation if not a parody. Why is there so little formal innovation in our biographies? Why no group biographies? No family biographies? No lives told from unlikely angles? Cut in at unlikely but telling moments?

Let me suggest a few reasons for our lack of playfulness as biographers. All too often we are hindered by our yearning to honor the Great Poet in Black. And as if that weren't enough to freeze the biographer's hand, this problem of the worshipful biographer often combines with that of portraying the Exceptional Negro or the Negro as Victim. Any of these can spell a deadly and wooden formula. Somehow, too, the tradition of writing biography has been a conservative one, despite the recent renaissance in the field.

What to do? Again, yes, use Freud. But also, perhaps more crucially, use the writer's *own* statements about who he or she is. These may produce fresher readings and more radical insights than any formula can anticipate. As critics, let us hold in our works both sides of the black American's much-heralded "two-ness": this time let us call the two sides "science" and "blackness." Here I come full circle back to Rampersad's most profound point, and Henry Gates's: That if there is something to call "black American literary biography" it exists and will exist through mastering master tropes (Gates might say the *master's* tropes) like Freud's—as well as those imbedded in black vernacular culture, which Houston Baker has aptly termed the "blues matrix." For me the most compelling challenge of the 1990s (and beyond) is to combine "science" with our own traditions of motherwit. Ellison once described his novel as mammy-made, an "ole Negro lie." We need to tell our stories without forgetting to weave an "ole Negro lie" into the basic fabric and pattern of the work.

As to motherwit: In my new work I am concerned with such "Africanisms" (really New World Africanisms or Afro-Americanisms) as improvising, with and against the group, in what William Harris has called "the jazz aesthetic." I am also concerned with *masking,* not just concealing or even disciplining the self or artist-in-training (in Yeats's sense), but with masking as the trying on of new identities in the Afro-

American tradition. American name-changes, Justin Kaplan has written, could be the subject of a book; if so, then a treatise on black name-changes alone could fill two books.

In a word, I do agree with Rampersad. More method, more science, of course; not just fact but form makes biography. Not just the rainbow, as it were, but the granite builds telling lives. And yet on the question of form I would say that what we need even more than more straight Freud is more artful playing with form. The biographer who is "trained" (in Houston Baker's wonderful use of the word to mean not just schooled but traveled through the briar patches of Afro-Americana) must know, in other words, all there is to know about Freud; but then he or she must be looking for something better. The something better is to be recovered deep in that briar patch, rusty with talk, as Toomer put it wonderfully, and singing with the blues. If all criticism, not just theory but even telling someone else's story, is a form of autobiography—as Baker has argued—then we need not see ourselves as beggars standing liminally between science and nothing of our own. In "science" plus the something of our own, in the long tradition of shaping lies that are truer than the facts can say, therein lies a tale richly worth the telling.

Afterword

Houston A. Baker, Jr., and Patricia Redmond

The process of book production has profited in recent years from word processing, computerized typesetting, and express mail. The delay between the idea of a book and its appearance, however, is long. The essays and responses of this collection—in all their energy and originality, pros and cons, and carefully considered phrasing—would undoubtedly be revised, emended, and supplemented by their authors if they were free to do so at this moment. In one sense, our authors' desire means that our book is already belated. In another and a far more positive sense, it means that the foregoing reflections represent a field that is so rapid in its development that the insights of a given moment can become readily accepted truths in a future scarcely removed.

It is, then, with both elation and caution that we hazard a few general reflections on the state of the art of Afro-American literary criticism and theory as it can be inferred from the present work and projected for the nineties. What we wish, finally, to outline are what seem to us the principal contours of argument and response in the volume and what such contours augur for work in the next decade.

First, it seems clear that the foregoing essays follow, in many respects, ideational and ideological lines that historically have marked the criticism of Afro-American expressive culture. From Henry Louis Gates's call for a privileging of the black vernacular as opposed to the Euroamerican "standard" to Arnold Rampersad's injunction to transcend vernacular pieties surrounding "the black life as written" and produce scientific literary biography, our volume reflects traditional issues.

Implicit in the essays of Gates and Rampersad are time-honored Afro-American literary-critical issues such as: "For whom does the Afro-Americanist write?" "How does the Afro-Americanist situate him- or herself with respect to hegemonic traditions and methods of scholarship?" "From whence does a truly empowering and comprehensive criticism of Afro-American expressive culture develop?" Inferable, as

225

well, from the essays of Gates and Rampersad is a transitional moment in the criticism and theory of Afro-American expressive culture.

Both authors explicitly address what might be thought of as a be-nighted past, one in which commendable efforts were made by men and women of good will but which, nonetheless, left comprehensive the-orization of canonicity and literary biography unachieved.

What is exciting about responses to the implied *creatio de novo* of Rampersad and Gates is their counterpointing. Respondents to both essays—particularly Gibson, O'Meally, and Fabre—suggest that our present generation of Afro-Americanists is not nearly so impoverished of useful precedents, reflections, or scholarly examples as we might believe. Gibson adduces powerful examples of Afro-Americanist, vernacular an-thologizing in the past; Fabre claims that an absence of attention to psychoanalytical modes of analysis may be less a matter of black culture's sacrosanct codes than a matter of that culture's considered rejection of the limiting constraints of psychology. O'Meally, in a manner comple-mentary to Fabre, supplies what might be thought of as the privileged routes, roots, and resources of what he would consider authentic, cultur-ally resonant modes of Afro-Americanist analysis.

Now, in these responses, there is a sense that a uniquely Afro-Ameri-canist genius is at work in the essays of Gates and Rampersad. This sense is combined, however, with cautions and addendums for the expansion and orientation of Rampersad's and Gates's work. What is most encour-aging about the exchanges is that they raise, reflect, and preserve an existing tradition of criticism and theory while, at the same instant, they gesture toward entirely new roads and bearings.

There is, in short, a kind of stability implicit in the exchanges, a welcomed stability since the telos of Gates's project is a *future* Norton anthology in its first stages of formation and Rampersad's biography of Langston Hughes is the only example of the psychobiographical ap-proach to the subject that he recommends. It is, thus, encouraging to be reminded that the overall worth and value of canonization or literary biography are determined, at least in significant measure, by a black past that has bequeathed an accountable legacy. The rage for a new order of black criticism and theory must be tempered by our serious attention to surrounding discourses, past examples, adept scholarly collaborations, and the sharing of knowledge engaged by Gates, Rampersad, and their respondents.

If Gates's and Rampersad's efforts are held to be theoretical, or, largely methodological, Houston Baker's work clearly joins their com-pany. His formulations on theory are intended as revisionist rejoinders to detractors who wish to uphold what they deem a historical "purity" of Afro-American expressive cultural criticism. Baker does not attempt to flee a past that he considers benighted. Rather, he sets out to reconstruct a past that he conceives as theoretically sophisticated and originary. Finally, he seeks to ally recent Afro-American feminist endeavors with his own constructions.

But as reasonable and energetic as Baker's attempts to situate "theory" on some common ground of a discoverable black past seems, the constructed and discursively interested nature of his attempt is decisively revealed by Mae Henderson's response. Unveiling the idealizing, essentialist, and scopophiliac cast of his formulations, Henderson offers a useful set of cautions about the "male gaze," especially a gaze conditioned by a "happy" or "gay science" of phenomenology.

Since Henderson takes up the general framework of Baker's claim for autobiographical theorization as a privileged domain, she seems to indicate that the *area* of "theory" is, indeed, a ground on which Afro-Americanists (even when gender promotes difference) can meet. Theory, then, manifests itself in the exchange between Baker and Henderson as an *active* site that gives birth to expanded notions of the nature and function of Afro-American expressive cultural criticism. Indeed, the accuracy of Henderson's response implies that theorization is always an endless process of complementarity—a perpetual filling in of details and strategic corrections designed to achieve useful analytical accounts.

Richard Yarborough and William Andrews seek to ground their work in archaeology. They both demand a counting of shards, remainders, and neglected wholes. Both are concerned to gaze steadily and scrupulously at what they think of as an identifiable and too often distorted (or ignored) lineage of Afro-American texts. They work like historians of a rather traditional stamp insofar as they claim an array (the vastness of which remains indeterminate) of texts as evidence. The concrete manifestations of Afro-American productivity represented by postbellum slave narratives or nineteenth-century fictional narratives by blacks call for inclusion in any analysis of these genres. There is, for both Yarborough and Andrews, an imperative to evidence, an incumbency of inclusion.

Like some of the responses already discussed, the actual essays of Andrews and Yarborough privilege the endeavors of a black past that seem either in danger of being flagrantly ignored or too scantly attended. In their missions of historical recovery, both authors suggest programs of investigation designed to alter the nature of questions and methods that have marked the study of their respective genres.

In one sense, the essays of Yarborough and Andrews can be called conservative, or preservationist. Interestingly, their conservatism produces precisely what one might expect in a dialectical scheme of presentation and response.

Radical sentiment marks the work of Sandra Paquet and Eleanor Traylor, both of whom seek to offer an epic (even a mythic) account of Afro-American life and expression rather than a traditionally historical one. What Paquet deems the epic and usable past of Afro-America is encoded by Traylor as a multivalent "I" of Afro-American expression—a *first person,* as it were, that reflects epic founding. Robert Stepto is less radical in his response, suggesting that the question of first-person narration may well be both more psychologically complex and, ironically, archaeologically accessible than Yarborough knows. Stepto's introduction of his own research example of Chesnutt offers a fine reminder that extant resources for our inquiry may well exist in the "in-progress" efforts of fellow scholars. Geneviève Fabre offers an account of what Afro-Americanist work on slave narratives has meant to the scholarly community of France.

The essays of Kimberly Benston and Deborah McDowell are correctives for past theoretical and methodological practices. McDowell seeks to indicate the limitations of a past essentialism in the construction of Afro-American feminist criticism. Assumptions of a unitary essence of Black Womanhood and claims that critics can determine, precisely, when that womanhood has been positively or negatively represented have led to detrimental constraints on analysis. The either-or mode of essentialist criticism must be replaced by a new dialogism that opens Afro-Americanist feminist criticism to the resonances of a host of discourses.

Benston seems to call for a similar openness of analysis when he locates a dialogism of contraries in Afro-America poetry itself as a first analytical step in his construction of a new poetics. "Performing Blackness" reveals the limitations of a traditional criticism of Afro-American poetry, a criticism that sought always to categorize the poetry in either "essentially" black or abstractly "universal" terms. The power of Benston's and McDowell's critiques lies in their critical explications of interpretations and problematics that come under interrogation in the responses that follow their critiques.

Michael Awkward and Cheryl Wall both take issue with the interpretations of, respectively, McDowell and Benston, and suggest that the critics' examples "work" because their problematizations are selective, and vice versa. Adducing, in revealingly dialogic fashion, other discursive evidence and examples, both Wall and Awkward provide possible cautions and interesting caveats. Spillers and Henderson, by contrast, move more in harmony with the broad formulations of the two principal presenters.

Our volume stages, therefore, both traditional Afro-American critical and theoretical issues as well as contemporary debates in the study of expressive culture. The collection should lead readers to ponder whether there is already sufficient historical evidence for preeminent claims that a new generation wishes, theoretically, to make. We trust that this collection will compel skeptics to admit that a diversified and energetically intelligent community of Afro-Americanists does, indeed, work in today's academy. We also hope that our volume offers an example of results that can be achieved by a community of scholars dedicated to setting an agenda in broad collaboration rather than in scholarly isolation.

Of course, we also recognize that the present collection reveals the problematic nature of all claims for "community," or an agreed-upon agenda. The variations among beliefs, methods, ideologies, and theories in this collection are sometimes quite sharp. Further, there can be little doubt that what we call a "community" is a selected array of scholars chosen preeminently for the demonstrated excellence of their work in particular subject areas. All of us were aware—some, such as Geneviève Fabre, were vocally aware—that important and influential scholars as well as important subject areas (such as drama) were excluded.

Moreover, we have come to realize that the underrepresentation of women as principal presenters at our conference signifies a relative neglect of feminist concerns that we must self-consciously seek to avoid as Afro-American criticism moves into the 1990s. The quality of women's contributions to our conference was impressive; the breadth and depth of feminist issues brought forth within the limited time allotted was also remarkable; but because we did not place women sufficiently high on our agenda, our treatment of Afro-American feminist criticism in this volume cannot serve as an outline of an agenda for the 1990s. It must serve instead as an inspiration to rectify a critical neglect.

Furthermore, we were aware of the diplomacy of our comings and goings. Our conference was thought of as a first effort at consolidation— under the new headings, achievements, and methods of Afro-American literary research—of gains in a specific field. We strove, therefore, self-consciously, to avoid stagings of internecine conflicts that are always implicit in the emergence of any new paradigm. Our feeling was that the media in combination with ever-present detractors would handle all advertisements of our conflicts.

What, then, is predictable from our proceedings?

First, we know that our conference was intended as the initial event of the University of Pennsylvania's Center for the Study of Black Literature and Culture. When the conference occurred, the center was, in effect, an announced idea. Currently, it is a well-financed and handsomely housed project at Pennsylvania, complete with a resident-fellows program funded by the Rockefeller Foundation. So we know that there is, at least, one established site for developing and carrying out whatever agenda is inferable from our volume.

Second, we know that our volume is the first publication in a University of Chicago Press series, "Black Literature and Culture." This series will publish scholarly works devoted to the literatures and cultures of the African diaspora. Its goal is the dissemination of new and revised assessments of key issues in African, Caribbean, and Afro-American intellectual history. Expressive culture is the series' principal area of concern. It is vastly easier to implement an agenda for the 1990s under the aegis of a series dedicated to the advancement of Afro-American scholarship.

Finally, we know that our collection will occasion controversy, critiques, and heightened critical exchange in Afro-American literary study. The promulgation of such energy is, finally, the best agenda we can imagine.

Contributors

William L. Andrews is Joyce and Elizabeth Hall Distinguished Professor of American Literature at the University of Kansas. His books include *The Literary Career of Charles W. Chesnutt, Critical Essays on W. E. B. Du Bois,* and *To Tell a Free Story: The First Century of Afro-American Autobiography, 1760–1865.*

Michael Awkward teaches English and Afro-American Studies at the University of Michigan. He is the author of *Inspiriting Influences: Tradition, Revision, and Afro-American Women's Novels* and editor of the forthcoming *New Essays on "Their Eyes Were Watching God."*

Houston A. Baker, Jr., is the Albert M. Greenfield Professor of Human Relations at the University of Pennsylvania where he also serves as director of the Center for the Study of Black Literature and Culture. His most recent books are *Modernism and the Harlem Renaissance* and *Afro-American Poetics.*

Kimberley W. Benston is professor of English and chair of the Department of English at Haverford College. He is the editor of the recently published *Speaking for You: The Vision of Ralph Ellison and the Achievement of Larry Neal.*

Geneviève Fabre is professor of English at the Université de la Sorbonne Nouvelle, Paris. She is the author of *Drumbeats, Masks, and Metaphors: Contemporary African Theater.*

Michel Fabre is director of the Center d'Etudes Afro-Américaines at the Université de la Sorbonne Nouvelle, Paris. He is the author of *The Unfinished Quest of Richard Wright* and *The World of Richard Wright.*

Henry Louis Gates, Jr., the W. E. B. Du Bois Professor of Literature at Cornell University, is the author of *Figures in Black* and *The Signifying Monkey,* which won the 1989 American Book Award for criticism.

Donald B. Gibson is professor of English at Rutgers University. He has written *The Fiction of Stephen Crane, Five Black Writers: Essays on Wright, Ellison, Baldwin, Hughes, and LeRoi Jones,* and *The Red Badge of Courage: Redefining the Hero.*

Mae G. Henderson is professor of English at the University of Iowa. She is the co-editor of *Antislavery Newspapers and Periodicals,* a two-volume annotated index.

Stephen E. Henderson is professor in the Department of Afro-American Studies at Howard University. He has published reviews, essays, and articles on black literature and is co-author of *The Militant Black Writer*.

Barbara E. Johnson is professor of English and Comparative Literature at Harvard University. She is the author of *The Critical Difference, A World of Difference,* and is the translator of Jacques Derrida's *Dissemination*.

Deborah E. McDowell is associate professor of English at the University of Virginia where she teaches Afro-American literature. Her publications include *Slavery and the Literary Imagination,* edited with Arnold Rampersad, and editions of Nella Larsen's *Quicksand* and *Passing,* Jessie Fauset's *Plum Bun,* and Emma Dunham Kelley's *Four Girls at Cottage City*.

Nellie Y. McKay is professor of American and Afro-American literature at the University of Wisconsin. Her publications include *Jean Toomer, Artist,* an edited collection, *Critical Essays on Toni Morrison,* and essays and reviews in various anthologies.

Robert G. O'Meally is professor of English at Barnard College, author *The Craft of Ralph Ellison,* and editor of *Tales of the Congaree*.

Sandra Pouchet Paquet is assistant professor of English at the University of Pennsylvania where she teaches Caribbean and Afro-American literature. She is the author of *The Novels of George Lamming* and is writing a book on West Indian autobiography.

Arnold Rampersad is the author of *The Art and Imagination of W. E. B. Du Bois* and the two-volume *Life of Langston Hughes*.

Patricia Redmond is a Ph.D. candidate in English at the University of Pennsylvania with a special interest in Renaissance and Afro-American Studies.

Hortense J. Spillers is professor of English at Cornell University. She is the co-editor of *Conjuring: Black Women, Fiction, and Literary Tradition* and has written for *Diacritics, American Quarterly,* and other journals.

Robert B. Stepto is professor of English, Afro-American Studies, and American Studies at Yale University. He has written *From Behind the Veil,* a study of Afro-American narrative, and co-edited *Chant of Saints,* a gathering of Afro-American literature, art, and scholarship.

Eleanor W. Traylor is professor of English at Montgomery College in Rockville, Md., and director of the Larry Neal Cultural Series at the Afro-American Historical and Cultural Museum in Philadelphia. Her essays have appeared in *Black American Literature Forum, Callaloo, Twentieth-Century Views,* and other journals.

Cheryl A. Wall is associate professor of English at Rutgers University. She is the author of essays on Zora Neale Hurston, Nella Larsen, and other women of the

Harlem Renaissance and the editor of *Changing Our Own Words: Essays on Criticism, Theory, and Writing by Black Women.*

Richard Yarborough is associate professor of English and faculty research associate in the Center for Afro-American Studies at UCLA. He has written widely on Afro-American literature and is the author of the forthcoming *Ideology and Black Characterization in the Early Afro-American Novel.*

Index